PRIMITIVE PRAGMATISTS

THE MODOC INDIANS
OF NORTHERN CALIFORNIA

NOLOGICAL SOCIETY

E. GARFIELD, EDITOR

VERNE F. RAY

PRIMITIVE

PRAGMATISTS

THE MODOC INDIANS
OF NORTHERN CALIFORNIA

INCORPORATING FIELD DATA COLLECTED BY
ETHEL ALPENFELS, EARL W. COUNT, IRVING GOLDMAN,
ALICE MARRIOTT, PHILLEO NASH, AND DAVID RODNICK

UNIVERSITY OF WASHINGTON PRESS · SEATTLE

684058

PREFACE

This is the story of the Modoc Indians of north-central California, a tribe at the crossroads of four culture areas: California, the Great Basin, the Plateau, and the Northwest Coast. The Modoc themselves were the northernmost of the Californians and their version of the culture of that area was so highly divergent that they would never have been admitted to the family by most of the tribes to the south.

Perhaps this exposure, on all sides, to extremes of cultural variation is why they typically insisted, "We'll do it our way." It may also help to explain the great freedom of choice allowed the individual and the conviction that right can be distinguished from wrong only by the test: does it work?

This is an ethnographic account. I have tried to report my findings in such a manner as to make quite obvious the patterns and practices, the beliefs and the ideals that characterize Modoc life and set their culture quite clearly apart from any other in the world, even from their immediate California neighbors. I do not, however, argue these points within these covers. In order that this book may be read as a story of Modoc life, rather than as an encyclopedia of cultural detail, and so that diagnostic complexes and beliefs may stand out in appropriate relief on the broader base of shared Indian culture—without spotlighting or labeling—I have abjured all subheadings and have incorporated within the text all useful comments and notations which more traditionally are offered as footnotes.

All that is presented herein is based upon original field researches, with minor exceptions, all of which are noted. This is

v

not a comparative study or a collation of available data. There are
numerous additional sources relating to Modoc culture, including
several of great value; these are listed in the bibliography following the text.

The research data utilized in the following pages were gathered
by five field workers in addition to the author: Ethel Alpenfels,
Earl Count, Irving Goldman, Alice Marriott, Philleo Nash, and
David Rodnick. These were the students who composed the 1934
field-training party sponsored by the Laboratory of Anthropology.
Dr. Leslie Spier, director of the party, chose the Modoc Indians
of Klamath Reservation, Oregon, for the summer's investigation.
In 1938 Dr. Spier turned over to me the field notes and accounts
from the field school with the request that I use the materials, to
the extent feasible, as supplementary data in the preparation of
my own treatise on the Modoc Indians.

The debt that I owe to the members of the field school is reflected by the listing of their names on the title page. I acknowl-
edge this debt but I must make it clear that the responsibility for
all statements and interpretations herein is mine and mine alone.
The great bulk of the raw field research data upon which this treatise is based was gathered by me and all of the student-gathered
information that I have used was checked in the field before incorporating it in this publication.

This field checking necessarily delayed the writing-up of the research materials. A nearly complete final draft was accomplished
in 1946. It was my intention to return to the field for further study
of certain topics before publication but administrative work and
other commitments interfered, and only as of this date has the
manuscript been completed. However, the bulk of the text stands
as written in 1946.

The many informants with whom we worked in the field undoubtedly included all those who were qualified to give reliable information. An incomplete list, with brief biographical information, is
given in an appendix. Almost without exception these generous and
cooperative Modoc friends of ours are now dead. They all wanted
the information which they had to offer about the old life to be pre-
served for their descendants and their fellow citizens who now
share their country. That is one important objective of this monograph. The other is to help us achieve a more adequate and valid
understanding of man.

Verne F. Ray

Bothell, Washington
1962

CONTENTS

ILLUSTRATIONS

Maps

INTRODUCTION

The Modoc Indians lived on both sides of what is now the California-Oregon boundary, immediately east of the Cascade Range of mountains. Their world was one of extravagant geographic diversity. Even within the bounds of their small tribal territory they looked upon perpetually snow-covered peaks and active volcanoes on the west, vast forests of Ponderosa pine on the north, barren alkali flats on the east, and near-virgin lava fields on the south. Numerous large lakes and thousands of acres of marshland were scattered over the plains of sagebrush and juniper. Isolated hills and minor mountain ranges created numerous drainage systems but all of the streams were relatively small. The greatest of these, the Klamath River, traversed only the northwestern portion of Modoc territory. Lost River was the stream of second order–"lost" because it rises in Clear Lake and flows into Tule Lake, which has no known outlet.

Along the banks of Lost River and most of the other streams were pleasant meadows blanketed with the green grasses which made these courses the favored grounds for villages and camps. Clear, cold springs provided drinking water, the alkaline properties of the streams rendering their waters scarcely potable. Bunch grass grew sparsely among the sagebrush in the adjoining hills and supplemented the grasses of the meadows as forage for Modoc horses. South of Clear Lake the bunch grass grew more prolifically and served as a significant resource, especially in winter, when other forage was scarce.

The watercourses belied their size by the abundance of fish– trout, perch, suckers–which they supplied to the Modoc larder.

The lakes and marshlands swarmed with ducks, geese, and swans in winter; and pelicans, loons, and gulls remained throughout the year. The former were of great importance in the Modoc economy and the latter were valued as supplementary resources during the lean months. The plains and hills provided rabbits, woodchucks and squirrels, the sage hen, prairie chicken and curlew; also the all-important antelope and deer. Mule deer also roamed the mountains, as did brown, black, and grizzly bears, elk, and mountain sheep.

Fields of camas flourished in the bottom lands. The Modoc dug the nutritious bulb in considerable quantities, supplementing the supply with many other tuberous roots which their lands provided, especially epos *(Carum* sp.). The lakes gave up a wealth of food in the form of water-lily seeds, an important item in the Modoc diet. Hills and mountains provided other seeds and nuts, notably the pine nut, but the Modoc depended far less upon seed for food than did most of the Indians of northern California.

The tribal territory of the Modoc was roughly four-sided, permitting the boundaries to be described in terms of the cardinal directions. The western line was that of the Cascade Divide, extending from the summit of Mt. Shasta northward to within two or three miles of the present California-Oregon border. The northern boundary ran from this point northeasterly to the region of Hildebrand and Yainax Butte, continued easterly to the region of small lakes south of Quartz Mountain, and southeasterly to Goose Lake, again at the Oregon-California border. The boundary emerged from the lake at its southern extremity, then followed a southeasterly direction to Mt. Shasta. Goose Lake was shared with the Yahuskin Paiute and the Achomawi. Only a part of the western shore was the territory of the Modoc.

This proximity did not mean that the three tribes were in close relationship, either socially or otherwise. The Modoc looked upon the Paiute as an inferior people whose personal characteristics and ways of life made social or commercial intercourse with them inappropriate and distasteful. With the Achomawi the Modoc were perpetually at war and from them they took a great many slaves. The Shasta they feared and hated. Only with their northern neighbors, the Klamath, was their relationship reasonably close and free. This relationship could not, however, be called friendly.

The Modoc shared fewer culturally diagnostic traits with the Klamath than they did with the Achomawi. However, borrowings resulting from proximity, similarities consequent upon occupancy of the same environmental province, and the sharing of traits common to all of western America made for a considerable degree of resemblance, and have led numerous observers to the erroneous conclusion that the Modoc and Klamath were culturally one. Both tribes depended partially upon water-lily seeds for subsistence, a trait not found elsewhere in the West. This was an ingenious utilization of a specialized environment which embraced many thousands of acres of marshland. These waters likewise produced tule and swamp grass in profusion, and the clothing of the two tribes was characterized by the use of these fibrous materials; also sagebrush bark from the desert areas they both possessed.

Cremation was the sole mode of disposal of the dead in both tribes. Neighbors all around them practiced burial exclusively. Cremation, however, was widespread in California even though absent immediately to the south of the Modoc. This is one of many bits of evidence which favors a central rather than northern California basic affinity for Modoc culture. Cremation is found archeologically far to the north in the central Plateau but this was not the source of Modoc-Klamath cremation, with its elaborate character and close resemblance to the central-Californian pattern. This is the principal Californian trait imbedded in Klamath culture.

A predilection for making artificial rock piles for religious or commemorative purposes and for attributing mythological significance to rock piles of unknown origin is characteristic of the two tribes, but not exclusive to them. More modest examples of this trait are found in various parts of the Plateau. The Klamath-Modoc practice appears to be an elaboration of the Plateau pattern.

Both tribes—at least in recent times—were vitally concerned with slavery. This was in no sense a simple sharing of a practice. The Modoc conducted slave raids and held slaves in a typical Californian way. The Klamath, on the other hand, bought slaves from the Modoc, and did some raiding on their own, so that they might engage in a slave commerce with the people of the Dalles on the Columbia River. They held and utilized very few slaves if any. In this they conform to a dominant Plateau ideal.

Another significant contrast was present in religion. Modoc beliefs and practices were Californian; the Klamath were typical of the Plateau. The acquisition and utilization of guardian spirits constituted a strict prerogative of shamans among the Modoc, a sharp contrast with Paiute and Klamath practice. The source of power was the dream, a Californian trait shared by the Basin. Most impressive was the congregation of spirits at a curing seance, a locally elaborated Californian concept. The initiation for the shaman was the announcement of professional practice accompanied by demonstrations of power, also Californian. The Modoc world view was dominated by the concept of an anthropomorphic bisexual culture hero. Warfare was well developed in the Californian style. Marriage patterns, birth practices, and adolescent ceremonies integrated with other northern and central Californian examples. These contrasted markedly with the Basin but not with the Plateau, except for details. The Modoc sweat lodge and sweating habits were a compromise between California and Plateau-Basin-Plains practices. The men's clubhouse was present but the heat was provided by heated rocks and steam rather than by fires.

Until recently clothing was typically Californian. Men wore little or nothing except a front apron in mild weather. The standard garment for women was the double apron or "skirt."

Houses were of the Californian earth-covered type with local elaborations. Canoes did not resemble the fine specialized forms of nearby northwestern California, but were typical of northern California generally.

Linguistically the Modoc and Klamath were an isolated unit. Their language was unintelligible to their neighbors in any direction. Formerly interpreted as a separate stock, called Lutuamian, it is now known to be a divergent brand of Sahaptin.

It was stated above that the Modoc looked upon themselves as ethnically unique and prided themselves on making their own decisions in all matters of cultural principle and behavior. This freedom extended to the individual, to the degree that cultural limitations permitted, which was considerable. Patterning was more prominent and distinctive than in most Californian societies, but orderliness, arrangement, and specificity of detail were not characteristic. For nearly any specific question about the cultural norms for economic activities, religious behavior, personal relationships, and the like, considerably varying answers were possible. In this the Modoc were consistent with many other Californian tribes, but the variability was not nearly as great as in the Basin. Compared to the Plateau, however, the looseness was extreme.

So much for the minutiae of culture, and interpersonal behavior. In tribal and intertribal matters there was much more formalization. Attitudes, policies, prerogatives, enemies, revenge, and such were so conceived and structured that response was consistent and uniform and the decisiveness of action by the tribe as a whole was impressive.

Modoc life was not, however, ruled by any dominant patterns, drives, or trends that might make for over-all cultural consistency or make available philosophic principles on which abstract judgments might be based. Unless pragmatism be such! The invariable test of the appropriateness and value of behavior–individual, family, or tribal–was the degree to which desired ends were achieved. The ends always justified the means, a conviction which made for intrigue, deception, and violence. This is sufficient answer, in itself, for the relatively low value which the Modoc placed upon affective relationships between individuals, for their social isolation in the intertribal community, and for their conviction that their ways of life were freely chosen or of their own invention.

PRIMITIVE
PRAGMATISTS

THE MODOC INDIANS
OF NORTHERN CALIFORNIA

⎰ ORGANIZATION

Modoc society was divided into three functional categories, each with its distinctive leadership. These were: warfare, religious affairs, and domestic affairs. Offices of leadership were clear-cut and officials bore unequivocal titles: respectively, war chief, shaman, and leader. Each of these terms is a literal translation of the native word. The war leader and the religious functionary bore titles which identified their specialized spheres of activity; not so the political figure. He was known simply and distinctively as "leader," the generic term being used without embellishment or restriction. With respect to his official privileges and responsibilities, however, there was ample specificity. His normal sphere was the domestic scene, his function political—no more, no less, save for the particular circumstances which sometimes raised such an official from his merely domestic role to that of a tribal or intertribal functionary. Even in such a case his sphere remained strictly political. As an official, he had no influence, to say nothing of authority, in matters of religion, kinship, war—or even economics unless it were a specifically political issue. Conversely, a war chief or a shaman, no matter how great, was never an authority in the political scheme, and was never called "leader." (In the Modoc language the title is *la ʻqi* which translates precisely as "leader"; hereafter I shall render the term as Leader without quotation marks, the initial capital letter being used to indicate that the term was a title.)

Only men could be Leaders. No woman, regardless of her wisdom, wealth, or following, was eligible for the role; indeed, the name itself was male-linked. The man had also to be the head of

a family and household. Beyond these basic requirements there
were three additional criteria which not only served to define the
community or tribal Leader but also determined the level to which
he was assigned in the hierarchy. These were oratorical ability,
wealth, and size of household. The last was a measure of the number of persons over whom he had domestic control. At least one of
these qualifications had to be met before a man could aspire even
to the lower levels of leadership. Top-ranking Leaders were invariably those who scored high on all three. Emphasis differed
with respect to the three, however. A man of great oratorical powers was recognized as a Leader almost without regard to wealth,
but wealth was more often the basis for claim to the title. (However, the Modoc were convinced that a man who "talks well" would
be economically successful because they equated oratory with intelligence and assumed that an intelligent man would succeed at any
activity he chose.)

Rank or level determined the size of the group over which control
was exercised and the amount of power which was wielded. The
lowest level was that of single-household control. Such control
made a man a Leader, in the most inferior sense, because there
were political implications in such domestic control. As commonly
encountered, the next higher level was that of Leader of a small
community, or the possession of modest power, along with other
Leaders, in the political affairs of a larger community. The highest level of leadership was that of the most powerful man in political matters of concern to the whole tribe.

It is impossible to say how many such Leaders generally were
found in a community of given size. The average community certainly recognized several men; a very small settlement might have
but one. If there were but one the question of political leadership
of the community was settled; it was this man's privilege and duty.
In larger villages any one of the Leaders might speak to, and in a
sense for, the group. One might harangue the people on a question
of the day; all would be expected to listen. Any Leader could call
the other Leaders of his village together for a conference, and they
in turn might call the Leaders of all the tribal villages into assembly. Indeed, any one Leader might call an assembly of his own
accord, but the people would weigh the influence of the man and the
importance of the question before deciding to attend.

Among a small number of Leaders the ranking was primarily a
matter of prestige and following. Special titles were not assigned.
However, it certainly was a prerogative of the people to give any
Leader a formally higher position if they so desired. This appar-

ently was done infrequently in early times, usually in the face of some critical situation. After the coming of the whites, when crises were numerous, the practice grew to the point that most communities designated one Leader as head or chief.

It appears that, aboriginally, once a Leader was elevated above his fellows, he might retain the honor even after the critical time which led to his selection was past. Especially was this true where the chosen man served his people well in the emergency. The fame of such a man spread to other Modoc communities and he came to be looked upon as a tribal Leader. If he presumed to call local Leaders from the various communities together to consider some tribal question, they were honored to accept. The powers possessed by the initiator of such a gathering were largely those of persuasion and oratory by which he might win over the local representatives. The latter, in turn, advised the people at home, where the final decisions were made. When selected by the local assembly as official Leader of the whole, a man had primarily the power of chairmanship. The people followed the advice of the Leader if it did not run counter to firmly held views; if so, his weapons were argument and oratory, which sometimes prevailed.

Hence the strong emphasis upon oratory as a qualification for a Leader. The Modoc repeatedly refer to the "good talker" in laudatory terms, emphasizing his importance in the society, and the esteem in which he was held. Whatever smoothness of function characterized Modoc society was undoubtedly due in large measure to these orators.

The qualification of wealth demands further analysis. If a rich man were "nothing else," he was a Leader, albeit of low order; but literally, if the head of a household were nothing else, he too was an inferior Leader. However, if one or the other were a great hunter, a clever gambler, or the like, he was so known. It was seldom that a rich man lacked other talents since his riches had to be acquired in one way or another and inherited riches were quickly dissipated unless replenished. The dissipation of wealth did give to the Leader a power not mentioned above. This does not imply bribery, but the extensive generosity expected of a man of wealth could not fail to enlist support for most causes that he might espouse. The rich man's house was large. Visitors were welcome; several guests were always to be found there. The hospitality of a meal was extended even to the casual passerby. This was true at any household, but the meals to be had at the home of a man of wealth were superior. The rich man could afford to lend horses because he usually possessed more than were necessary for his own purposes. The possession of slaves gave him freedom to devote his time to his guest in gossip or games and to be present at all local gatherings, however casual. If, in addition, the man were of tolerable disposition he could hardly fail to gather numerous loyal followers.

The third criterion mentioned above, size of household, is not to be confused with size of house. The latter was an aspect of wealth. The former refers to the number of persons directly dependent upon or associated with a man. A relatively old man, especially in a small community, might have a large enough number of relatives closely associated with him to constitute a significant percentage of the total population. The importance of such a following is obvious but this factor is distinctly third to those discussed above.

Other qualities possessed by a man were brought into question especially when the assembly debated the selection of a formal Leader. Most important of these was sound judgment according to cultural standards. Ability to act with promptness in an emergency was emphasized. Also affability and diplomacy were desired. The man need have no particular talents in the crafts or economic pursuits. A good hunter or gambler was at no advantage. He need not be a warrior; this is unequivocal. A coward would hardly be selected but ability in the formal pursuit of war or past participation in war were in no sense qualifications.

There was no inheritance of leadership, even though wealth, an important qualification, might be inherited. Each man had to establish his own position regardless of the fame of his father or other relative.

The activities of leadership were set by the qualifications. Most important was keeping of the peace within the community, and maintaining the respect of other communities for one's own. Oratory, haranguing, casual advice—these were the principal mechanisms. At irregular intervals the Leader spoke to the community in a highly formal manner. The occasion might be a threatened disruption of community peace, neglect by the people of economic duties, or merely the feeling of an old man that advice was needed by the younger. At such a time the Leader arose before sunrise, stood on the ladder outside his house, and addressed the people in groups: men, women, then children. He spoke in a loud voice so that he might be widely heard, and expressed himself in carefully chosen phrases. If the village were large he might move on to another quarter, stand before a large house and repeat his remarks. This was continued until all in the village had heard him. The people addressed remained in the houses, abed, and listened attentively. A particular man might not perform thus more than two or three times a year, but a large village heard various men at frequent intervals. Sometimes an assembly was called in this way but usually it was merely advice that was given. The people were reminded of quarrels that had occurred in the past and the disastrous results; they were asked to put their differences aside. Listeners were admonished not to gossip or quarrel, to work assiduously at the food quest so that none might starve in the spring, and to arise early to such purpose. Children were urged to treat their parents with respect; parents were advised to act kindly toward their sons and daughters. The speaker never talked in a belligerent fashion; neither at this time nor any other did he demand that he be obeyed.

The speaker was served by no spokesman or assistants. However, the Leader sometimes accepted one or two young men into his home where he informally educated them in the responsibilities of an adult Modoc. These boys, who came at the time of puberty, apparently were relatives who had lesser opportunities at home. They worked with a will for their proctor and were respected by the community therefor. The host taught the boys Modoc values, responsibilities, and history during long talks just after retiring. Such boys established homes of their own after marriage and in no sense succeeded to the Leader's position.

It was expected that a village Leader would attempt to terminate disputes between individuals or groups of individuals whenever he could do so within the proper scope. He would urge the persons concerned to get together and arrange a proper payment for the wrong so that they might be friends again. It was preferable that the disputants make their own arrangements and settle the matter without an outside arbiter if possible. But if this failed of realization, the Leader might attempt direct arbitration, serving alone or together with other Leaders. In affairs so serious that two or three persons already had been killed, he might even call an assembly to consider the threat to the peace of the community and to put pressure on the participants to settle the matter amicably. An individual sometimes approached a Leader and requested that he carry demands to a supposed wrongdoer. In these cases the Leader did not specify the amount of the settlement. Determination of this was left to the litigants but he might strongly urge the wronged one to accept the proffered settlement. These services were sometimes furnished by a man other than a Leader, if the dispute were local, but if the adversaries were from different villages or tribes, it was proper to the dignity of the affair that a Leader from each side be present. The Leaders served only as arbiters; they did not have police power or other executive prerogatives, in this setting. If the sides could not agree, bloodshed followed.

A Leader received no compensation for services except gifts freely given when he served successfully as a mediator. It was customary for both parties to the dispute to show their appreciation in such manner. The Leader profited indirectly from his position in other ways. Favoritism was shown in the distribution of meat, for example, when hunters returned with an especially large bag. The possession of a loyal group of followers was, however, the most enviable possession of the Leader. Regardless of his actions, such a man could depend upon the support of a considerable number of villagers. This advantage was infrequently exploited, but the assurances of support gave the Leader self-confidence and freedom of mind. In a crisis resulting from some personal misstep the Leader might assume a bold front and refuse to disturb himself with explanations, excuses, or indemnities. (Oratorical powers were not used in one's own behalf.) The loyalty of the man's following made this possible; there is no doubting the reality of this support. To be sure, a Leader could not transgress cultural standards habitually, or even frequently, without losing his following and his honor. However, the knowledge that one might assert his immunity when either merely suspected or patently guilty, no matter how improbable the event and hence the need, was a possession the value of which is hardly to be overestimated.

In the event that two Leaders came into conflict the immunity vanished. It was then a question of which one possessed the larger following. If there were a notable difference the one with lesser resources must necessarily meet the demands of the other. If there were a near balance—this was frequently the case—physical conflict between the two groups was highly probable. Again, the Leader was not immune to the attacks of a shaman via supernatural channels. However, the layman might accuse the shaman of witchcraft and achieve his death on such grounds.

As stated earlier, a Leader need not be a great warrior. In fact, he was seldom a warrior at all. He remained at home; it was thought proper that he protect himself from possible death. Leaders had a voice in the selection of the war chief, nevertheless. They, together with the warriors, made the selection.

2 LEGAL PROCESSES

An important legal mechanism was the community assembly. However, it was highly informal in character and lacked any fixed code of procedure. Despite this looseness, it was the highest and final authority in Modoc political life. No formal tribal assembly existed; tribal action resulted only when the various communities reached a common decision in consequence of assembly discussion, if the matter were controversial. On many questions, especially in the smaller communities, the holding of an assembly was unnecessary for the determination of opinion. Village gossip might easily indicate unanimity or near unanimity of view. In large towns, unity of the several local Leaders indicated a numerical following amounting to a safe majority, and a majority was all that was necessary. Formal voting in the assembly was seldom or never resorted to, but the verdict was reached when the attitude of the majority became obvious. Such a decision was not always accepted in good spirit by Leaders of the opposition, especially if accustomed to victory through a relatively large following. Seldom, however, did the minority revolt, for they recognized the democratic principle ("even in mythological times the society was democratic") and equally recognized the physical strength of the majority.

All adult men and women were accepted in the assembly. Anyone spoke who cared to do so. Courtesy demanded that his views be heard, no matter how circuitously presented or long extended. Women or men, young or old, were equally entitled to the floor. Naturally the local Leaders were the most voluble, and the most influential, in consequence of position and experience at oratory.

9

The community as a whole never concerned itself with the griev-
ance of an individual. Action toward the resolution of any personal
injury, including murder, had to be initiated by the individual or his
family. This applied alike to purely local affairs and to those that
involved persons from different communities. Indeed, it extended
to intertribal torts when the tribes represented were friendly.

Homicides were categorized as follows: intentional murder (including deaths attributed to shamanistic witchcraft); death resulting from a dispute or brawl; murder committed in a fit of rage with
due cause, especially the killing of an adulterer; the wholly accidental killing of another. The first two types called for retaliation
or compensation. The last two were not considered grounds for any
retaliatory action.

Intentional murder was usually followed by further bloodshed.
The relatives of the dead man were expected to make an attempt
upon the life of the murderer and were justified in doing so. Should
they fail to seek revenge it did not, however, affect their social
reputation. Absence of action by the injured family was doubtless
interpreted by the community as failure in secretly attempted revenge. Avenues available for action included the waylaying and
summary dispatching of the guilty man, decoying him to his death
with the connivance of another, the hiring of another man to do the
killing outright, or the hiring of a shaman to attack him by witchcraft.

Any relative of the dead man could take action of the direct nature. All other approaches required the services of someone from
outside the family. Such services were not available without substantial compensation; consequently only families of means could
avail themselves of these devices. The notably rich man usually
hired someone to act for him. In such a case the paid killer was
not considered guilty and the rich man was more or less protected
by his position. A decoy arrangement was frequently utilized if the
man sought were a member of a distant group and consequently
difficult to reach without suspicion being aroused. If a Klamath
had killed a Modoc, for example, the family of the latter might
pay some neutral Klamath to entice the murderer to the Modoc
village on some false pretext, where an attempt on his life would
be made. Well-known men such as local Leaders sometimes assisted in such schemes. A man was less apt to be suspicious if
the invitation came from a prominent man. Most frequently of all,
however, retaliation was sought through the agency of a shaman.
This was the most secret way, and less expensive than hiring a
man to kill outright. In a sense it was the safest. The affair was

less apt to develop into a feud if the murderer died from some un-
certain illness. Yet prolonged feuds, if they may be so called,
were carried on by shamanistic witchcraft. The point is that they
were physically much less serious than far briefer objective feuds.

Deaths resulting from disputes, fights, or brawls might be settled
immediately upon proper action by the guilty man. He might go to
the family of the deceased, explain that the death was unintentional,
that he very much regretted it, and that he would give to the family
a certain amount of goods. If the offer were generous it was usually
accepted; it was proper to do so. With the payment the matter was
terminated. However, a man of moderate means might have to offer all he possessed before the amount be considered properly generous. If a man did offer his entire fortune it was invariably accepted, unless he were a "poor man." In such case he would make
no gesture at all because he knew that refusal was inevitable. Hence
the poor man and the man unwilling to lose all or the bulk of his
resources found themselves in the same position as the intentional
murderer. Their lives were sought in compensation. The poor man
could do nothing but keep on the alert against an ambush. That he
sometimes succeeded can only be attributed to the dulling of emotion for vengeance after a time. The economically more fortunate
individual was in a better position. The injured family might lessen
their demands or, failing that, the murderer's family or a local
Leader might convince him that he should pay despite the amount.
If a man guilty of an unintentional killing made no gesture at all
toward the family of the deceased, either he might be considered
guilty of intentional homicide or, rarely, the bereft ones might
take the initiative and demand indemnification. A Leader might
advise them in this respect, indicating the proper amount to demand.

Murder within a family was not subject to legal action, as is
doubtless obvious from the basic principles enumerated. If a man
killed his son, or vice versa, the bereft and the injured were one
and the same. Incensed relatives might, of course, turn upon the
murderer, but it would remain an intrafamily affair. If a man
killed his wife, or the reverse, the parents or other blood relatives of the murdered one might take action on legal grounds. It
is improbable that this was done, however, if the family were long
established and the husband the culprit. A considerable proportion
of the murders remembered from earlier generations were intrafamily affairs.

An adulterer caught in the act might be killed with impunity by
the injured man, at least in principle. If the family of the deceased

took action, despite the code, they were considered the aggressors and retaliation was approved. However, the adulterer's family might consider it safe to enlist the services of a shaman against the man who killed their relative.

A clearly accidental killing, the result, e. g. , of a stray arrow during a hunting venture, demanded only an explanation to the kin and the expression of condolences. Witnesses were necessary for corroboration only if the men involved were at odds.

A sharp distinction was made between murder and all other torts. Blood revenge or heavy indemnity was due only to surviving kin. An altercation resulting in serious physical injury to one of the participants did not entitle the latter or his family to make an attempt upon the victor's life or to seek compensation. In order to avoid the pyschologically inevitable antagonism of the injured one, the victor might offer presents to him. It was expected, however, that this gesture would be reciprocated. This resolution of the affair would occur where the feeling leading to the fight was not of long standing. When tempers flared, men were apt to draw their bows. The formal apology for the consequences was, "My arrow slipped." When words exchanged between men, indoors, reached a critical point, one of them might grab his bow and arrows and run outside, shouting, "I'm going to shoot somebody." The other was expected to stay indoors; if he went out a duel ensued. Otherwise the angered man merely stamped about for a while and then returned to the house. This procedure was considered the proper release for emotion on the part of men of good judgment.

Theft and slander complete the list of serious torts. The victim of theft was expected to demand return of the stolen goods if he could ascertain the guilty one. If the latter complied with the demand the matter was terminated. Restitution relieved him of guilt; this point is unequivocal. If he refused, force might be used but in this event it was important to have witnesses to the accused man's possession of the goods and to his refusal. Otherwise, in case the accused man was killed, his relatives might deny his guilt, or his resistance, and treat the accuser as a murderer. It is improbable that theft was at all common under aboriginal conditions but its existence and a pattern of reaction accord with the Modoc emphasis upon wealth.

A man guilty of slander was asked to retract and apologize. If he complied he was warned against further acts of the kind and the matter usually was dropped. Sometimes the culprit was forced to pay a small indemnity. If he refused to retract or to pay as demanded, a fight was certain to ensue. Here again it was important for the accuser to have witnesses for reasons similar to those in accusations of theft. However, a slanderer was not required to make a public retraction.

Feuds were mentioned above but only with reference to their incipient stages. Reactions to retaliatory measures and treatment of feuds which reached serious proportions may now be described. When a murderer had been killed for his deed, the two families involved were free to resume friendly relations. Not always, however, were they emotionally ready or willing to do so, particularly the family suffering the most recent loss. To counteract the tendency to prolonged bitterness with the attendant danger of further deaths, friends of those involved urged them to announce formally the end of hostilities. Particularly was it felt that local Leaders should exert their influence at this time to bring the affair to an end. If these gestures were successful, a time and place were set for the formalities. The arrangements were usually made by the third party, friend or Leader, but sometimes one of the two families took the initiative and plans were made by common agreement. The date was set sufficiently in advance so that all residents of the community, particularly all relatives, might be notified and arrange to attend. The meeting place was outdoors if weather permitted. This might be at or near the home of one of the two families if convenient in location.

On the day chosen the spectators and principals arrived not later than mid-morning. A formal seating arrangement was practiced; the opposing sides sat facing each other in parallel lines. The friend or Leader stood between them. He represented neither side; his sole function was to insure the resumption of peaceful relations. Toward this end he talked at great length, directing his remarks to the opposing lines, but speaking in a loud voice so that all might hear him and using phrasings, emphases, and enunciations of formal oratorical character. His words were of the character of the following:

"I do not want you people to quarrel, to be angry with each other. You have many relatives. Do not be mad. Do not live in this way. If you have anything, give it to the other, and be friends again. I do not want you to fight and to make trouble.

"Now today you want to talk together; you want to become friends. It is right that you should be friends again. It is a bad thing to live as you do, as enemies all the time. All of us will feel good when you two families are friends again. Each should give to the other

the best things you possess. Now talk it over. Your relatives will
feel good again when you are not angry all the time. The way you
are now living looks bad."

The two families discussed the matter at length. An amicable
termination was indicated if the remarks tended to emphasize the
former friendship of the groups and the futility of brooding over
past wrongs. From time to time the mediator spoke further, con-
ciliating, commending, and urging. Spectators participated also
but their remarks were informal. As soon as the two families
agreed that they were "even," and peace was desirable, the exchange of gifts occurred and the affair was terminated. The gifts,
in this instance, were merely good-will offerings. They were not
great in value and the quantities exchanged were roughly equivalent. Both sides presented the mediator with presents in appreciation of his services. Other persons present might also exchange
presents. The formal ending of the ritual was indicated by a remark from the visiting family, "Now we go back"; and the reply,
"Yes, yes, now you go back." Occasionally, however, the visitors
remained for a few days as guests of their late adversaries.

The above description typifies the settlement of a simple affair
of short duration. When complications entered, the procedure was
modified accordingly: one family might demand substantial compensation before agreeing to settlement and the consequent exchange
of presents. This family was usually the one suffering the first
death. It was argued that the whole conflict was started by the first
killer and that the greater guilt thereby attached to his family. In
this instance the mediator urged that the demands be met if he felt
that no other procedure would be successful. He did not, however,
specify amounts or in any such way enter into the bargaining. These
negotiations were carried on exclusively by the opposing families.
Occasionally both sides remained adamant and the attempted settlement failed. The sides retired, often more antagonistic than before, and subsequent attempts at revenge were inevitable. Prolonged feuds, other than those conducted through shamans, were
not common, however. The pressure of the community was the
more strongly felt the more prolonged the feud. The participants
were more apt to settle upon a second attempt than at the first,
even though the factors involved were less evenly balanced than
before.

A rich man was at a great advantage in an attempted settlement.
His resources were adequate to cover any necessary indemnity.
He could stand fast in any demands he might care to make over an
economically less fortunate adversary, since he had a large fol-

lowing and could easily pay others to assume the risk in a prolongation of a feud. He would not accept an offer of mediation if the opponent were a very poor man.

Feuds were carried on between families, not between groups of unrelated persons or between individuals. No instance is remembered of a brawl leading to several deaths and wholesale feuding.

When a notoriously evil and aggressive man was killed, his relatives might make no attempt to avenge his death.

Quarrelsome persons were numerous but public criticism was the only action taken against them. Quarrels between women often started with children's disputes; jealousy was a second prominent cause. Rocks were thrown at one another, with the head as the target. Men did not fight with rocks; mild altercations involved hair pulling.

③ WEALTH

At this date it is difficult to assess the role played by wealth in aboriginal Modoc life. That the concept was present is certain; that economic stratification was a reality is equally certain. The range of economic variation is, however, difficult to ascertain. Except in terms of slaves and, recently, horses, the range was probably not great. It is certain that no social classes resulted therefrom; nor were any correlated therewith, for social classes did not exist. The rich man was not socially superior to the poor man in any formally recognized way. The advantages enjoyed by the man of wealth in achieving leadership, or in personal relations and disputes, are discussed elsewhere. These were the significant rewards of riches as we have seen in the preceding chapters. The Modoc attitude can be better understood in such terms than in any enumeration of the objective nature of riches. However, a few further remarks on the ramifications of the concept may help in understanding the amorphous Modoc view.

Food was not an item of wealth. The rich man did not necessarily enjoy a better board than the poor man. The former's possession of slaves, however, gave him an advantage in the quest for food, and enabled him to serve guests most generously. Slaves, as mentioned, were an important criterion of wealth but, curiously enough, wealthy men possessed slaves only as the result of purchase. Slaves were obtained by Modoc warriors; rich men did not go to war. "It was too much of a risk!" Slaves were not long held or in great numbers. The wealth with which slaves were bought from warriors was usually the profit from earlier transactions with the Klamath, to whom most slaves eventually passed. Thus a rich man was, at least in part, a successful tradesman.

A man might become rich through success in hunting. Most articles mentioned as criteria of wealth are those so achieved: buckskins, furs, and clothing made from these materials. Beads, bows, arrows, and baskets might also be considered in economic reckoning. The rich man had better furs and more of them than the poor man. "The poor man has just one of everything: one shirt, one pair of moccasins, one dog, and so on; the rich man has more. A poor man has a rabbitskin blanket; a rich man one of wildcat. The poor a buckskin; the rich a bearskin. The poor a skunk cap; the rich a beaver cap. And the rich man takes good care of his possessions and prides himself on fancier clothes. And he has a large house and many people live with him."

A simple dichotomy was recognized: a man was either rich or he was poor. It is certain that a poor man, with good fortune, might become rich, but the process by which it was determined, at a particular time, that he had moved from the one category to the other was highly ambiguous.

Men of wealth not infrequently abused the privileges they possessed in consequence of their economic station. They might refuse to arbitrate a feud, although in the wrong. If some object possessed by one economically less fortunate were desired, it might be seized, with little danger of retaliation. Instances of the seizure of poor men's wives are recalled but this probably occurred only if the women were willing.

The concept of rich versus poor was culturally more significant and functional than the reality of material differences in goods possessed. The difference was always thought of in categorical terms, not in the dimensions of an inventory, either actual or imagined, of the possessions of a person in question. Hence, there was more than ample room for adjusting the criterion of rich versus poor to accord with noneconomic evaluations of a man's prominence—his intellectual qualities, his oratorical ability, his cultural conservatism, his capacity for leadership. Indeed, the only term applicable to the rich man *(la ́qi)* was also the designation for Leader, as we have seen.

4 WORLD VIEW

In the meager cosmogony of the Modoc the world was characterized as a flat disc with its center located at a point on the east side of Tule Lake. At this spot is situated a small hill which was the original earth matter. Starting with this the culture hero, Kumookumts, expanded it, in somewhat the manner of weaving a basket, until the present size was reached. The sun, moon, and stars were assumed to be already existent and no attempt was made to account for their origin. Likewise the existence of mythological beings, including the culture hero, was accepted without explanation. However, the first human beings were brought into the world by action of the culture hero, perhaps with the help or at least agreement of other mythological characters. One interpretation credited Kumookumts with creating the various tribes by an act of "scattering seeds over the world." Another version was that the culture hero plucked hair from his arm pits and thus created human beings. Races other than Indians were also created by Kumookumts, but at a later time. For an indefinite period the two types of beings, human and mythological, lived together. The latter had the forms of animals of today and could not assume any other appearance except by disguise. However, they spoke the language of the human beings "just like Modoc today," and even conversed in this way with the heavenly bodies. The human population of this time was distinguished from the people of the later epoch by a specific name, but the two were lineally related and identical in appearance, language, and ideals. In some quite indefinite manner, apparently involving a council of all mythological beings, the mythological period came to an end and the historical period ensued. There now

18

appeared the spirits which were nonexistent before. To them were attributed many of the characteristics of the mythological beings but they were not rationalized as a transformation of the latter. Kumookumts apparently ceased to exist. At least no prayers were offered to him, no contemporary phenomena were attributed to him, and he was always referred to in the past tense.

Kumookumts was simply the greatest of the mythological beings, not an entity of a different order. He was conceived as part male, part female, in view of the emergence of an infant from his knee. He traveled about in the guise of an old woman, and wove baskets but never finished them. He performed tricks and was the victim of many tricks. The latter often led to his apparent death but his hipbone was never damaged and this made it possible for him to regain life each time. Stories were told of his eroticism but in this he was outdone by some of his contemporaries. His contributions to human beings included knowledge of edible and poisonous plants, instructions concerning shamanism, and the introduction of the sweat lodge. The name he bore was meaningless, not an animal name like the majority of his fellow beings. In casual remarks the Modoc pictured him as of human appearance, but this view was rejected when thought was given to the matter since human beings existed as the work of his hand and he was not one of them. Although Kumookumts disappeared his tracks remained on the earth; many geographical sites were named in terms of his activities in the respective localities and his dwelling place was specifically located. These were cited as validating data for the former existence of the culture hero.

Certain other mythological figures partook of the pseudohuman rather than animal conception and likewise disappeared at the inception of the historic epoch, notably an erotic character named Aisis. Coyote also belongs in this category in that phase of his character in which he acted the trickster. In other connections his name and actions placed him with the animal-like characters.

The principal animal-like beings were Medford Eagle, Mink, Weasel, and Spider. These achieved the most remarkable of the supernatural feats, and of these Medford Eagle was the greatest. He looked down from mountain tops and his field of vision extended as far as the ocean. When he flew overhead the beings below "lived well, fought well, and gambled well." He was all-knowing and the fleetest of all birds. His home was near Sprague River. If anyone came to him for help he gave it. It was he who named all the other animals. Weasel's power came from his ability to travel under water, over land, or from tree top to tree top. Spider could rise

straight into the air and move as fast as a bird. None of these beings ever was killed by his enemies.

Comparative lengths of winter and summer were determined by
all the mythological beings at a great and lengthy council in which
the matter was discussed and a decision reached more or less
democratically. Through similar procedure it was determined that
human beings should die rather than be immortal. Kumookumts
rebelled at this decision when his human daughter died. He went
westward to the land where the dead lived and attempted to return
with his daughter but after five failures he gave up.

The land of the dead of mythological times and that of the historical period were designated by quite different names, as was
true of the human beings of the two epochs. Both, however, were
located in the west and separated from the world of the living by
a mountain. Since the world of the living in the earlier period was
conceived as being in the territory of the Modoc today, it might
appear that the distinction in the lands of the dead was merely
nominal. But in the mythical land of the dead the occupants were
conceived as following a definite pattern of existence in which
everything was done in a way opposite to that of the living, and the
dead were pictured as aggregations of bones or skeletons; whereas
the contemporary land of the dead was ill-conceived, possessed
no definitive characteristics, and the skeleton was the mark of the
ghost which wandered on earth, unable to reach this land. Possibly
light is thrown on these concepts by the recent development of a
distinctive curing procedure for infants in which the illness is diagnosed as due to a physical attachment by a cord to the mythological land of the dead. Evidently that land is still existent and
separate from the contemporary counterpart. Or perhaps the infant's tie is with the supernatural world generically.

A deluge myth is remembered today in meager fragment. After
the flood, which caused much loss of life, a single canoe, perhaps
with Kumookumts as occupant, landed on the top of a hill.

The summary of mythological concepts presented above is not
an abstraction from the myths themselves but represents rather
the views and attitudes of informants on these subjects.

Prayers played an important role in Modoc religion. The powers addressed included the sun, moon, stars, and earth. An individual selected one or another of these as the object of his prayers
depending upon the circumstances and individual bias. No one was
necessarily more powerful than another but the sun and earth were
most frequently chosen. In addition to these natural wholes, parts
of the earth were frequently addressed. The range of selection

was wide, including almost all natural features. Most often called
upon were mountains and bodies of water. These aspects of nature
were addressed especially when specific requests were made; for
example, a prayer to the mountain where hunting was to be done
for luck on that particular venture. Also, animals were prayed to
for good luck in hunting.

Either generalized or specific prayers were made to heavenly
bodies. Generalized prayers called for good luck, the implied
spheres being health, wealth, and personal relationships. Specific requests involved aspects of these categories or temporally
particularized pursuits. A person did not pray that he might kill
a specified number of rabbits, or achieve the affection of a particular girl, or win a particular robe in gambling. Instead, he
prayed for luck in hunting, luck in love, and luck in gambling. Or
luck in hunting rabbits tomorrow, in love making at the next puberty dance, or in gambling at the next village. Weather changes
were not sought through prayers.

An example of the generalized type of prayer follows: "You,
rocks! You, mountains! Give me my deer. I am hungry. I don't
want to starve. You are going to help me. This is my country; it
is here for me. I don't want to be naked or hungry. You're not generous. [But you should be.] Help me. Give me food, venison, clothing."–Mrs. George.

(Additional examples of prayers are presented in the Illustrative
Data at the end of this chapter.)

It is now necessary to give attention to the altar at which these
prayers were uttered. A strange altar it was, by western standards. Even so, a linkage may be found, in the Christian tenet that
"cleanliness is next to godliness," for the Modoc altar was a sudatory which served the dual purposes of cleansing the body physically and spiritually.

The sweat house, as it is familiarly designated in both the collo-
quial English of the Modoc and the technical language of the ethnolo-
gist, was a humble but efficient structure. Its architectural variations are described in a later chapter. Essentially it was a tiny
hut, nearly airtight, in which the temperature could be raised to
near the level of toleration while at the same time achieving near
saturation of the enclosed atmosphere. This was done by bringing
into the hut rocks which had been heated to near redness, then
sprinkling water on them from moment to moment.

The sweat lodge itself was not thought to have a supernatural
personality, as was the case with some Plateau tribes, but served
merely as the altar at which prayers were offered.

Traditionally the practice of inducing sweating was originated by the culture hero Kumookumts upon the death of his daughter's child. "You are weak. You are unwell from grief. I will build for you a sweat lodge. You must use it for five days. If you sweat for five days you will feel good once more." Thus sweat bathing was most basically associated with mourning and functioned as an indispensable part of mourning ritualism, but its associations were much broader. Sweating helped to cure illness, brought luck in hunting and gambling, revived the enervated, and purified the woman after menstruation. Luck was gained and illness cured, not directly through the bathing but through the spiritual communion achieved in the sweat house. Prayers were addressed to the rocks which furnished the heat and to the earth itself, of which they were a part; and to supernatural forces generally as represented by fire and heat, water and steam. The heavenly bodies were also addressed, as noted above, with prayers either generalized or specific.

Prayers were uttered either before entering the sweat house or during sweating. Early morning and dusk were favorite times for praying, perhaps because these were the times chosen for sweating. However, lack of desire or opportunity to visit a sweat lodge did not deter one from offering a prayer.

The sweat bath was also used for the mundane purpose of cleansing the skin; this was its least important service.

The functions of sweating thus fall into three quite distinct categories: mourning ritualism, communion with the supernatural, and body cleansing. It is worthy of note that sweating was not associated with crisis quests, shamanistic quests, or puberty rituals, except incidentally.

Yet this is not the whole story of the sweat lodge in Modoc culture. Sometimes the shaman treated patients in the sweat house! The audience, which assisted the shaman by singing, was disposed both inside and outside the lodge. This could not have been the lodge of meager dimensions alluded to above. A former utilization of the large sweat house of north-central California is implied. Also, men sometimes spent the entire day at the sweat lodge, often the whole afternoon. The structure was not used for sleeping at night but daytime naps were indulged in there.

Other artificially constructed piles of stones, in addition to those used to supply heat in the sweat lodge, were the recipients of prayers. These were the piles which slowly accumulated along trails as passers-by each added a stone. These piles of stones were started long ago; new ones had not been begun within the span

of memory. The stones were all quite small, which distinguishes
them from the rock piles made on crisis quests. Also the total
bulk was much greater; one large pile measured four feet in height
and six feet in diameter. When a traveler approached one of these
piles he ideally stopped and threw bits of food in the four directions, uttering at the same time a prayer in which he might call
upon the sun, earth, mountains, and water. If he had no food he
threw a small stone on the pile as a substitute. If no stone could
be found a stick sufficed.

Similar offerings of food were made at every halt on the trail
by a party during summer movements, and at every spring where
water was obtained. Prayers and offerings were likewise made
before evening meals in the summertime. In winter the throwing
of bits of food was omitted but the prayers might be continued, especially when guests were present. The directions were faced in
the order east, south, west, north. The power addressed at each
direction varied with the supplicant.

Dreams were of great importance to the shaman, the dream
doctor, the pubescent girl, and individuals engaged in crisis quests.
The dreams associated with each of these activities and conditions
are discussed in the appropriate contexts. All other dreams were
treated quite casually, although attention to dreams was favored
by the conditioning of formalized dreaming. Individuals varied
greatly in the prophetic significance they attributed to dreams. One
Modoc woman stated that she always had prophetic dreams, but
the example that she gave was a dream told by one of her uncles,
in which he purportedly saw an incident from the Bible before the
whites had yet come. Some thought that a dream told to others before breakfast was apt to come true, but most persons told their
dreams at any time in the day without hesitation.

The most undesirable type of dream was that by a relative of a
recently deceased person in which the latter appeared as if he were
yet alive. Such a dream was not dangerous but it was considered
unnatural and unpleasant. Every possible effort was made to forget
a dead person once he had been cremated. All his personal possessions were disposed of; the principal object of this was to eliminate visual reminders but it was thought, doubtless correctly, that
the incidence of dreams would be reduced as well. If dreams occurred despite these precautions, the experiences were highly dis-
concerting. But it was not thought possible to exert any further
control over the dreams. As one man put it, "if you want to stop
dreaming you have to quit sleeping. Everybody has dreams, even
an infant."

The concept of soul was weakly developed. The life force was identified with both the heart and the breath. During life the locus was the heart but upon death the "breath left the heart and escaped through the top of the head to become just air." Correlatively, the head was never allowed to face the west, direction of the land of the dead, during sleep, but a corpse was placed on the cremation pyre with head to the west. The soul might leave the body during sleep but its safe return was assured if the head faced other than west. It returned before awakening; the person was unaware of its absence. Whether dreams were caused by wandering of the soul was a question not pondered.

Illness was not caused by soul absence or loss unless the affliction in infancy, mentioned above, be so interpreted. The child was bound to the supernatural world by a cord, the breaking of which brought relief. The soul may have been involved but the concept appears unique, in any case not soul loss.

Spirits and ghosts were moderately elaborated notions but they functioned almost exclusively in the shamanistic complex and are discussed in that connection. There was no guardian spirit for the layman nor was any other type of personal spiritual power available to him. The shamanistic complex included not only true shamans but a class of pseudoshamans called dream doctors who communed with the world of spirits.

Dangerous beings were recognized as a supernatural type and catalogued by a distinctive name but their role was exhausted in a few anecdotal tales. "They ran around the world making trouble for people." An anecdote, told to explain why Modoc women did not leave their infants untended, relates the experience of a Paiute woman who returned to the neglected cradle to find a dangerous being in the place of the child. Another account tells of a dangerous being that appeared in the guise of a saddle flying through the air.

ILLUSTRATIVE DATA

Beliefs concerning animals. Mysterious and unusual qualities were attributed to certain animals of the contemporary natural world. These beliefs do not fall into patterns. A few examples follow:

Bears have human intelligence. "A bear had dismembered a man. It listened to the man's heart to see if he were dead. Then it slapped him heavily and listened again, repeating until it was sure the man was dead, whereupon it covered the man with branches." (The man was rescued and recovered.)–Peter Sconchin.

Snakes of all kinds are immortal because they shed their skins. In the council of mythological beings which discussed mortality versus immortality for man, Watersnake wanted men to shed their skins likewise but was overruled. Waterweaver said, "There are too many people to step on me now and I don't want any more." So people today step on waterweavers whenever they can and say, "We are glad to do this."–Evaline Sconchin.

Dove is known as "the chief mourner." He cries like a person. "Once while Dove was engrossed in playing a game he was told that his grandmother had died and he must mourn. He replied that there would be plenty of time to mourn later, and continued playing. He has been mourning ever since."–Evaline Sconchin.

"Meadowlark is called a lazy bird. He sings only when it is cloudy and calls a curse upon people by saying: 'What difference do you make, there are lots of us, too.' "–Evaline Sconchin.

"When it appears that many coyotes are howling at night it is really just one."–Evaline Sconchin.

Numerous beliefs were current concerning the animal, frog, but these merge with notions of the spirit, Frog, so that they are difficult to segregate. The following ideas presumably relate to the animal.

Frogs bring good luck; they should not be killed. Boys may play with them, since frogs are female, but girls must not touch them, especially small ones, lest the mother come in the night in search of the young one and fill the girl's mouth with tiny frogs. When a frog dislikes a person it makes a noise indicating the fact. If a frog be killed, the spring in which it lived will go dry. Prayers are addressed to the frog and food is offered when people stop at a spring to get water or to set up camp.

(Some of the beliefs mentioned above, and in the section below, may be examples of recent acculturation.)

Omens and signs. Omens, like beliefs about animals, were of heterogeneous character. The majority of them dealt with death.

An individual's death is presaged if he is followed around by a barking coyote or a howling fox; or if he kills a young bull snake. Someone is expected to die: if an owl hoots near a house at night; if a dog howls at night in a manner suggesting lonesomeness; if a loon is heard in the early evening making a sound like the neighing of a horse; if a person remembers that he cried in a dream; or if stars are arranged in a certain way with relation to the moon. The death of a noted person is foretold by the falling of a large star; that of a child by the falling of a small star from a position near the moon, many such indicating multiple deaths. The direction toward which the star falls indicates the locality of the death. A relative's death is presaged by the twitching of an eye. An arm twitch indicates that a sore will develop at that spot. Hiccupping means that something is to be received by the person. When one sneezes he knows that someone is talking about him; a boy sneezes when a girl talks about him.

If one dreams of grizzly bears he will have an enemy. If a water-snake winds itself about a person's leg he is assured of a long life.

Good luck charms. A few good luck charms were recognized, including the desiccated body of a humming bird or mole, or the tail of a squirrel. Young girls strung mole's teeth to form brace-lets which were worn until puberty to assure luck in subsequent root-digging activities.

Eclipses and phases of the moon. Eclipses were caused by Bear's attempt to swallow the sun or the moon, as the case might be. Whenever he tried this, Frog urinated on him and caused him to desist. Frog could be seen as the dark spot on the full moon. The people assisted Frog by shouting loudly during the eclipse, but no other action, such as the shooting of arrows, was taken. The moon was said to die as it waned, but it was the same moon that re-turned again.

Excerpts from cosmogonic myths. The mythological beings held a council which lasted for five years. First they made the night, and determined that following night would be the morning. They put the moon in the sky to shine at night. Moon said, "All right, I will shine at night." Then they determined the length of the day, and the length of winter, and the length of summer. Coyote wanted a winter twelve months long, but the others said that that was too long. Most of them wanted a winter three months long. They agreed on that. "How long do we want human beings to live?" was the next question. Some said, "We want them to live forever just as we do." Watersnake said, "I want them to shed their skins as I do and be-come young again." But the majority said, "We want them to grow old and die." Mole said, "I want them to grow old, and get cold when they sit down and shake and die. Flowers, trees, and every-thing living must die or the world would get too full." It was agreed. —Peter Sconchin.

Kumookumts went to the land of the dead to visit his daughter. He found everybody there gathering swans' eggs. Kumookumts did likewise. Everybody gathered them in baskets with holes in the

bottoms. All of them filled theirs except Kumookumts. His eggs
always fell through the hole until he stuffed it full of tule. Then
he filled the basket but when he got back to camp it was empty.
Everything in that land is reversed; even night is day.
The next morning Kumookumts went to gather the bones of his
daughter and his relatives and his friends. He put them in the basket and started home. He climbed the hill separating the living
world from the land of the dead. When he was half way to the top
something began to pinch him and to tickle him all over. He paid
no attention; he just kept going. But just before reaching the top
he could stand it no longer. He dropped the bones; they all rolled
back. Then he went back again, to get at least his daughter. He
gathered her bones the next morning. The same thing happened
again. This time when he went back he was determined. The people
from the land of the dead didn't want to go back. So he had the
same experience again. He tried five times, then he gave up.—
Celia Lynch.

Further examples of prayers. All the prayers recorded here
were furnished by Peter Sconchin. Other informants agreed that
prayers were important to the Modoc but were reluctant to give examples or unable to do so; personal interest was slight. Sconchin,
on the other hand, was absorbed by the subject, prayed a great
deal himself, and developed an overwhelming personal interest in
sun worship. His more elaborate prayers must not be taken as
typical.

Sweat house prayers:
"Mountain, give me good luck, give me deer. Earth, give me
good luck in hunting. Give me plenty of deer."
"Sun, give me good health. Help me in all that I do. I will also
pray to the earth to help me in my life."

Stone pile prayers:
"You see me give you something. I bring this rock for you. Help
me now to have the luck to get anything that I want."
"My good helper, stone pile, you give me good luck. I am going
out to hunt now. I give you this. Help me to have good luck hunting
deer. That is what I want you to do."

The following is a prayer to a slain animal, in which Sconchin
talked "for the animals" ("I talk as if I were this animal so he
can notify the others and they can find out what happened to their
brother. This makes all the animals talk that way. Other animals
don't hear you but they come to you to be killed."): "I want you to
know, all you animals. Open your eyes. Find this man [mythical
human being] who killed this animal. Find out what happened to

this [specified] animal who is our friend, and whom this man killed.
We'll go out to meet him; let him kill us. We don't want to live
when this big animal, who is our brother, is dead. All of us animals will meet this man and find out what became of this animal."

A prayer said before the first meal in a new summer camp: "We
are glad to be here. We are going to give our food to this our country. Make us strong; make us lucky. Keep the women in good health
so that they may dig camas and other roots in plenty for the winter.
Sun, you give us what we want so that we may be happy. Sun, you
are all-knowing. You want us to have a good time and to live well.
Now, great sun, you know everything because you are over us."

The following narrative suggests that Sconchin's sun worship
was stimulated by his father's blind brother: "My father's brother
was born stone blind. He never saw anything. When he was a young
man he used to pray before eating. 'Now, sun, look after me. Look
at me. I want you to help me in my eating. I am going to eat now.'
He never saw the sun but he would say, 'You are up there, sun.
Give me good food.' When he went visiting he first prayed to the
sun for help, 'Help me, sun. Guide me to this place.' Before he
returned, he prayed, 'Give me luck that I may get home. Lead
me.' He walked straight to his destination. He could see nothing
because he had no eyes."

In the following prayer Sconchin's individualism and Christian
influence are blended: "Earth, look up to me, know who I am; I
will ask you for my wants. Give me all that I ask when you hear.
I am a man. I want to know all these things: the right way to do.
Teach me what I am to do. You know better than I, so I ask you to
tell me as much as I, a man, may know. Help me in all things I do
on this earth. You are my land; I was reared on you. I want to know
everything so that I may be like others. I want to know all man's
ways and do things in the right way. Also you, my sun, you see
me every night and day. Give me light so that I may see everything. The sun is with me so I can do all that a man can do. I want
plenty to eat and drink. Give me all that and I'll be like your child.
You are over all. Some men do wrong, some men do right. I want
to do right. In many ways I see people pulled down by another's
hand. I want you to put your hand upon me so that another can not
pull me down. I want to live on this earth under your care. I know
you have given me already that which I live on. I ask you about all
that I need. What I use you know about. I know what you have done
for me already, since I was old enough to know. How good I have
felt when the sun has shone on me and warmed me on a cold day.

I am very thankful for your care. You made all that on earth which is my food. So I just want to say: Gaze down upon every man living under you. You know what they need. Give it to them. Then we shall live on this earth. Give us a good life, a strong life, plenty of everything, good times; and allow all of us to be what you want us to be. You are our great sun, so we ask you to give us strength."

Lizzie Sconchin, Peter's wife, offered the following as her philosophy of death: "Water evaporates, trees die. I used to think it was too bad to get old and die; but I see everything and everything grows to maturity and then dies. So now I think it is all right. Trees mature, and they fall, and new trees spring up."

Dreams. Following are observations by two Modoc women: "When my oldest boy was killed, I used to dream about him. I dreamed that I was lying on a bed beside another bed with a sick woman on it. My boy appeared and asked, 'Why are you lying beside that sick woman? You will get sick too.'

"Some time later I was caring for a Paiute woman who was very ill. My bed was about three feet from hers. My other son came in and asked, 'Why are you sleeping beside that woman; you will get sick too.' It was just like the dream. So my bed was moved out. The Paiute woman died.

"Was that really my son? No, that was just a dream. You can't raise the sky. When a stick is broken it can't be made whole again."
—Lizzie Sconchin.

"I always had prophetic dreams. I always knew when something was going to happen.

"Before the whites came and before I was born my father's brother, Ulysses Grant, lost his wife. He went on a mourning quest. He had a dream as he slept in a cave. He dreamt he saw something coming on a jack rabbit with very long ears. A man was on the rabbit; he was so bright the sun seemed to be shining behind him. The man had bronze or reddish hair that was curly. The rabbit walked across the water and carried the man to shore. The man wore a blanket. A voice said to my uncle, 'This is the day that is coming. Your descendants will know this man.'

"My uncle told me this dream in Oklahoma, when he was old and blind. That man was Jesus, he said, riding a mule and coming into Jerusalem."—Jennie Clinton.

Dangerous beings. This is the account referred to on an earlier page: "An old, old man once told me that he had two older brothers who died from seeing a dangerous being. They had gone westward to trade and were returning. Near Medicine Rock one suddenly

heard a peculiar buzzing or humming coming from high in the air.
Soon the other heard it. The older brother said, 'Look out! Stand
beside me; we must keep out of sight.' They flattened themselves
against the rock. In the air appeared a great saddle. Nothing else
could be seen. It swung past the rock and then faded into nothing.
"The brothers hastened home and told the people of their experience. Then they lay down together and died."–Lizzie Sconchin.

5 ACQUISITION OF SUPERNATURAL POWER

Power derived from spirits was the possession of shamans exclusively. It was received through a series of experiences which uniquely linked the dream and the quest; neither, alone, was efficacious. Properly, the initiative rested with the spirits rather than with man. The latter, in his eagerness to acquire power, sometimes assumed the initiative but failure was certain unless the spirits were particularly well disposed toward him.

A man was subject to spiritual call at any time during the mid-years of his life, that is, from the time of marriage or shortly thereafter until old age approached. A woman might be chosen only during the relatively few years which separated menopause and old age. Consequently many fewer women became shamans than men, but the nature of the sponsorship and the degree of power achieved did not differ. The spirits did not select individuals on the basis of any culturally recognized standards. The rich man, the prominent man, the talented man—none of these was more apt to be chosen than a little known and otherwise unimportant individual. It did not even matter that he may have neglected his puberty training, or that he might be an orphan or a slave.

The Modoc cannot account for these facts in cultural terms but they are easy of explanation in a subjective analysis. First it must be understood that the individual did, in fact, make his own decision to become a shaman. The "call" came in a dream which was markedly vague in character. Many spirits appeared in kaleidoscopic transition. Upon awakening the dreamer did not remember the identities or characteristics of the spirits, even though the guises in which they appeared were presumably those of animals

familiar to him. He understood that the spirits wished him to sing
but as yet he had no songs. Dreams of this character continued for
several nights–the pattern was five–but not necessarily consecu-
tively. If young he now sought the advice of his parents; if older
he came to his own decision. To become a true shaman several
further steps were necessary, all requiring definite action on the
part of the dreamer.

We may now interrupt to note the psychological factors operat-
ing. The "call" was a dream of indefinite and variable character.
Almost every man had such dreams; this was inevitable in a hunting culture, especially to the young man attempting to make his
mark in this most important of all economic activities. The sub-
jectively variable factors of significance were the frequency of
such dreams and the interpretation made. The man whose prime
ambition was to become a shaman, he who pondered the matter during many of his waking hours, could not fail to experience dreams
which could be interpreted as spiritual, and these repeatedly. The
man who was already successful in other lines of endeavor, or he
whose conditioning led him to recoil at the thought of a shaman's
life–these would not be led to interpret any dream as spiritual in
character or to induce by cogitation the repetition of a questionable
dream. He who did not desire to possess shamanistic power was
even further protected by a cultural mechanism for counteracting
proffered spiritual association. A man might rub upon his body a
smear of menstrual blood, or carry such in a pouch around his
neck; he then need never fear the approach of spirits. (The strong
antagonism of menstruation and all supernatural manifestations
likewise accounts for the restriction of female shamanistic practice to the postmenopause period.) In a word, the man whose associations and experiences had resulted in a point of view and personal characteristics favorable to shamanism–coupled, in some
instances, with lack of success in other endeavors–was the man
who became a shaman. The call of the spirits, in psychological
aspect, was in no sense involuntary. It should be added, perhaps,
that dreams were never induced by any culturally determined pattern or action.

Another aspect of shamanism in which the cultural phrasing ran
counter to psychological fact was the assumption that the practitioner was but a tool–a "servant"–of the spirits, doing their will
and lacking entirely in personal volition. This will be illustrated
later; we now resume the description of acquisition of spiritual
power.

Immediately following the dreams, five days were devoted to a

quest in which personal contact with the spirits was sought. Visits
to various spirit locales were made at least once every evening—
preferably twice each day, during the early morning and late evening. The places visited were traditional; specific instructions were
not given during the initial dreams. By far the most important of
the spirit abodes were the deserted house pits where deceased shamans had lived or performed rituals. Upon the death of a shaman
his spirits deserted his former haunts, particularly his home, for
about a year. If the house were not rebuilt or reoccupied they then
returned. The spirit seeker frequented such pits, one after another, during his vigils. Or, if he thought it wiser, he returned
repeatedly to the pit of a famous and powerful shaman. Kinship
with the former shaman did not predispose to success. All deserted homesites were tribal, not family, property and a man was
entitled to make use of any or all as he chose. Other spirit sites
were the former gathering places of mythological beings, and certain pits and depressions other than those of deserted houses. The
latter were spiritually notable for one reason or another, e. g.,
the presence of snakes (of a harmless species) or of mythically
monstrous beings. None of these was of importance compared to
the house pit. Other sites of apparently similar character, such
as cremation places, deserted sweat houses and caves, were never
utilized. House pits chosen by a man for his vigils were within a
short radius of his home.

The visits to these spots were brief and the procedure simple.
The man lay down in the pit and "slept." His dreams were similar
to those earlier, but more vivid. During the course of these dreams
all of the spirits of the universe appeared to him but they did not
speak. Most of these appeared in animal form, but some looked
more like men, women, or children, often of miniature size—"not
larger than one's finger." Each spirit was of a definite sex; the
male and female of a species appeared successively where both
sexes were represented. Some types were exclusively male, some
exclusively female—notably Frog—and at least one was always conceived as a male child, the "Boy" spirit. Small mountains were
female, large, bald-topped ones, male; earth, female; springs,
female; rivers, male; sun, female; moon, male; small stars,
female; large stars, male; rain, female; snow, male; cumulus
clouds, male; nimbus clouds, male. Different songs were associated with each sex of the paired spirits. Upon awakening, the
dreamer could remember the appearance of none of these with sufficient accuracy for an adequate description. A divergent and de-
tailed description given by one informant may have been taken from

the Shasta: "The spirits are butterflies and yet they are human. Their bodies are small, somewhat larger than butterflies. They have small waists and are crystal clear. You can look right through them."

Nor did any one or any group play a more prominent role than the others. These dreams functioned merely to acquaint the subject with the spiritual world; he did not acquire his familiars at this time.

By the evening of the fifth day all had passed in review. Then came the most dramatic event of the quest. As he stepped into the pit, the seeker fell "dead," that is, unconscious. A fleeting glimpse of a half-human form was had, a figure that resembled vaguely a skeleton. The vision disappeared and a stentorian voice was heard. The remainder of the experience was wholly auditory. "Now you have seen all of the spirits in this universe, except me. I am the last one. Now you know you will be a doctor. I am the spirit of all ghosts, of all the people a long time dead. I control all of the spirits and I'll be around to help if they fail. I am always 'round and about. In the evenings you will hear my cry, first in the west and then passing along to the east, and then all gone. Your body will feel cool and you will know that I have been near. But you will never see me, only hear me. Now I have some orders to give to you. I want you to be careful about everything that you do. You are getting ready to be a doctor. Don't eat in the morning or in the evening—only when the sun is high. Do not sleep with your wife. And don't try to doctor until after your initiation dance. Now I give you this song. . . . " The visionary awakened with blood flowing from his mouth. He sang the song he received and thereby regained normalcy. Thus ended the second phase of the making of a shaman.

The partial fast and continence dictated by the ghost spirit had already been observed during the preceding five days. Everyone knew that this was required. No mention was made to relatives or friends of the experiences or progress of the quest. The midday hours were spent inactively, for the most part, but not abed. The sweat bath was frequently used but not as a formal part of the quest. At night the shamanistic aspirant slept in his own bed in the family house.

The third period of the quest, also of five days duration, followed immediately. The subject remained at home, observed the taboos already established, and awaited the appearance of specific spirits. They came, according to the invariable pattern, in dreams. These experiences occurred at night while the man lay in his own bed. He did not sleep during the daytime nor did he return to the house pits. The spirits which came now were far fewer in number than during earlier dreams. Furthermore, they appeared individually and spoke to the dreamer directly. The experience was wholly auditory. Each one thus heard became a specific familiar of the shaman. The spirits came in pairs, male and female, one being heard after the other. After identifying itself the visitor spoke somewhat as follows: "Now I have lots of doctoring to do. I want you to help me. I want you to be my interpreter; I will speak through you. When I doctor I want you to tell the people what I see and tell them what I say. I want you to sing my song for me when I am doctoring. You will have to be very careful and do just what I say. You can't say anything unless I tell you. You will be my interpreter. Now I give you this song. . . ." In addition to the song each spirit gave the aspirant certain specific instructions. The latter usually concerned the fabrication of some symbolic object which was to become a part of the shamanistic paraphernalia of the man. No dance step was conferred, nor were specific statements made concerning the curing power conveyed. After each such visitation the subject awakened singing and the other members of the household joined him. All remained abed. Each aspirant received many spirits during the course of the five days. It is impossible to establish figures for either the mode or the range, but it appears that the five nights were in effect periods of continuous ritualism as one and then another spirit appeared to establish relationship with the man. Yet the collection thus obtained by one shaman differed from that of any other one and no one man possessed more than a small fraction of the total number of spirits. Comparatively, some men received few, some many. It may be that the acquisition of some spirits caused bleeding from the mouth as did the ghost spirit. This is a controversial matter among present-day informants; it may represent individual variation. It is clear, however, that in Modoc belief the appearance of the ghost spirit, both initially and subsequently, was invariably accompanied by this phenomenon. Incidentally, the ghost spirit was fully acquired at first appearance. It did not return during the following period.

The quest proper was concluded with the end of the third phase just described. Each period was characterized by a specific function; first, the spiritual call; second, acquaintance with the spiritual universe; third, acquisition of shamanistic familiars. There remained only the initiation, which occurred at a later date, before practice might be assumed. Indeed, some shamans, contrary to spiritual instructions, practiced before or even without the initiation. The success of these men was very limited and it may be that this aberration existed only during recent years. It is proper to add that the relatively sharp pattern of the quest was not necessarily followed in detail by all aspirants. The ever acceptable excuse for a variation was that a spirit so requested. However, the cultural pattern stood and the variations discernible in anecdotal material do not fall into types.

A man never attempted a second quest to obtain additional spirits. Those he received during the five days determined the amount of his power. Shamans differed, not only in the number of spirits possessed but also in the efficacy of the particular combination. Some spirits were more powerful than others. More important, perhaps, was the representativeness of the collection. A shaman was the more fortunate the wider the range of characteristics and talents possessed by his spirits. The effective measure of a shaman's power was the number and variety of songs he might sing; it was of no value to possess a particular spirit if he could not remember the song it conveyed.

A shaman might return to the house pits, or to any other spiritual site, at any time during his life at the instigation of one of his spirits. This, however, was not to gain new power although it might serve to renew and make fruitful the talents already possessed. Ordinarily, however, such an act was performed simply to carry out instructions from a spirit, particularly one being used in a cure. Spirits often directed that novel, difficult, or even highly dangerous exploits be carried out and it was incumbent upon the shaman to do so. Otherwise he was subject to severe illness and even death.

The person who received a summons to embark upon a shamanistic quest was also subject to illness if he failed to accede or to take proper counteractions. Nevertheless it appears that an occasional individual gained pseudoshamanistic power in consequence of the dreams alone. The critical factor here seems to have been the failure to obtain the ghost spirit with the accompanying symbolism of mouth bleeding. Where significant dreams persisted the person was called a dreamer and gained power to cure in a minor sort of way by laying his hands upon the patient. No specific familiar or shamanistic songs were obtained but the communion with the spiritual world that the dreams involved gave the person power which must be termed spiritual, however generic. These persons are here called dream doctors, a fairly literal translation. Their activities are described in a later chapter.

6 INITIATION OF THE SHAMAN

Spirit quests were conducted during the spring or summer seasons. In the late fall the initiation ceremony was held. This was arranged by the novice himself. It was he who made the preparations, issued invitations, conducted the ritual, and defrayed the expenses. It was essentially an announcement ceremony; a mechanism by which the novice made known to all the people that he now offered his professional services, the potential value of which he demonstrated by singing the many songs which he had obtained and by the performance of feats of supernatural power. Other shamans took no part in the ceremony; indeed, it would have been dangerous for the novice had they done so. The initiate was assisted by four laymen, whose functions are noted below.

In preparation for the ritual the novice prepared a ceremonial pole to be erected at the dance house. This was about nine feet high, a slender but substantial pole from which all limbs and bark were carefully removed. It was then painted with red in a spiral design, or with vertical stripes, or sometimes in solid color. To the top was fastened a cluster of feathers, the tail feathers of a hawk, taken intact and spread fanwise. Less commonly other feathers were used, sometimes an entire stuffed bird. Fixed also to the top was one or more streamers or pendants, three or four feet in length. These were of cordage or long strands of grass. Along the length of the cordage were tied brightly colored and symbolic feathers, such as the red plumage of the woodpecker. To the ends were secured objects of traditional ritual significance together with others symbolizing the spirits of the shaman. Characteristic of the former were small discs formed of tule, with a pair of feathers

on either side of the string by which the disc was attached. A dozen
or more might be used. These were vaguely associated with Frog,
a ubiquitous spirit. The specific spirit symbols had been gathered
or fabricated immediately following the quest. These assumed
many forms: bits of fur, feathers, stuffed birds, grasses, and
miniatures of such objects as bows, arrows, baskets, and musical
instruments. The symbolism was sometimes quite obscure but
there was no hesitancy in revealing the meanings. These objects,
as noted, were added to the pendant cords on the ritual pole. Properly one was provided for each spirit possessed, but practice fell
short of this ideal. Sometimes a second pole, of similar character, was prepared and placed, at the time of the ritual, in one of
the house pits the shaman had frequented during his quest. It could
be explained that spirit symbols not present on the dance-house
pole were to be found on the other. Five ceremonial wands were
also necessary to the ritual. These were of willow, about a foot
long, and painted in solid red.

A great quantity of food was accumulated. It was necessary to
serve five meals, one each night, to the scores of guests that would
assemble. The difficulty of obtaining sufficient food led sometimes
to the postponement or neglect altogether of this ceremony of announcement.

Several days before the date set for the ritual, messengers were
dispatched to extend invitations. These invitations were not individual, but general. Spectators often arrived from considerable
distances.

The ceremony lasted for five nights if the food proved sufficient.
Traditionally the same pattern was followed each evening except
the last. However, individual shamans, hoping to gain greater
prestige, varied the routine or introduced novel elements. The
traditional form will now be described.

An ordinary dwelling house was used for the ceremony, usually
the shaman's own. The ritual pole was not placed inside, as might
be expected, but was fixed in the ground outside the house and to
the right of the doorway. The height from the ground was seven or
eight feet. Around the base, in circular pattern, the five wands
were thrust in the ground. At dusk, after the guests had assembled
indoors, the five principals gathered outside the door. They wore
no special regalia. They arranged themselves in file: first, the
shamanistic novice; second, the shaman's spokesman; third, invoker of the spirits; fourth and fifth, the imitators. The spokesman's service to the shaman was comparable to that of the shaman
for the spirits. When the spirits spoke the voice heard was that of

the shaman. But to the layman the words were unintelligible. The spokesman interpreted, speaking out in a strong clear voice. The duty of the invoker of the spirits was to call the spirits to assemble and to entreat them to use their powers toward the shaman's ends and for the welfare of the people. The imitators repeated the cues of the spirits, five times over, and led the singing and dancing. The imitators were selected for the occasion and might be any of the laymen present; however, the tendency was to select those who had performed before in such a capacity at initiations or curing seances. The more important assistants, spokesman and invoker, were men who served in this capacity for a number of shamans. In a small village there was commonly but one man who served in each of these capacities. These men were old rather than young and were well acquainted with ritual routine. They were not paid for their services in an initiation ceremony but received compensation for assistance at curing.

The group made a counterclockwise circuit of the fire, which was in the center of the room, before assuming their places. Sometimes five such circuits were made. The song chanted at this time appears to have been that referring to the ritual pole: "The pole waves from side to side; the wands march in single file." Throughout the march of entry the audience stood and danced in place. A simple steplike motion was accompanied by up and down movement of the outstretched arms. The position taken by the shaman was near the fire, somewhat to the right of the path from the door to the fire. The spokesman was a short distance to the right of the shaman, facing him. The invoker stood at the left of the spokesman. Behind these two were the imitators. The audience occupied the periphery of the room. Men and women were intermingled; children were not permitted to attend.

From his position the invoker called the spirits to assemble. As they approached their cries were heard and repeated by the imitators. From this time forward the spirits were heard from time to time talking to each other and to the audience. This occurred particularly in the periods between songs. In the meantime the novice had taken a reclining position which he might retain for the remainder of the evening. No further dancing was to be expected on this night. Soon the shaman started to sing his first song. After he had gone through it once the imitators joined in and the audience followed suit. The songs were very short but were repeated several times. Some of the songs were novel to the audience, some familiar, especially to the older people. The former were songs conferred by a spirit for the first time; the familiar

songs were those used at an earlier time by a since deceased shaman. A man used the old song only when reconferred by the same
spirit; he could not assume it otherwise. To put it properly, when
the old song was heard the audience knew that present in the dance
house was a particular spirit possessed earlier by another shaman.
The spirit and song were the same as formerly; but the medium of
expression, the shaman, was changed. It need not be doubted that
this opportunity for the use of old songs was extensively exploited
by the shaman inept at composition.

During the progress of the evening one after another of the shaman's songs were sung; never was there a repetition. During the
intervening periods the spirits explained, through the shaman and
his spokesman, the symbolism of the songs and of the spirit objects on the ritual pole. They urged the audience not to hesitate to
call them when ill, since they were eager to help and the patient
was sure to get well if they were summoned, but was sure to die
otherwise. They discussed the dance in complimentary terms,
predicted the weather, and conversed with one another. All of the
principals were much occupied at such times since each had his
part to perform. About midnight the singing ceased and preparations were made for a modest feast. The food was brought in from
its place of storage nearby, and placed before the shaman. The
spirits spoke, saying, through the usual channels, "I'll sample
this food; I wouldn't want any of you to become ill. Yes, this is
good; this will not poison you." A small bite of each kind of food
was taken by the shaman, then women passed the dishes, one at a
time, from person to person. The shaman ate little. He observed
a partial fast until the last night. Fresh meat and fish were taboo.
At the end of the meal the guests reclined or dispersed and the
ceremony of the initial evening was terminated.

The procedure on the second, third, and fourth nights duplicated
that of the first, except that new songs were sung each evening.
On the last night there was more dancing and the shaman demonstrated some of his supernatural abilities in fields other than curing. Also, a larger feast was provided, if possible, and the shaman ended his fast. The shaman danced while singing on this evening, moving slowly around the fire. When he finished the audience
danced, in single file, following the same route, counterclockwise
around the room. This was usually repeated with each new song.
But intervals between songs were apt to be long as the shaman's
repertory approached depletion. Some unfortunate novices found
this occurring on the third or fourth nights. At such times the audience was entertained with shamanistic demonstrations of power.

The tricks employed were few in number and elementary in character. Prior to the performance of a trick the spirits contested
with one another for the privilege. The one finally winning was assured of the assistance of the others if he fell into danger from
failure. Most dramatic was the purported swallowing of arrowheads. After the shaman had apparently gulped them down he addressed the audience, requesting that they remain silent and motionless. He assured them there was nothing to fear. Soon arrowheads began to drop onto the floor from various parts of the shaman's body. Members of the audience heard them drop but did
not see them. The details were described by the spokesman, who
gathered up the points, placed them in a basket and shook them
about. Another trick was the familiar swallowing of fire. Five
small bundles of pitch wood faggots were handed to the shaman.
One by one he lighted the sticks, plunged the burning end in his
mouth, then removed it flameless. He explained that the fire was
being consumed by Bear.

It was proper for a shaman to offer this five-day ceremony each
year for five years. Recently this has not been done. It is probable
that even in earlier times this was more of an ideal than a reality.

A few negative aspects may be mentioned. No musical instruments of any kind were used. Cures were not effected at the ceremony. Shamanistic tricks did not include the enticing of spirits,
the removal of sticks thrust in the ground, dancing near the fire,
or any of many other familiar feats. The ritual pole was not used
again. After being stripped of the symbolic objects it was hidden or
buried, but not burned. The spirit objects were carefully wrapped
in buckskin and secreted in a safe place. If a layman were to find
or touch them he would become ill. The place of safekeeping differed from shaman to shaman: sometimes indoors, in or near his
bed, sometimes outdoors in a secret place.

Details from the initiation ceremony of the last great shaman
("Dr. George," see Appendix, *Informants*) illustrate individual
variation from the traditional pattern. This initiation was recent,
in fact the last such ritual. Between one and two hundred persons
were present. Apparently no imitators were utilized. Dancing
occurred the first and second evenings but not on the remaining
three. George's dance was a side step, clockwise (?) around the
fire. The audience did not dance. George sang fifty songs the first
night (?). The words of the first three were as follows: "A long
circuit I made on my trip" (Black Fox); "I am the squealing mink";
"The world to my echo reverberates" (pestle).

7 SHAMANISTIC PRACTICE

A shaman was a full-fledged member of the profession as soon as his inaugural dance was completed. His powers were as great as they would ever be; as noted earlier, he did not embark upon further quests during his career. He might gain one or a few additional spirits through theft from other shamans but this proportionately small accretion did not effect a practical increase in professional ability. He might become a smoother ritualist as he gained experience but native evaluation, it must be remembered, was in terms of spirits possessed; only they could project illness or effect a cure. It is true that a shaman would fail if he did not call the proper spirits for a particular illness, or call them in the proper order, but the patterns were relatively simple and traditionally known. Furthermore, he had the assistance of an experienced invoker and a trained spokesman. A shaman who failed in these elementary matters could never establish a practice.

By no means were all shamans of equal ability, since the number and combination of the spirits represented by them differed considerably. The poor shaman had few spirits upon which he could call, these were weak in character and certain important spiritual categories were unrepresented. Another man, with no larger number of spirits, was much more capable if his familiars were well balanced and representative. The strongest shaman was the one with many spirits representing each aspect of spiritual power and including all of the most powerful spirits. Female shamans, though fewer in number, were quite as capable as men. They obtained supernatural sponsorship in the same way, observing the same type of quest, and curing by the same methods. This did not take place, of course, until after menopause. This may explain the failure of women to give the inaugural dance, the one discrepancy between the sexes. The maturity of the woman, the wide knowledge of her character and her established position in the community probably rendered such a ceremony−essentially an advertising mechanism−superfluous. The same ought to apply to a man if he embarked upon his professional career equally late in life, but it appears that men seldom waited this long. In the one known example the inaugural dance was not observed.

The only case of Modoc transvestitism known today was that of a man who at the age of thirty began to affect the clothes and manners of a woman and at the same time started practicing shamanism. His healing powers were considerable; in addition he was especially adept at the trick of swallowing fire.

The shaman was not set apart by distinctive dress. Even when treating a patient his regalia were meager: a distinctive cap and sometimes a bear-claw necklace. He used no rattles, drums, or other instruments. He often brought a buckskin band to which were fastened a number of feathers; this he merely laid beside the patient. In his home many kinds of feathers were displayed on house beams and walls. The feathers and other objects he had used at initiation were kept hidden away until his death at which time they were buried. If touched by a layman they caused illness; if burned at his death a storm ensued.

A shaman was an influential and respected individual in the community. He was the one person holding a specifically recognized public position of unequivocal character. Even so, he was not charged with the public welfare in any civic sense. He recognized no public duties or responsibilities. The ceremonialism of the inaugural dance was enjoyed by the audience and the food provided was available to anyone who might care to attend. But the whole affair was essentially private and selfish in motivation. The shaman's only object was to improve his personal future. The dance was not repeated after he had established a practice even though he was thenceforward in a better financial position to give it. The extent to which a shaman utilized his powers in a curing ritual was determined entirely by the fee offered. Even a brother or a son had to pay in order to obtain treatment. A shaman was believed to be capable of changing the weather, but he attempted this feat, not for the good of the community but for his own purposes or when paid by another to do so. Each shaman attempted to give his patients the notion that he had little but contempt for the abilities of his colleagues and that antagonism characterized all their relationships. But his patients as well as others knew that this was mostly a pose. Although in theory each shaman, through his spirits, was pitted against all others in a struggle which might lead to death, in actuality the relationships were much more cordial and cooperative, as will appear in later descriptions. Two prominent shamans of recent times went so far as to agree to joint use of each other's spirits. Although wholly contrary to the principles of Modoc shamanism, this association was accepted by the community. Even when one shaman accused another of causing an illness, and demanded that he withdraw it lest he be killed, the accuser was in fact doing the accused a favor for the latter could then collect a fee.

A doctor was invariably secure economically but he was seldom a rich man. He was well paid by his clients but his activities were specialized. Unavailable to him, or at least little used, were the profitable pursuits of commercialism, gambling, and intensive hunting. He was not socially superior to other men nor was he patronized as was the wealthy man. He was subject to the legal processes of the community to the same extent as anyone else. A death from witchcraft was a murder nonetheless. The injured person might fear to take direct revenge, though justified in doing so, but he could always utilize the services of another shaman.

It was a folk conviction that a man who killed a shaman would die within the year. Personal histories apparently demonstrated the truth of the belief. But it was also believed that a shaman invariably died a death of violence. Equally impressive documentation was available. Some man, sooner or later, was sure to take direct action for a wrong, real or assumed. Clearly, shamanism was a hazardous profession. No one questioned this and many men frankly asserted that they would never accept the risks involved, no matter how great the prestige or profitable the pursuit.

While anticipating a violent end, the shaman faced many other dangers. The commonest was the accusation by the spirits that their orders and remarks were being incorrectly interpreted. Another criticism was that the shaman was showing favoritism; a group of spirits resented the relative neglect of their talents while other familiars were being frequently called upon. Illness resulted from these accusations but not necessarily for the shaman. Any member of the doctor's family might suffer the penalty, especially his children. Often the offended spirit or spirits openly demanded that the father give them permission to take the child by death. The parent usually offered the life of a dog instead. This alternative was sometimes accepted, whereupon the dog died and became

a spirit. If the life of the child was insisted upon the shaman had
no recourse. The child's ghost did not, however, become a spirit.
A shaman's child also became ill if he broke any one of the many
taboos relating to the person of the doctor. He might not walk behind his father's back, cry or fret in his presence, or play in the
ashes of the fireplace, lest illness and possible death result. The
difficulty of training the young child to respect these arbitrary
rules was clearly recognized. The deaths of two sons and two
daughters of Dr. George were attributed to such breaches. To protect children from the dangers of transgression they were sometimes sent to the homes of relatives to be reared. For these reasons a shaman's household was usually small; also because he
preferred it so. Some doctors lived entirely alone for periods of
time. Spirits were more frequent in their visitations under such
circumstances. They kept the shaman better informed and he was
able to use them more effectively. The doctor traveled little, partially for reasons already cited; also because he feared that "someone might put poison in his food."

Other children were likewise subject to harm if the shaman's
personal taboos were broken. Further, it was thought that a shaman often expressed his antagonism toward the parents by making
a child ill. Consequently children were forbidden to attend the inaugural ceremony, were seldom taken by parents when visiting a
shaman, and were sent away or highly restricted in their actions
when a shaman was present in their own home. Adults were equally
subject to these rules of conduct but it was easier for them to avoid
a breach. Dust, particularly that of ashes, was abhorrent to the
shaman, causing blood to flow from his mouth; hence no one swept
a floor or stirred a fire in his presence. Association with a shaman carried risks beyond these obvious ones, however. The doctor
was capable of causing illness quite without objective provocation.
Furthermore there were dangers from the spirits associated with
the shaman even though no volitional act of the latter was involved.
Often the doctor himself was unaware of the mischief being wrought
by his spirits.

A shaman's spirits were available to him at any time. He needed
only to sing the proper song and the spirit appeared to him, or
rather, its presence was felt, he heard it speak, and he could
speak to it. The immediacy of the relationship did not vary with
the seasons; there was no necessity for periodic re-establishment
of rapport. Yet it is hardly proper to speak of the spirits as being
physically associated with the man, except when specifically called.
Before a seance they had to be summoned from the four quarters

of the earth, the zenith, and the nadir. Yet at the patient's house each spirit which responded occupied a specific position in the room. When one spirit abducted another it was carried to a hiding place specifically localized in Shasta territory.

The circumstances under which a shaman exercised his powers to commune with his spirits were, however, determined by tradition, not personal caprice. The occasions were the inaugural dance, the curing seance, the plotting of sorcery, and self-illness. The time in all cases was night. Certain other circumstances led the spirits to appear of their own volition. They came to inform the doctor of activities being conducted in his behalf; to request services of him; to accuse him of improper shamanistic procedure; or to tell him of accidents just suffered or illnesses newly contracted. Others in the household knew of these visitations because the doctor immediately began singing and the others joined him. If he wakened with blood on his mouth they knew that someone of the community had suffered violent injury.

Certain spirits were possessed by all shamans. Included were Eagle, Fish Hawk, Frog, Pelican, Crow, Rattlesnake, and the ghost spirit. Without these no diagnosis—essential to a cure—could be successful. In most cases some of these commonly held spirits were indispensable for the cure as well. By the same token they were the most used spirits. So well known was the pattern of spirit selection and sequence of use as applied to the average case that even the lay spectators sometimes called the shaman to task for omissions or variations. Such being the case it is not surprising that some spirits were neglected and caused the shaman to become ill in their resentment. But when the patient exhibited unusual symptoms these little-used spirits were invaluable. The shaman with the greatest number upon which to call was most certain to succeed in diagnosis and cure since selecting the proper spirit was largely a random procedure.

That the process was not wholly haphazard, even in common illnesses, was due to a degree of specialization in the disease-causing, the diagnostic, and the disease-curing abilities of the spirits. A rough correlation was drawn between the characteristics of the animal or object whose name the spirit bore and the objective symptoms of the disease. Thus Buzzard, since the bird circles over its prey, might be responsible for an illness characterized by dizziness. A correlation was likewise drawn between the characteristics of the spirit and the nature of the curing technique. Thus, if an intrusive object were to be removed, a grasping and tenacious spirit such as Hawk (through analogy with the bird) was used.

Some spirits were known as strong, some as weak. The evaluations were of limited significance since a spirit, no matter how strong, could not function outside its proper realm. Hawk was a strong spirit; it could remove an intrusive object but it was of no special value in diagnosis. Frog, a strong spirit, was powerless to remove illness caused by Weasel, a weak spirit. The latter's weakness was in curing; in causing illness it was highly effective. As might be anticipated, there was a high correlation between strong spirits and those extensively utilized.

A dangerous category was recognized, including all those spirits that were most frequently responsible for illness. Frog was classified here as well as among the strong; Weasel, here as well as among the weak. The ghost spirit was characterized as powerful, dangerous, and malevolent. It was principally responsible for the shaman's frequent and characteristic bleeding from the mouth. Its realm of action was broader than that of any other spirit. Although associated with death it was capable above all others of curing the apparently fatally ill patient. No malevolent category was segregated: "All spirits are mean but some are worse than others."

Of major importance were the differences in power among the various spirits of a single species. For example, nearly all shamans possessed Rattlesnake familiars. But each of these was individually distinct from every other one and no two conferred upon their shamanistic associates exactly the same amount of power with regard to the functions of the Rattlesnake spirit. This factor must constantly be borne in mind since the use of the categorical term—a legitimate translation—for both the individual spirit and the species invites confusion.

It was believed that spirits, with respect to themselves alone, were peaceful; that they bore no enmities and sought no revenge. Only contact and association with man brought them into conflict. This concept did not accord with the belief that the shaman was but a tool of the spirits, but the conflict was not seen, or at least not found troublesome. Although the spirits were not recognized, in theory, as a construct of man, the Modoc did not, in fact, recognize any spiritual activity or incident in which man was not involved. One spirit might abduct another, either of its own species or of a different group. This was sometimes at the instigation of the shaman; upon other occasions he was "ignorant" of the act un-

til informed by his spirit. The theft could not have occurred except
in service of the shaman. When a shaman became ill because one
of his spirits was dissatisfied with his actions, others often remained loyal and contested with the complainant. Spirits were
pitted against one another when one shaman attempted to remove
from a patient an intrusive object which had been put there by another shaman, those of the guilty shaman vying with those of the
treating shaman.

Various types of illness have been mentioned in connection with
the descriptions of spirits and shamans. But other categories remain and an all-inclusive analysis is now in order.

The two broadest classifications were the supernatural and the
natural, in terms of causation. All illnesses of supernatural origin were amenable to shamanistic treatment. In addition, some
natural illnesses called for like attention. A logical inconsistency
here is obvious, since a shaman's powers were wholly supernatural in character. In terms of curing procedure, however, the conflict is less apparent since, as will be seen below, the symptoms
of the natural diseases subject to shamanistic ministration were
similar to those of the supernatural category.

The supernatural were further subdivided into the spiritual and
the nonspiritual. So far as the layman was concerned, one might
say "intrusive object illnesses" in contrast to all others, since
the only form of spirit-caused illness was that involving an intruded object. However, the very important distinction between
diseases volitionally caused and those otherwise incurred would
then be lost. Further, the special case of the shaman would be
neglected; he was subject to other illnesses of spiritual origin.
These were spirit alienation and spirit loss. Obviously the layman was not subject to the latter since he possessed no spirits.

Most important of the nonspiritual illnesses were those caused
by the breaking of taboos: puberty, menstrual, death, and the like.
So-called taboos respecting the behavior of individuals, in the presence of the shaman, for example, belong in the earlier category.
Breaking of these led to retaliation by the spirits of the shaman.
In the case of violation of a true taboo, illness resulted automatically; the agency was not personal or spiritual.

The remaining nonspiritual illnesses were those caused by fright,
and by soul loss. Fright might accompany experiences involving
spirits and resulting in spiritually caused illness. But illness resulting exclusively from fearsome circumstances is the type here
involved. The concept of soul loss was known but played a distinctly
minor role.

No other causes of supernatural illnesses were recognized. Some of those mentioned merit fuller description. Intrusive-object illness resulted when a shaman effected the intrusion through one of his spirits, or when a spirit did so of its own accord. In the latter case the shaman remained ignorant of the fact until informed by the spirit in a dream, or when the offense was discovered by another doctor while treating the injured person. A shaman initiated an intrusion for one of several quite definite reasons: because he bore an enmity toward the victim, or toward the victim's parents; because he had been hired by another person to do so; or because he hoped to collect a fee from the victim for removing the illness. The enmity mentioned might have resulted from any of the numerous situations which breed that emotion, but one in particular must be singled out, not because of its importance but for its distinctive character. This was the custom mentioned above, of protecting the doctor and his spirits, in any social gathering, by a wall of restrictions regarding his person. The transgression of any of these led to use by the offended doctor of his power to cause intrusion.

An adult knew the rules with respect to the shaman and could therefore protect himself fairly well. But this was not true with reference to illness caused directly by spirits. Ordinarily spirits were invisible to the layman but occasionally one would be seen in the form of a quite ordinary object, for example, a fish lazily swimming in a pool or a rabbit crouched in the grass. Illness resulted even though the observer were wholly unaware of the anomalous identity. Usually, however, some obscure cue was given by the spirit, causing the person to worry about the experience. The appearances and actions of the spirits were wholly capricious, a trait quite characteristic of them. Certain related experiences with spirits differed in that man was better able to insure himself against injury because the situation was traditionally known to be fraught with danger. For instance, it was always safest to avoid a whirlwind as far as possible, since some of these were manifestations of the whirlwind spirit. Also, a person who drank directly from a pool was inviting illness from the Frog spirit associated with the pool. Immunity was insured by drinking water from the cupped hands. To see a ghost or to hear the rattling of its bones was perhaps the most threatening and dangerous of all these experiences. Although each ghost was individual in character, the collective singular was used in speaking of them and the concept was that of a genus or type. The ghost traveled only at night. Fear of it was so great, especially among children, but including many adults, that to leave the house after dark was a traumatic experience. It was described in various ways by those who had had the unfortunate experience of seeing it, but always the rustle of bones and the cry "sqo--qs" was heard. Specific descriptions included: a "bone"; a skeleton; a skeleton with a hump on the back and a bundle at the side. An elaborate description came from two skeptics who boasted that they were not afraid of the ghost and were going in search of it. A friend reluctantly accompanied them. It should be noted that the account was given by him. "We started out on horseback in the afternoon. Jeff carried a revolver, Ned a hunting knife. I was unarmed. Toward evening we saw a blazing fire as high as a mountain and colored blue-green and white. We could see the ghost squatting by the fire with his scrotum touching the ground. Jeff thought he saw two men at the fire. Suddenly the flame began to move across nearby Tule Lake. A strong whirlwind came up. Something grasped for Ned's foot; Jeff was lifted in the air from his saddle. The horses shied and refused to move. Jeff tried to shoot but his gun had jammed. Ned found that his knife was bent double. We gave the horses free rein and they raced toward home. I discovered that my hat had been seized by the ghost. When we reached home we noticed a spotted hand. Jeff said it had tried to seize his saddle. Jeff's mother died that evening. When we reached Jeff's house we found a group of shamans there. They already knew what had happened. The next morning I returned to the scene and found that the field had been all ploughed up. Jeff and Ned were sick for a week."

As implied in the preceding descriptions, the intrusion of the foreign object sometimes occurred in the course of a momentary glance, or via the auditory organs upon hearing a certain sound. More often entrance was through the mouth in the course of drinking or eating that which normally would be harmless. The extensive emphasis upon the Frog in curing was because of that spirit's ability to analyze seemingly harmless foods that had been eaten. The nasal apertures were not considered possible routes of entry. Where a shaman was the instigator, two steps in the intrusion were involved: his overt action and the subsequent entry, sometimes at a much later date. Regardless of the selected mode of entry, the shaman needed only a momentary glance at the victim for his part. This means, of course, that this slight cue was all that his spirits needed. Since the spirits knew the shaman's thoughts and emotions they sometimes appeared in a dream and questioned him. One might ask "What do you think? What shall I do? Shall I go down there and kill that person?" If the shaman indicated his approval the spirit effected the illness. A shaman could not injure one unknown to him; the range of his spirits' acquaintance was identical with his own.

The shaman was theoretically subject to intrusive-object illness, but in practice this seldom occurred. He was less susceptible to the capriciousness of spirits than the layman and of course the layman could not attack him by intrusion. Sometimes in swallowing the object removed from a patient during a curing treatment the shaman became ill and required the services of another shaman. This occurred if the spirit whose role it was to take the object from the shaman's larynx failed in the task.

Illness from spirit alienation or spirit loss was the shaman's really serious personal concern. Alienation occurred when a spirit was offended because the shaman was neglecting its services in his practice, that is, showing favoritism among his many spirits, or when the spirit or spirits disapproved of the invoker or spokesman or their procedures, or when the doctor was considered by them to be incompetent or careless in his techniques. (The diagnosis was made by another shaman, of course.) Upon such occasions all of the sufferer's spirits were called together by him; they discussed the difficulty and devised a solution. They might exact from the doctor a promise to reform or, at the opposite extreme, acceptance of the death of one of his children.

Actual loss of a spirit led invariably to the shaman's death. When one shaman sought to harm another it was almost invariably an attempt to steal one of the other's spirits; that is, to lead his spirits to abduct one of his rival's. When successful the victim became seriously ill even though ignorant of the circumstances. He remained ill until the discovery of his loss, as revealed by a colleague's diagnosis, whereupon he died. There was nothing that the victim or the diagnostician could do to avoid the death. Even the death of the guilty shaman would not restore the lost spirit and the patient's health. To call upon the offending shaman for help would be equivalent to clutching for a straw. He would surely refuse; furthermore, he would find himself unable to help if his spirits refused to give up the captive, as they usually did.

The abduction was conceived as a physical act of carrying away and secreting the stolen spirit, effected by the rival spirits acting as a group. Two or three spirits remained to guard the captive until the death of the shaman. Because concerted action was necessary to success, the shaman with few spirits was incapable of using them in this manner. Efforts frequently failed. The proposed victim sometimes eluded its pursuers and hid in a safe place until rescued by other spirits of the same shaman. The latter learned of the circumstances in a dream and sang to bring all his spirits together.

Successful abductions were also limited in number because spirits were ordinarily well hidden from one another. Had they been easy to find "no doctor would have lived many days." Abducted spirits were called "slaves," and called themselves by the same term. The "slave" spirit was added to the doctor's retinue after the death of its former possessor. Henceforth it was used as any other spirit might be; it was no more or less powerful than before.

Most nonspiritual illnesses resulted from broken taboos. These breaches resulted in internal ailments that sometimes appeared years after the transgression. The symptoms were usually vague, requiring a shaman's diagnosis. The latter sometimes explained that a morbid growth had developed within the body. This was usually localized in the chest and conceived as a grapelike growth. Superficial symptoms were those of influenza or tuberculosis. The spirit used in treatment broke up the growth and the doctor sucked it out. The eating of tabooed food, such as meat from animals killed by an eagle, caused a bilelike accumulation in the stomach which was removed by sucking. The symptoms in this case were dizziness and delirium. After the removal of the accumulation the doctor gave the patient a bit of eagle flesh to eat. One might eat such food without ill effect if it were first whirled about the head in a counterclockwise direction. Fright sometimes led to conditions of general functional disturbance, apathy, or mental illness. Sucking treatment was used, with removal of foreign fluids.

Dreams did not cause illness, except through fright or in infants, as described later. A dream in which a shaman appeared presaged an illness caused by that shaman but not by the dream.

Natural illnesses included body injuries such as wounds and broken bones, the common cold, the common headache, indigestion from obvious causes, and many other specific types of minor ailments. For some of these household remedies alone were used; for others a shaman was called if the illness were prolonged or acute. Two distinct concepts were involved in the treatment of natural illnesses by a shaman. First, what appeared to be an accident might have been caused by a spirit. For example, a bone lodged in the throat was usually the result of carelessness in swallowing, but if coughing and swallowing did not serve to remove it, spirit causation was feared and a shaman's services were sought. In the second category were ailments such as an arrow point imbedded in the flesh or the reactions to natural poisons. No spirit

or shaman was suspected as responsible, but a shaman was called
because by sucking he could remove the foreign matter.

All requests for shamanistic treatment were made through the
shaman's invoker. An adult member of the sick person's family
went to the invoker, who served for all the local shamans, and
explained the circumstances. Sometimes a specific shaman was
named; at other times the invoker's advice was sought. The invoker conveyed the message to the shaman's spokesman but waited
until evening to summon the shaman, since treatments were restricted to the hours of darkness. An exception was made only
in the most critical cases; even so, darkness in the house was
achieved by closing all outside apertures and extinguishing the
fire.

The invoker visited the shaman's house alone. He stopped outside or stood on the roof to perform the first act of the curing
ritual. Raising his right hand palm downward to his forehead in a
formal gesture, he called loudly in a ritual monotone, summoning
the shaman's spirits. A traditional formula was used. Facing first
north, then, in turn, east, south, and west, and finally looking
down to the earth and up to the sky, he implored the spirits from
these various directions to gather. He spoke of the illness of the
patient and the urgent need of spiritual assistance. Each invoker
developed his own wording, varying the details to fit the particular case. Only the outline content and method of presentation
were fixed. Two fragmentary examples, freely translated, follow:
"Come to the ill, birds of the sky; make ready your powers, birds
of the sky; make ready your powers, lower ones . . .; make ready
to fight with death to lose or win. . . ." "Hear us, spirits that live
in the north; you too, pray, in the east; hear us where you live; you
too, pray, in the south . . .; you who live in the west . . .; you
too, pray, in the sky, you that fly. . . ." Upon concluding, the
invoker entered the shaman's house and explained his mission.
Apparently the shaman never refused to accept the case, at least
after the spirits had been summoned. It seems probable that the
invoker would have consulted the doctor before the summoning had
there been any doubt of his reaction. The shaman gathered his
meager paraphernalia. Most important was his professional cap.
This was a skullcap of buckskin, perforated in a regular pattern
and adorned with woodpecker feathers, clustered at the top and
pendent from the rim. Usually the buckskin was painted red. He
might also take some of the small objects symbolic of his spirits;
this was optional. He then proceeded to the patient's home. The

invoker accompanied the shaman or preceded him. The spokesman was expected to be present at the time of the shaman's arrival; likewise the imitators if the shaman had ordered their presence. The functionaries just mentioned were the same as those serving at the inaugural ceremony and their duties were of the same character. Exigencies sometimes forced the shaman to dispense with the services of the imitators. They were essential only if demanded by the spirits. Substitute imitators might be chosen from the audience but untrained men were apt to make errors. Women never served as assistants to the shaman, even though the latter were a woman.

Spectators were numerous. As soon as word spread that a shaman had been called, relatives and friends began to drift in. They came to observe the ritual but their presence was necessary to the procedure. They formed the chorus and carried out numerous odd chores for the doctor. If children were present they were permitted to sing with the adults but had to be careful in their actions not to offend the shaman.

When the shaman entered the patient's house he looked in the direction of the patient but his glance was directed upward. Hanging from the beams above the bed were the goods offered for his services. Bulky or animate offerings were symbolically indicated; a rawhide thong, for example, designated a horse. The shaman evaluated the goods and determined, but did not specify, the amount of service that he would give in return. If he considered the fee a meager one, he would treat the patient for but half the night. If the payment were especially generous, two entire nights would be devoted to the cure. The amount offered had been decided upon by the family of the patient as the result of considerable discussion. Three variables were involved: the seriousness of the illness, the goods available, and the reputation of the shaman. Perhaps it was sometimes realized that a large payment would mean a slower diagnosis and protracted treatment, regardless of the character of the illness. There was no discussion of the fee between the family and the shaman, to say nothing of haggling. The doctor accepted whatever was offered without a word. It must be added that he received his fee whether the patient was cured or not. Instructive, too, is the folk observation that rich men offered small fees because they disliked to part with their wealth, while poor men paid liberally because they wanted the patient to become well. A bag of camas, or a few beads was a very small fee; a horse or slave, a large fee; more than this was considered handsome payment. The spokesman and invoker were paid small sums by the family, but these were not designated. The patient lay with his head toward the wall but not toward the west for this was the direction of the land of the dead. The spokesman stood near the patient's head, his back to the wall. The shaman seated himself at the foot of the bed facing the spokesman. The invoker stood on the opposite side of the room with the audience ranged between him and the wall. The imitators stood with the audience nearest the spokesman. Sometimes a semiformal chorus of a few women, noted for their singing, stood in front of the other spectators. Everyone present assisted the shaman in his songs but these women led the chorus.

Three steps were involved in the ritual: the shaman's preparatory acts; the diagnostic procedure; and the curing procedure. The first period was brief. The shaman lighted his pipe and smoked in a manner which had been dictated by his spirits. He sat motionless as he smoked, or performed certain acts, according to his custom. He might blow smoke upon his hands, or direct puffs toward the patient's body. The latter procedure was purely ritualistic; it did not affect the illness. The parts of the body toward which the smoke was blown and the number of puffs varied from doctor to doctor. The head and feet were usually included. The pipe was put aside and the doctor turned to the patient. He laid his hands upon various parts of the body to ease, but not to cure, the pain. The patient was thus relaxed so that diagnosis might proceed smoothly. Sometimes an aspersion was used for this purpose. The water was taken from a basket which had been provided meanwhile. No words were exchanged between the patient and the shaman. No questions regarding the illness were asked; no information was volunteered. The silence and pantomime were broken as the doctor covered his eyes with his hands and directed a few words to his spirits. His muttered remarks were repeated in a loud clear voice by the spokesman. The shaman had indicated that he was now ready to serve the spirits in their attack upon the illness.

The second phase of the ritual, the diagnosis, began with the summoning of the spirits, one by one, to the bedside. The doctor accomplished this by singing the appropriate song for each. The spirits were hovering nearby as the result of the invoker's earlier prayer. From the many the shaman chose those he felt would be most useful in diagnosis. As mentioned earlier, the selection and sequence came to be somewhat stereotyped. Those not called remained in the background as a sort of guard to protect the spirits being used and the shaman against attack by spirits associated with unfriendly doctors. Spirits were particularly vulnerable to abduction while engaged in treatment of the ill. "They were too busy to be cautious." Most important in this service, and certain to be present, was the ghost spirit.

The first spirit to be called gained no precedence, but was thus honored as a strong spirit. Frog was perhaps the most frequent choice for initial call. The logic of the selection was this: most illnesses are caused by an intrusive object; food is the commonest means of entry; and Frog is a keen analyst of foods. Or if Lightning were chosen: the task is to find the source and nature of this illness; the possibilities are many but Lightning makes even the night as bright as day and spreads everywhere; surely Lightning can help. Comparable reasoning was used in selection of the score or so of spirits assembled for the diagnosis. The opinion already formed by the doctor regarding the character of the illness led to choices that would not have been made otherwise.

The summoning of each spirit dramatically correlated the activities of all persons present. The shaman sang the brief verse of a song; as he repeated the audience joined him. As the song was continued the invoker oratorically entreated the spirit to obey the summons. Soon the shaman allowed the chorus to continue without him, as he became the voice of the newly arrived spirit. The spokesman carried the shaman's words to the audience. When the spirit finished speaking the doctor clapped his hands and the chorus ceased singing. (Sometimes he gave a like signal before the end of a song to indicate dissatisfaction with the performance of the singers.) With each new song the sequence was repeated. The invoker's prayer was similar to that uttered earlier but now directed to the particular spirit whose song the doctor was singing. For example: "Now, you in the north, Frog; your talent is to make people well; you never fail; you always make well those who are ill; come now, see this man; find out what is wrong; examine him so that he may become well. Now I call upon you!" The doctor shaded his eyes with his hand and peered in the direction from which the spirit was expected to come. The invoker discussed the probability of response to the call and spoke of the distance to be traveled. (If this were incompatible with presumed earlier gathering of the spirits, the Modoc were either unaware of it or unconcerned.) Once the spirit had accepted the call, the invoker kept the audience informed of progress to the destination. Its arrival was made known by a call, symbolic of the spirit, uttered by the invoker. The imitators picked up the call and repeated it five times. If these functionaries were not present, the shaman himself repeated the sound. The spirit spoke briefly: the audience heard the voices of the shaman and the spokesman. The following is an example: "I am ready; I give water in the pool; give him drink." The spirit occupied a particular position in the room and remained there until called upon to take an active part in the ritual. The spirits were invisible to the audience. The shaman was capable of seeing them by concentrating upon the task, but for the most part he was content with merely auditory reminders of their presence.

When all the selected spirits were assembled the second or active phase of diagnosis ensued. The earlier orderliness of the affair gave way to a confusion of voices as the spirits discussed and argued with one another as to the cause of the illness, the identities of the guilty spirit and the implicated shaman, and the proper and most effective procedure to follow. The invoker added to the confusion by urging the spirits to exert their best efforts, and by hazarding guesses as to the unknown factors. The shaman and spokesman were hard pressed in their vocal services to the various spirits. The shaman did not speak an esoteric language; his voice was clearly audible. But his phrasings were meaningless to the audience for two reasons: the phrasings were symbolic, and he omitted articles, connectives, and adjectives. The spokesman's interpretations supplied the missing words; his remarks sounded like everyday speech. But the symbolism was maintained and phrases which were individually meaningful were joined to form sentences which were quite meaningless. The auditors knew that they could not understand the shaman. They thought they understood the spokesman, but they did not long remember what he said. The shaman followed no set formula; his remarks differed considerably from seance to seance. But the general source of all his recitals as indicated above, was the discussions held by the spirits. Each spirit offered an interpretation of the illness. Some were in agreement, some differed. The differences were eventually resolved and the diagnosis complete. Upon occasions when agreement appeared impossible, the ghost spirit was called. This was a hazardous procedure because of this spirit's representation of death, but there was no choice since the patient would die if a diagnosis could not be made. The ghost spirit's interpretation was accepted as valid without question, even though it ran counter to that favored by a majority of the other spirits. During the active diagnosis the chorus was called upon from time to time to sing the song of the spirit speaking, or leading the discussion, at the time.

Several hours were consumed by the diagnosis; sometimes the entire night. Upon conclusion a recess was declared and the shaman either rested and smoked his pipe or went home to resume the following evening. Often he declared at this point that he could do nothing more for the patient, and his services were terminated. Such declaration resulted from the offering of an inadequate fee or complete failure in the diagnosis. But more often the break was indication that the shaman, having ascertained the identities of the sorcerer and his spirit, was unwilling to attempt a cure because of probable failure or the danger involved.

Great was the fear of a shaman of retaliation by the spirit of the sorcerer. Even a strong and famous shaman hesitated to engage in conflict with the spirit of a less powerful colleague, since the strength of the spirit, rather than that of the other shaman, was the critical consideration. He could never be sure that his own spirits, however numerous, would be certain to bring him victory. The spiritual complement did not act as a group but selected one member to attack the adversary. Consequently, defeat was always possible and retaliation by the victor certain. Hence the usual procedure upon discovery that a patient's illness was the result of action by another doctor was to make the fact known and retire from active participation in the treatment. Indeed, it was commonly said that the only doctor who could cure an illness was the one who had caused it. However, the diagnostician often remained as an observer to make certain that his successor proceeded in an ethical manner with the treatment.

The new practitioner was called in the usual manner, the invoker being sent to solicit his services. If he refused to come, which was not uncommon, close relatives of the patient called upon him and begged his aid. The first shaman sometimes added the weight of his entreaties, or if necessary, threats. The doctor whose services were sought knew that these threats were not idle ones, since causing illness did not entail the dangers that did the treatment of illnesses caused by another. Ordinarily threats were not necessary since no stigma attached to the doctor responsible for the illness. It is true that he might intentionally have caused the disease, through malice or for gain. Doctors often visited illness upon their enemies, or for a fee caused their spirits to attack any person designated. Also, those whose property was coveted might be made ill so that the property might be collected as a fee. But regardless of the actual history of the case, the shaman could always say that his spirits had caused the illness entirely without his knowledge or approval. This explanation, cul-

turally valid in some instances, made it possible for the shaman
to appear unabashed before the patient, and, if the fee offered was
satisfactory, to proceed with the treatment. Refusal to treat a patient occurred when the shaman considered the condition hopelessly
fatal, if he felt that his reputation would be damaged irreparably
by the death. He did not so decide, however, without realizing that
the relatives of the patient might seek revenge for the death, which
they would interpret as resulting from the doctor's refusal.

The treatment was identical, whether performed by the diagnostician or the guilty shaman. Sucking was the only technique used;
the only theory was that of an intruded object or matter. All in-
trusions were caused directly or indirectly by spirits, but the latter never entered the body.

In preparation for the sucking the audience and assistants disposed themselves about the room in the same manner as during
the diagnosis. The shaman knelt beside the patient who lay naked
except for a robe covering. Nearby were placed two baskets, one
containing water. Before active treatment the shaman sometimes
smoked his pipe in silence. Then instructions were given to the
audience. The spirits which were to effect the cure had made themselves known to the doctor who specified the proper songs and the
order in which they were to be sung. This was necessary since
the intensity of his activity and reactions during the treatment
sometimes made it impossible for him to speak. Complete loss
of control of muscular reactions was common upon final sucking out
of the intrusive object. In anticipation of this a volunteer was sought
from the audience to stand behind him and grasp his shoulders when
this occurred. Any strong man could serve in this capacity.

With all in readiness the shaman dipped his index and middle
fingers alternately into the basket of water and into his mouth several times. This prepared his mouth for sucking. He then started
a song but soon placed his mouth on the patient's body and began
to suck while the audience continued singing. The lips were placed
against the skin and the sucking was accompanied by explosive
sounds. Sometimes biting was resorted to but care was taken not
to break the skin. Areas commonly selected for sucking included
the temples, the top of the head and various areas on the upper
torso, but not the limbs. Sucking at one spot continued for about
a minute, then the process was repeated at another point. The object was to suck in the locale of the object to be withdrawn but
some exploration was necessary and sometimes several objects
had to be removed. Details of the procedure were determined by
the spirits; the doctor was merely their agent. Each spirit acted

individually while his song was being sung; the order had been determined by the group as a whole. Inactive spirits stood by, observing the progress of the treatment and making suggestions through the spokesman. The invoker urged the performing spirit to exert his best efforts and called upon the others to be on the alert against the spirits of other shamans that might well choose this time to abduct one of them, particularly the one performing the treatment since under such circumstances he was unable to protect himself. Meanwhile the audience shifted from song to song as the leaders sensed the proper moment for a change. Experienced as they were they knew when the actions of the shaman called for a transition. All of the spirits performing were noted for sucking ability or tenacity, such as Pelican, Buzzard, Fish Hawk, Eagle, and Coyote. But some were especially proficient in the earlier stages, others at later stages in the sucking process.

The intensity of the shaman's actions and reactions increased as the treatment proceeded. His breathing became labored, and choking and gasping occurred. He might suddenly turn to the empty basket and discharge from his mouth a quantity of blood. If this were done the spectators knew that success was near. The final song of the series, that of the spirit which was to effect the actual removal, was begun. Often this was Pelican. At the critical moment the doctor raised his head slowly from the patient's body. When twelve or eighteen inches away, his head was thrown back with a violent jerk and he fell backward as though pushed with great force. The intrusive object had been removed. The assistant was ready to grasp his head and shoulders and help him gain control of himself. Often the doctor indicated to the spokesman that aid was needed to keep the object from escaping from his throat, whereupon the spokesman thrust his finger in the doctor's mouth. Sometimes this was done during the period of slow removal of the shaman's mouth from the patient's body. After a few moments, with the completion of the song, the doctor regained control of himself and the assistant stepped aside. The shaman held the back of his right hand over his mouth and uttered a gurgling sound. Relief was felt by the patient immediately. He knew the doctor had actually removed the object because at the critical moment he had felt a sharp pain, sometimes described as a biting sensation.

Before removing the object the shaman sometimes invited guesses from the spectators as to its character. Various guesses were made, not in terms of the physical form of the object only, but with reference to its symbolical significance, the identity of the offending spirit. It augured well for the rapid recovery of the pa-

tient if the correct guess were made. Identifications were erroneous if the doctor remained silent upon hearing the suggestion.
Some shamans permitted the guessers to place their fingers in his
mouth to feel the object. At other times the guessing was not called
for at all, or not until the object had been removed and shown to
the audience. The thumb and forefinger were used to extract the object; it was placed in the palm of the left hand and the fingers closed
over it. Even now there was some danger of its escape. When
spectators were allowed to examine the object they peered through
the doctor's slightly opened fingers. Hundreds of distinctive forms
were possible, ranging from bits of animal skin or fur, bird feathers, hair, claws, and other organic matter, to stonelike material.
The most distinctive of the latter was a sliver of yellowish quartzlike stone which was typically associated with diseases localized in
the chest. This was perhaps the most oft occurring specific object.
It was not associated with any particular spirit. Although certain
objects were indicative of specific spirits, many others were common to all.

Sometimes the object was not shown to the spectators at all. The
excuse for this was that the spirit in question was jealous of his
prerogatives and methods, and demanded secrecy. Or it was said
that the object was too dangerous to be shown, it might possibly
escape and cause illness to someone present. In such cases the
doctor removed the object as indicated but immediately returned
it to his mouth and swallowed it. It will be recognized, of course,
that this secrecy, or, alternatively, examination of the object
through the doctor's partially opened fingers, fully insured the
shaman against failure or inadequacy of his techniques.

The objects were invariably disposed of by swallowing, burying,
or, rarely, burning. Breaking or cutting was never resorted to,
nor was the object ever used for retaliation. Burial was a satisfactory method of rendering harmless an object which had been
shown to the audience. Otherwise swallowing was employed. Burial
was commonly outside the house; if performed in the house the spot
chosen was at the edge of the fireplace. (In either case it would
have been difficult to disinter the object.) When swallowed, the
object was returned to the mouth directly, or put in the basket of
water which was then drunk. In this case the shaman had "eaten
the spirit," to use a literal but highly misleading translation. As
earlier indicated, the native term for spirit *(swi̇́is)* means song, as
well as spirit. Thus an equally literal translation would be, he has
"eaten the song." By extension of the concept, the phrase meant,
in this instance, he has "eaten the object sent by the supernatural

power spirit-song." But even this is not the whole explanation. As the swallowing took place a song of a scavenger was sung, perhaps Crow. The scavenger spirit was waiting to grasp the object before it reached the shaman's stomach. The spirit was not inside the shaman; its supernatural power made it unnecessary to be so located in order to perform the feat. Thus the spirit was not in any sense or at any time intrusive. The intrusive-spirit concept, clearly defined elsewhere, was unknown here.

The treatment was not yet concluded. Sometimes two or three objects were removed, involving repetition of the whole procedure described above. But in any event, it was customary to suck further at the point where the object had been extracted in order to remove the contaminating matter associated with the object. The matter thus removed was described as a thick, green, bilelike fluid. It was deposited in the basket provided, wherein the blood had earlier been placed, later to be washed into a hole and buried. Meanwhile the appropriate songs were sung, those identified with the spirits performing this part of the cure.

Finally the shaman indicated his prognosis to the audience and the patient. Immediate recovery was seldom promised. The identity of the offending shaman was discussed with the patient. The latter always agreed with the shaman in his interpretation. Sometimes this was because the ill person had had a dream in which the guilty shaman had appeared—information which the treating shaman had appropriated by indirection. At other times the patient agreed merely because he had been convinced during the curing procedure. Before departing, the shaman sometimes called for certain food to be given to the patient. The latter was instructed to take five bites. While eating, the spirits, through the shaman and spokesman, discussed the probable reactions to the food, and gave advice for succeeding meals.

The audience dispersed and the doctor departed, not, however, without collecting his fee. He did not need to wait to determine the outcome of the case since the fee was due without regard to the patient's recovery.

The description above refers to the treatment of illnesses where the diagnosis indicated that a shaman was responsible, and consequently an intrusive object was involved. By far the commonest diagnosis, this was not however the only possibility. Two further categories amenable to shamanistic sucking were illness resulting from the breaking of personal taboos and those caused by natural poisons. In both instances the procedure duplicated the above except for the aspects of the intrusive object. Only blood and the bilelike matter were removed; these alone were responsible for the illness.

A spurious similarity to the intrusive-object case was characteristic of the treatment of arrow or bullet wounds. The arrowhead or bullet, ostensibly removed, was treated exactly as was the spiritually intruded object. In all these cases the diagnostician also performed the treatment since there was no guilty shaman to ferret out.

In either type of case, however, the patient's family might call several doctors in succession to perform independent diagnoses in order to avoid any possible error. Shamans did not resent such checking of their findings; they received their fees regardless. Indeed a doctor sometimes discarded his diagnosis in the light of a colleague's differing interpretation. The shaman performing the earlier diagnosis sometimes remained to observe his colleague's work and hear his findings, but never worked together with him. Of his own accord a doctor sometimes called another to take over the case. Then the payment was made to the original shaman who in turn paid the substitute.

In English the word "pain" is occasionally used to designate a crystal-like intrusive object mentioned above. The word further implies a pleurisylike ailment. The disposal of this kind of intrusive object differed, at least at the hands of some doctors, from the procedure used for other objects. The crystalline slivers were removed in pairs; the doctor appeared to thrust one into his forehead above each eyebrow. When doing so he declared that these would enter and kill anyone who tried to murder him. This minor complex, poorly integrated in Modoc shamanism, was obviously borrowed from tribes to the south.

The treatment of children differed somewhat from that of adults. Diagnosis was similar but in the sucking the mouth was held a slight distance away from the skin. Since a shaman's enmity toward a man often led to the selection of the latter's child as a victim for sorcery, the doctor who refused to treat a child was at once a suspect. If he persisted in his refusal and the child died, the father was almost certain to seek the doctor's life.

A treatment for infants, highly specialized in character and bristling with innovations, is reputed to have been the invention of a particular shaman three or four generations ago (Dr. Charley, *tokta ʾmts*). The treatment was designated by a phrase which means "to take away the illness caused by a parent's dream." Some shamans adopted the procedure as soon as they learned of it; other contemporaries shunned it. But it flourished in varied forms until the breakdown of Modoc shamanism.

Variable features included the use or neglect of the traditional invoker and spokesman, the conduct of the ritual at either the patient's or the doctor's house, and the degree of emphasis upon specialized songs and spirits.

Diagnosis was relatively unimportant since illnesses of the type were limited to infants of a few months of age and were marked by constant crying. Such ailments reputedly baffled shamans prior to Dr. Charley's discovery. He declared that the child was suffering from an irritation of the heart caused by that organ being linked by an invisible cord to an object in a supernatural world, "the twilight land." This object was a black sphere of the size of an eye and possessed of the winking characteristic of that organ. Each time the object winked a tug on the cord, and consequently on the infant's heart, occurred, greatly to the irritation of the child.

The condition was invariably attributed to a dream of the father or mother, particularly the latter. The special type was a crisis-type dream occurring to the mother during the five days following the child's birth. But by extension it included other nightmarelike dreams of either parent. The dream was one experienced but un-remembered. The relating of the apparently supernatural dreams and the supernatural twilight land was undoubtedly suggested by the infant's very recent appearance from a supernatural world, the crying indicating an emotional attachment to that land, not yet broken, and the cord symbolizing this attachment.

The doctor's task was to capture the offending object and to break the cord. Since the object was obviously not within the patient, the sucking technique was useless. A new procedure was employed for obtaining the object but in other respects the treatment was that customary for intrusive objects. While the audience assembled the doctor sat quietly with the palms of his hands covering his eyes and face. When everyone was present a cord was passed from hand to hand until it extended around the room. The ends were fastened at either side of the doorway. During the treatment each spectator held the cord grasped in his right hand. Many songs, or few, were sung; the length of the ritual varied accordingly. Two were critical and necessarily included: the Dog and the Frog songs. This means, of course, that the Dog and Frog spirits were present and active in the cure.

Replacing sucking as the mode of attack was a journey to the twilight land by the Dog, where he ferreted out the evil object and

proceeded to pursue it to the house where the ritual was being conducted. The progress of the journey and incidents occurring en
route were described to the audience by the spokesman or shaman,
as the case might be, and symbolized by dramatic actions. All the
while the Dog song was being sung; at the end of each phrase the
shaman barked loudly. Facing west, he danced in place: his arms,
bent at the elbows, were upraised; his feet were lifted alternately.
The spectators squatted rather than sat so that the Dog would have
free space in which to run when he arrived and so that there would
be no niche in which the pursued object might hide. As the spirit
drew closer the shaman danced faster and faster and began to shout
instructions: "Look out! Here he comes! He's here now; watch out!
He's under your feet. Don't sit down!" Suddenly the doctor seized
the object, as if from the air, by clasping his outstretched palms
together. At the same instant the spectators pulled hard on the
cord and broke it into as many pieces as possible. The object was
thereby permanently disengaged from the infant and the cure was
immediate. The crying ceased, it is said, at the moment the cord
was broken. But the object had yet to be brought under control by
the doctor. Meanwhile he was running about the room, bumping
into one person and another, as the object blindly carried him forward. Control was gained after a time, aided sometimes by plung-
ing the object into a basket of water. After displaying it to the audience the doctor disposed of it by swallowing. Now the Frog song
was sung because in this instance it was that spirit which effectively swallowed it.

In the meantime several large baskets of cooked water-lily seeds
had been brought into the house. Preparation of this food had been
begun early in the afternoon preceding the ritual. The latter, as
usual, took place after sunset. During the Frog song the doctor
pushed the baskets with his foot, a gesture which implied that he
was calling for Frog's judgment of the food. "Yes, that food is all
right," the audience heard the spirit say, through the agency of the
spokesman or shaman. Whereupon everyone, including the doctor,
feasted on the seeds and thus concluded the ritual. The doctor then
received his fee and departed.

The serving of water-lily seeds was a marked departure from
traditional curing practice, where no food of any kind was allowed.
Another distinction was the shaman's omission of any special regalia, paraphernalia, or facial paint. Variable aspects, in addition to those mentioned above, included the order of the songs and
the postures assumed by the doctor. The Frog song, for example,
was sung first, or last, or both at the beginning and at the end of

the treatment. Sometimes the shaman started the singing while
lying quietly on his back, later to rise and start dancing.
An intriguing innovation was the use of inverted speech. When
the food was served the shaman first ate a bit, then began a song
during which the spectators joined in the feast. The spirits said,
"I do not watch you eat," but the meaning was the opposite, "I am
watching you eat."

Shamans occasionally attempted to control the weather, particularly to bring mild weather and rain to end a protracted cold spell.
The shaman called his spirits in the evening and sang at length as
in the diagnostic portion of a curing ritual. Guests were present
and food was served. This was done when someone hired him for
the task, as might a cattle owner, in recent times, whose herd
was suffering. Likewise, cold or unusual weather could be brought.
During the Modoc War a shaman smoked his pipe and called his
spirits. Then he ran wildly about the camp with blood coming from
his mouth. Soon a heavy fog settled over the lava beds and lasted
for many days, protecting the Modoc against the nearby troops.

Shamans claimed little clairvoyant ability but by using the Dog
spirit they were sometimes able to find lost or stolen objects and
people. After starting the song the doctor was led by the spirit on
a physical journey to the location of that which was sought.

The acquisition of pseudoshamanistic power leading to dream
doctoring has been mentioned earlier. It remains to describe the
practices involved. The essential distinction between shamanistic
treatment and dream doctoring was that the former used the sucking technique while the latter merely involved the placing of hands
on the patient. Types of illness subject to dream doctoring were
ill-defined, but generally speaking they were minor and nonspecific
in character. Diagnosis was not practiced by the pseudoshaman
and treatment was uniform in character. Consequently the typing
of ailments was not developed. Furthermore, the dream doctor
was an unimportant practitioner. But since there were a good many
persons who claimed such power, and since they charged small
fees or none at all, their services were frequently solicited in the
hope that a shaman would not have to be called.

Parallels with shamanism included the use of spirit songs, with
an assisting chorus, and the occasional use of aspersions. But no
invoker or spokesman was employed nor did the spirits congregate,
and of course no intrusive objects or matter were withdrawn. The
practitioner laid the hands, or sometimes the foot, on the patient
and sang. The repertory was small as compared with that of the
shaman. The performance was brief and the audience was not re-

stricted by shamanistic rules of conduct. Children as well as adults were treated, the former with particular success.

Dream doctors were noted for their clairvoyant powers. They saw in dreams future events concerning both themselves, others, and the tribe as a whole. When one dreamed of a death it would not occur if he took care not to mention it until after the morning meal.

Among the spirits figuring in dream-doctoring songs Ant was the most common. The dream doctor usually assumed a new or additional name based upon his first or most important spirit dream. This was not true of the shaman, and it must be added that dream-doctoring power was in no sense a step toward shamanism.

Skepticism with respect to the powers of shamans was not at all uncommon. In recent years Peter Sconchin, an old Modoc warrior, has been the most notable disbeliever.

ILLUSTRATIVE DATA

"In the ancient times described in myths the doctors really cured people, but now they just fool them. When I was old enough to remember, my father and another chief wanted a doctor to kill a man forty miles away. The doctor agreed. But I know for sure that he didn't kill that man. Even when a doctor tries to kill a man living nearby he always fails. But when someone does die the doctor wants all the credit and claims that he killed the man.

"During the Modoc War the strongest doctor was supposed to be Curly-headed Doctor. He took a long cord and painted it red and put it around the whole camp. He said that the federal soldiers would fall down and die if they touched the string; they would never be able to cross it. The people believed him and danced with him all night, singing all the while.

"A few days later we saw soldiers coming toward our camp. As they came closer we saw that one of the leaders had a sabre. Behind him two other leaders were followed by the troops. As they came close to the string the leaders shouted, 'Mark'; the soldiers dropped to their knees. They shouted 'Fire' and the soldiers shot all around. They then ran over the string. The string did not kill the soldiers; Indian bullets did that. I saw it with my own eyes. After that I didn't believe any more.

"The doctor claims he can make rain. He can make the strongest wind, too. He can make heavy snow. He can stop wind, rain, or snow. My father once asked a doctor to stop a bad storm. The doctor agreed. But with all his singing and dancing for two nights the storm didn't cease. Sometimes a doctor will sing and dance for five nights and still the bad weather continues. The people are disappointed that the doctor can't change the weather. But they try to believe him, and they try again sometime. Even though they know the doctor can't make it rain or snow they still believe in him. If the rain comes in two or three days, the doctor says that he brought it. If the storm stops the doctor says that he did it, and everyone believes him. As far as I can remember a doctor never stopped rain or wind.

"My father, John Sconchin, was an intelligent man. The last time my father believed in doctors was when the soldiers crossed the string. He said, 'This is the last time that we will believe in doctors. We'll ask them no more.' Then my father and the others discussed the many times they had asked doctors to kill other people and it never happened; how many times they called doctors to cure and they didn't cure; and how many times they asked for rain and didn't get it. They spoke of how the doctors always claimed they were responsible when these things did happen. My father and the others were badly disappointed in the doctors.

"But most people still believe."—Peter Sconchin.

"My brother-in-law once offered a woman doctor a team of horses if she would make it rain. She agreed to do it but failed."—Anderson Faithful.

"One very bad winter a man named Jackson, who had 800 head of cattle, came to see my father, Dr. George. The cattle were dying in large numbers. He hired my father to make it rain. Two days and nights of rain were needed to remove the snow. Jackson gave my father ten dollars and told him he would give him more later. My father and all the family sang all night. Dr. George didn't dance or do anything unusual. Then the rain came and the snow melted. Jackson brought flour, meat, sugar, coffee, and money. In the old days food wouldn't have been accepted for payment."—Usee George.

"Jakalunus *(dzaqalu⁀'nuc)* was the greatest, wisest, and most patient of Indian doctors. Once when Warm Springs warriors came to Modoc country and killed a few men this great doctor sent his spirits to combat them. The invaders wondered why their men died without an observable cause.

"Once war broke out with the Snake Paiute. They killed women and children but this doctor's spirits killed all of the Paiutes but two or three who were left to go home with the news.

"I don't know what would have happened to the whites if he had been living then.

"Jakalunus always brushed his hair at noon with a porcupine brush; in that way he knew if anyone was coming. In his house he had strands of small round plaques, several rows of eagle feathers and red-headed woodpecker's feathers, and also stuffed jack rabbits. When anything unusual happened one of these would jump around as if it were alive.

"He had the largest pipe ever seen. After he filled it with tobacco it would light itself. A Klamath doctor wanted to trade for the pipe. He was told that the pipe wouldn't stay with him but he was confident of his ability and the trade was made. When the Modoc man returned home the pipe was there. Later the Klamath doctor called and inquired about it. The Modoc said, 'I gave it to you. What did you do with it?' 'It disappeared.' 'Well, it got to my house before I did. Here it is. You should have listened to me. Even if you held this pipe in your hand it would leave and come to me. My spirits do that.'

"'Why can't it serve me in the same way?' the Klamath inquired. 'I don't know,' the Modoc answered. 'My spirits determine that.'

"A few days later the Klamath shaman died. Jakalunus' spirits had caused it. The Klamath people wanted the Modoc to kill Jakalunus. They offered many furs and blankets.

"An old woman was once buried alive by her children because they didn't want to take care of her any more. Jakalunus immediately went out to dig her up; his spirits had told him about it. While he was busy the Klamath came and filled him full of arrows. He didn't die right away. First he killed many Klamath by snapping his right index finger at each of them. They dropped and died almost immediately. This happened about a hundred years ago."– Jennie Clinton.

"The most powerful of all Modoc doctors was Jakalunus. He had more spirits than any other doctor that ever lived.

"One day he was in a boat on Tule Lake. Other people were around fishing. The doctor took out his stone pipe to smoke but dropped it in the water. The others tried to find it but failed. When the doctor returned home he found his pipe in the usual place. He lifted it and found that it was already lighted. His spirits had done that."– Celia Lynch.

"My mother's father was the great doctor named Jakalunus. He didn't believe the spirits could hurt a white man. A white man is just like a frog, he said, arrows go right through him. Poison goes right through him and never stops. I remember when White

Sandey [the transvestite shaman] tried to kill Brandenburg, the white school superintendent. His spirits failed him."–Anderson Faithful.

"Dr. George, with his wife, went to a town in Pit River country to buy himself a hat. On the return he decided to stop at the home of a Pit River shaman and steal a spirit. When the two met they shook hands, then the Pit River man suddenly seized the new hat, put it on his own head, and walked off. Dr. George lighted his pipe, said, 'Yes, now I'll try you,' and blew smoke toward the man. The latter became ill immediately. A little later a Pit River man came to Dr. George and asked him to attend the stricken shaman. Dr. George refused. When the messenger returned the shaman was dead."–Anderson Faithful.

"Dr. George's spirits killed all of Henry Jackson's children. Jackson arranged for four men to waylay Dr. George and kill him. The men succeeded but all of them died within a year. Jackson, who hadn't taken part, lived for two years."–Anderson Faithful.

"Curly-headed Doctor died in Oklahoma. He was killed by his spirits because he couldn't do anything for them. That day the Pigeons, his spirits, came in great flocks: the trees were filled with them. The doctor said, 'Don't kill these birds or you may suffer. They have come to bid me farewell. As soon as I die the spirits leaving me will cause the greatest storm you have ever seen.' As soon as he died came the worst storm we had ever seen.

"He did not want to be buried, but cremated. It was the most unusual fire ever seen. The flames were of many colors and very high. We children were not allowed to witness the cremation."–Jennie Clinton.

"Modoc Henry was hunting rabbits with his shotgun. He sat down and shot at a rabbit. It jumped high and fell to earth but when he looked for it it couldn't be found. Next he shot a large rabbit with an enlarged belly. When he skinned it he found no young, nor any intestines. It was full of evil-looking matter.

"The same evening Henry's daughter became ill; she died within a week. That was caused by the first rabbit. Now Henry became ill with a stomach ailment and soon died. The second rabbit had caused that. Some doctor had caused the deaths through the power of his Rabbit spirit."–Usee George.

"Long before my father was a real doctor he was a dream doctor. One night he just happened to dream about Frog and got a song: 'I cause the north wind to blow.' When he wakened he began to sing and everybody in the house sang with him. While he sang he repeatedly blew on his hand and made a sweeping gesture with it. He was imitating the Frog in making the north wind.

"My father was known by a name he got from another dream-doctoring song: 'I carry [pull] the world around.' He used that name before he was a doctor."–Usee George.

"After the Modoc War a dream doctor dreamt that a great hail-storm that would destroy everything was coming. A large dance house was built. The people sang the dream doctor's song: 'Cloud-bursts are descending on the house.' "–Celia Lynch.

"Dream doctoring is mostly encouraging people."–Usee George.

THE GIRL'S PUBERTY DANCE

A dance of notification was held individually for every girl, rich or poor, upon attainment of puberty. The ritual was essentially a way of publicizing the fact that the girl was now ready for marriage. The cultural rationalization, however, was of quite different character. The ritual was declared to be a device for keeping the girl from sleeping at night for the duration of the menstrual period. This was necessary, it was said, because any dream experienced by the girl during the nighttime sleep would come true, leading to illness and death for the girl or others, since her dreams at such a time revolved around such subjects. Daytime sleep, on the other hand, was harmless because dreams experienced during these hours did not come true. Another unphrased function of the dance was to provide a period of social pleasantry, love making, and sexual experimentation for young men and women, particularly the unmarried.

The dance lasted for five nights and was properly repeated for the same length of time at each subsequent menstruation until ten had passed. Practice often fell short of this ideal. The ritual was a rather expensive one and only rich families could afford so many repetitions. Even the poorest family, however, managed with the help of relatives and friends to provide one ritual period for each daughter. Arrangements were made for orphan girls by relatives of either parent or both. A girl sometimes experienced great embarrassment in telling her mother or other female relatives of the onset of first menses, but she knew that she must do so.

Although the dance lasted only five days the food and isolation taboos for the first period lasted ten days. Only dried roots and berries were eaten; meat and fish were specifically taboo. Quantity was not specified but the girl was expected to eat lightly. Water, perferably warm, was permitted without restriction of quantity and without the use of a drinking tube, nor were special dishes used for her foods. She was forbidden to scratch the head or body except with a deer rib, or a bone or wooden scratcher which hung from a string around her wrist or neck. She wore a headband and wrist and ankle bands of woven buckbrush. Her hair was braided, then covered with buckbrush or sagebrush, to hide the strands. No head covering was worn but the girl walked with bowed head and took care not to glance directly at any one. Her hair was not combed nor was her body or face washed during the first five days but these rules were relaxed during the second five. In the five days of the dance her face and the back of her hands were blackened with charcoal. This was commonly rubbed on pitch which had been applied to the skin but at other times was mixed with oil or grease to make a paint. The black covering was thought to be a safeguard against dreams. Ordinary clothing was worn during the ritual period. In summer a sagebrush skirt was worn without an upper garment. In winter a twined rabbitskin robe which covered the whole body was preferred. If a belt were needed one of sagebrush was worn. Guests wore ordinary garments and used no paint or special regalia except that singers sometimes brought deer dew-hoof rattles.

The pubescent was isolated in a hut while she slept or rested in camp. This was not specially built unless necessary; a storage hut or other existent shelter usually served. The dance was held in the open or within a circular windbreak of sage or juniper brush in the summer. In winter the dwelling house was used. This was usually adequate since the audience at a puberty ritual was not large. Invitations were not issued except to relatives and a few singers. Others were welcome if interested. The older men and women attending were mostly relatives. The bulk of the spectators consisted of young people; men and women were not segregated. The girl's father did not attend nor did he engage in hunting or fishing activities during the period. To have done so might have caused the daughter to dream of hunting accidents, which then would have occurred. The girl was careful not to go near her father's weapons and implements.

The dance began immediately at sunset. A fire had been built in the open or in the middle of the enclosure or house. The girl took her place by the fire, facing the east. The spectators formed a semicircle in the westerly quadrant. Between them and the girl stood the singers, one of whom the girl's mother designated to step forward and serve as ritualist. The latter, usually a woman, held a staff with deer dew hoofs attached to the top. She kept time for the dancing and singing by moving the vertically held staff up and down, the lower end striking the ground. The ritualist selected the songs which were to be sung and determined the length of time each was used. The pattern called for repetition of each song five times but there was considerable variation. Some songs were repeated for as long as an hour at a time. Among the songs used only two were invariable: the opening song, and the closing or morning song. Sometimes a special song was sung at midnight. Others were chosen from a large repertory of traditional puberty songs. New or private songs were not used. The texts referred to the aspirations of the pubescent, the proper roles for women, and love affairs. Many were sexually suggestive. Some were cynical or mocking in character.

The opening song: "Evening now take something off"; sunrise song: "Daylight now little bird"; midnight songs: "Minnows I don't like; elk ribs I like"; "Bring something your way with a stick"; other songs: "Kanamatsa lost his breech cloth" (repeated with other names); "White geese crawl up to the young boy" (a mocking song).

The girl danced along a path extending east and west. The dance was a rapid shuffling step forward followed by a slower movement backward over the path. Each song lasted only during one forward and one return dance. At the end of each the girl hesitated briefly beside the fire, which was located to the right of the dance path at the inner end near the audience. Her eyes were directed toward the ground rather than the fire but there was no taboo against viewing the fire. The ritualist stood or sat near the fire. The girl did not sing or speak; the spectators sang but did not dance. Intermissions between the series of dances were brief. The girl's task was intentionally strenuous so that she might be kept from thought of sleep. If she so much as felt drowsy she might dream momentarily between dances, a condition to be avoided at all costs. When her physical strength failed to the point where it was feared she might fall, a woman—a relative or friend—danced with the girl, supporting part of her weight by the arm. Two or three women might alternate in giving such assistance. It was common practice for such an aide to guide the girl for the first hour or two of the initial night's dancing. It is said that some girls never felt sleepy or needed assistance. The ritualist's task was an exhausting one also. She might sit down part of the time but spent most of the hours on her feet. She had to be ready with a new song each time one was needed and was expected to sing in a strong clear voice so that the audience could easily follow. The ritualist was often replaced by another before the night was over, and succeeding evenings usually found different ritualists officiating.

The girl was accompanied by her mother if she left the dance house. Sometimes she remained absent for an hour or two but during that time she walked about in the vicinity; she did not stop to rest.

The fire was kept burning by men or boys who assumed the task. Water was brought to the guests at least once during the night but the girl did not drink at that time. Composition of the audience fluctuated as some left and others arrived or returned. The audience was noisy with conversation but not rowdy. Guests were not permitted to drowse or sleep.

Sometimes a light meal was served to the guests at midnight or, more commonly, at dawn. The girl did not participate, of course. After the closing song at dawn she left for the woods or hills where she spent most of the day. When at least a mile or two from home she lay down to sleep. She arose, preferably by midmorning, and started wandering about, selecting a route that would take her through unoccupied country. When she encountered water she drank if she felt thirsty. She might eat roots or berries but usually depended for food upon that which she got at home. In the afternoon she returned to the camp. On the way she gathered wood to be used for the fire at the dance. After depositing it she went to her designated hut. In all of her movements about the camp she took care not to encounter anyone. At the hut she rested or slept until late in the afternoon. At that time her mother visited her, bringing food and water. The two discussed the affair of the preceding night and the plans for the present evening. After the meal of roots and fruit the girl went out to gather more wood for the dance fire. After accumulating a sufficient quantity she returned to the hut to remain until her mother called for her at sunset. She did not engage in any activity during the hours in the hut.

Following the fifth night the ritualists and principal singers were paid. Beads or buckskin were usually given. Later, when money was used, five dollars per night was average. The women who assisted the girl in her dancing received no compensation.

The pubescent took a sweat bath, combed her hair, and returned to the hut for an additional five days, if it were the first ceremony, or to her home if it were a subsequent one. After the final ritual the symbolic buckbrush bands were burned and all taboos were ended. No special ceremony marked this event. At the sweat lodge the girl was alone and she returned to her home without accompaniment. Henceforth her dreams were harmless either to herself or to others. Marriage was permissible at any time thereafter but usually a year or so elapsed before this occurred.

During subsequent menstrual periods the woman, single or married, isolated herself in a special lodge or in a storage hut. For five days she did no cooking for others. Meat and fish were forbidden in her own diet. Other women might freely visit her or work in the same hut. Men conversed with her but remained outside the door. Her male relatives were not restricted in their hunting, fishing, or gambling. The menstruant carried wood for herself and for the main house, but not water. Unlike the pubescent girl, she was not required to use an implement for scratching. On the sixth day she took a sweat bath and returned to the family house.

If a menstruating woman were to eat food obtained with a bow or gun the bow would no longer project an arrow accurately and the bullets would jam in the gun barrel. If she sat behind a gambler he was sure to lose. If a gambler succeeded in putting menstrual blood on his opponent's blanket the latter could not help but lose. A horse became lame if ridden by a menstruant.

Menstrual contamination was treated with an aromatic plant (ma´s). After associating with a menstruating woman a man rubbed his body with the juice of the root. A contaminated bow, gun, or horse was treated similarly. Or the horse might be made to breathe the smoke of the burning plant after being exercised so that it would breathe deeply. The plant was also used for these purposes in the form of an infusion.

⑨ CRISIS QUESTS

Certain crises in the life of the individual were occasions for observance of a quest involving fasting, isolation, strenuous artificial activities, and ritual bathing. The occasions for such ritualization were puberty, the birth or death of one's child, and consistent and serious losses in gambling; also, occasionally, chronic illness, or the death of one's spouse. The basic ritual pattern was identical for all; each was designated by the same term *(spu ʻdo)* preceded by a distinguishing adjective.

The framework of the ritual was a quest in which the individual wandered about the woods and hills in areas isolated from human settlements. That which was sought in the quest was a prophetic and satisfying dream. This was achieved by engaging in energy-consuming but economically worthless activities, followed by a short period of sleep. In all but the puberty ritual preparation for the dream required swimming in pools or streams significant because of their mythological associations.

The puberty quest was the first crisis ritual in which the individual engaged. The quest was open to both boys and girls upon reaching puberty. Some parents encouraged their boys, particularly, to prepare for the quest by going out for brief periods prior to puberty. Upon such occasions the lad departed at sunset for a few hours of wandering in nearby forested or brushy country. He was not told where to go but his father or mother instructed him to keep constantly moving and to engage in certain tasks: to break the trunks of shrubs as he passed, to twist and uproot small trees or to strip them of their bark, to tie knots in limbs, to make bundles of brush and tie them up, and to collect and pile rocks. All activities were physically strenuous; repetitive tasks such as plucking needles from pine trees were not demanded. In a practice quest the boy returned home after a few hours of such activity. A boy might repeat this routine many nights during prepubertal months if he were ambitious or if his parents were insistent. Of course he did not upon these occasions achieve the dream experiences with which true crisis rituals culminated.

The girl seldom engaged in prepubertal excursions since opportunity for ample practice was hers during the days of her puberty dance ceremonies. During that time she was required to be away from the village most of the day and to dance throughout the night. During her daytime wanderings it was proper but not essential for her to perform the activities mentioned above. In addition she engaged in the useful labor of collecting and carrying in firewood. Like the boy, she experienced no characteristic dream. At this time the girl's daytime dreams were considered meaningless; nighttime dreams were dangerous and to be avoided at all costs.

If a boy had been practicing, his vigils worked gradually into a true puberty quest—gradually because of the indefiniteness of attainment of puberty in the male. He stayed out longer, finally remaining to sleep during the predawn hours at the top of a mountain or other remote spot that he had reached. After completion of her puberty dances the girl might do likewise. Indeed she must if she were to achieve the coveted dream. Girls seldom if ever remained away for more than one night but the ideal for the boy was a five-night vigil. On such a prolonged quest it was customary to include ritual bathing in the activities. A complete fast was prescribed, even on the five-day quest.

It should be noted that not all boys went on repeated excursions but nearly all made some attempt to gain the dream. Relatively few girls observed the quest. All ritual quests served a dual purpose: they helped one over the crisis and afforded him an opportunity to gain a kind of supernatural power. At puberty the boy was unaware of any crisis to be bridged but was acutely conscious of approaching manhood and the need for talents which would gain him a respected place in the adult world. Consequently, by him the ritual was viewed as a quest for talents, for power. The situation was quite different for the girl. For her the physiological crisis was distinct and significant but she felt little need for supernatural aid in taking up her role as a woman. The puberty dance, although culturally phrased as a notification of marriageability, nevertheless functioned for the girl as a bridge over the crisis. She felt no great drive to complete a successful dream quest.

Girls who did participate followed the same pattern as boys. They piled fewer rocks but spent more time breaking and gathering brush. Rocks were piled in a typical manner: a large one at the base, a somewhat smaller one surmounting that, continuing thus until the pile was as high as could be built. These rock piles were erected wherever the material was to be found. Running to the top of a mountain was an additional form of prescribed activity.

Every full-scale quest included ritual bathing. The acceptable bathing places were spots where some unusual event had occurred in mythological times. Consequently no obvious characteristics distinguished these as a group from other possible swimming places. Some were at confluences of streams, some were backwater pools, and others were pools formed by springs; still others were at fish spawning grounds. The proper activity at each was distinctive, however. At one, where five round boulders, called "rabbits," lay in a row at the bottom of the stream, the swimmer was expected to swim under water and touch each one in turn. At another location the pool was located in swampy ground. Although small it appeared to be dotted with islands. In reality these were floating patches of reeds and grass which sank if stepped upon. The pool was very deep and still but when the dream seeker approached it, large waves might appear or a whirlwind sweep over causing a waterspout to form. When swimming in the pool a horse typically materialized underneath the swimmer and carried the latter on its back as it swam to shore. Without a sound the horse disappeared; without a word the swimmer climbed ashore and continued his quest.

Only one bathing place was visited each night; the swimming was always coupled with the other arbitrary tasks mentioned. The usual sequence was swimming, brush breaking, mountain climbing, and sleep. Favorite sleeping places were the tops of hills or mountains.

All active phases of the crisis ritual have now been described. The procedure was basically identical for boy or man, for pubescent or aged mourner. Superficial differences included duration and selection of the quest site. Variations in the length of the pubertal quest have been mentioned. The mourning ritual ordinarily consumed five days for men, beginning immediately after the cremation. Women seldom observed the mourning quest; when they did it was usually for a shorter period. Gamblers seeking to regain their luck seldom stayed out for more than two or three days.

Some bathing places were specialized. The first one described above was used by boys and girls at puberty. The pool with the horse was visited only by gamblers. Other specific sites were useful only to mourners. To a lesser degree mountain sites were of specialized use.

The dream was experienced during the brief sleep that followed the night's activities. Just before dawn the dream seeker sought a spot to lie down, preferably at a traditionally used spot which, like the swimming sites, was significant because of mythological associations. The sleeping place was sometimes a shallow depression in a meadow or a niche among rocks. A brush windbreak might be thrown up but a fire was not built. Suffering from exposure was rare since quests were not undertaken during the winter. One always lay with the head toward the west, the direction of the supernatural world. At other times this position was carefully avoided. Despite discomfort, sleep was not long in coming to the exhausted and hungry man. The Modoc were practiced dreamers; in addition to this, the conditions were ideal for the inducement of dreams. The returning vigil keeper never complained that he had not been able to dream. His concern was rather with the content of the dream.

There was no typical dream pattern; only a pattern for the interpretation of the dream. Even the latter was of very general character. A dream, quite ordinary by objective standards, could be interpreted as highly significant in terms of quest objectives. These objectives differed in specific character depending upon the type of quest. But all were variations upon three themes: good luck, good health, and long life. All dreams were prophetic in that they indicated the kind of fortune, the health, and the degree of longevity that could be expected. Apparently all dreams were favorably interpreted but some were more auspicious than others. The particular concern of the pubescent was good fortune in the typical pursuits of the adult. He expected an indication of the kind of pursuit in which he would be most fortunate, such as warfare, gambling, or hunting. The gambler naturally was particularly concerned with his luck at gaming. The mourner sought indications of health and long life. The father of a newborn child was hopeful of experiencing dream symbols which would insure good health and longevity for his child.

The interpretation of dream symbols was relatively straightforward. If the pubescent dreamt of furs, buckskin, or meat, he would have good luck at hunting. If he smelled deer grease the interpretation was similar. If he heard the rattling of gambling bones it augured well for his success in gambling. The gambler that was carried on the back of the swimming horse expected to dream about horses. He would then win many of these valuable animals as gambling stakes. Any dream in which the stakes, implements, or activities of gambling were present was significant. The mourner hoped to dream of the experiences of his youth or of activities typical of young people. For example, for a man to dream of his puberty quest or a woman of her puberty dance was an indication that the dreamer would remain young for a long while.

Spirits did not figure in any way in these dreams. Animals seen were those of the everyday world. Even the mysterious swimming horse and other animals that performed unusual feats were emphatically nonspiritual. It will be noted that the horse represented that which was to be won, not the agency of success. Shamanistic power was never achieved in these quests nor did success in a dream quest predispose to shamanism. The shaman, as such, never engaged in this type of quest. He might, however, be a gambler or mourner as well as a shaman; in the former roles he might embark on such a quest. Not only were spirits wholly foreign to the quest, but the seeker obtained no sponsorship or continuing presence of any kind.

Rich men, it is said, did not go on quests since they were secure in their positions and fortunes. As mourners they might well have participated, however, since bereaved persons recognized that the quest helped them to forget their sorrow. There was considerable individual variation in the observance of quests. The usual occasion for a mourning quest was the loss of a child, but some persons went out upon the death of a spouse. It may be that those suffering from chronic illnesses sought relief in a quest when toleration of suffering reached a critical point. Ordinarily individuals interpreted their own dreams but pubescents sometimes consulted their parents. Most quest sites were within Modoc territory but sometimes distant trips were made. Crater Lake, in Klamath territory, was not infrequently visited.

In at least one instance the mythological associations of a quest site called for symbolic re-enactment. Near a ritual bathing place used by gamblers lay two large stones, one with vagina-shaped aperture. The plain stone bore the name of a mythological character; the other was called his wife. After swimming it was customary for the gambler to rub against the male stone, then simulate coitus with the other.

10 MARRIAGE

Marriage usually occurred within a few months after puberty for both boys and girls. Seldom was the delay greater than a year or two. This does not mean that mates were always matched in age; sometimes one of the mates was a widow or widower. Personal qualities were emphasized above age in the selection of a mate, both by the parents and by the principals. A woman should above all else be industrious. The ability and willingness to spend long days at root digging was the best criterion of industry. It was said that a girl who was efficient at root digging was always beautiful. The girl should be quiet, retiring, and serious. If a poor man's daughter should exhibit these qualities, she was more desirable as a wife than the unindustrious or frivolous daughter of a rich man. The qualities sought in a man were strength of character, bravery, and wit. He should also be a reasonably capable participant in the economic pursuits of men.

The qualities emphasized suggest that the choice of a mate was made by parents rather than the individuals involved; this was quite true. Some parents paid no heed to the wishes of the children, especially the girl. Others consulted with the youngsters but the object was to win their agreement, not to capitulate to opposition. Opposition was seldom strenuous. The children had been reared in a culture in which parents made the choice, and they were yet very young emotionally when the match was arranged. Not much opportunity was found during the months between puberty and marriage for the establishment of ties of affection. The activities of girls during this period were quite carefully guarded. Boys were allowed full freedom, but they were most interested in the company of other boys or men and in the vigorous outdoor activities of the adult male. Their days were spent in hunting, fishing, canoeing, and such pursuits. The supervision of the girls was largely to avoid clandestine meetings with boys which might result in an illegitimate birth. The elders did not fear that these brief affairs would establish undesirable emotional ties. The daughter of a rich man was not more carefully guarded than that of a poor man.

The basic pattern of the marriage ceremony and associated practices was rigid but much variation was permitted in the details. When a boy's parents felt that his marriage to a particular girl was worth serious consideration, they made known to the boy their intentions and proceeded with plans for a visit to the girl's parents. A quantity of food considerably in excess of that necessary for the anticipated meal was accumulated. At the time selected for the visit this food was carried to the girl's home by the boy's parents and close relatives. The boy did not accompany the party, nor did the girl remain in the house after the visitors arrived. The food was presented to the host upon arrival and the women of the house immediately prepared a meal. The affair that followed differed in no way from a casual visit except that more food had been brought than was usual and the ensuing meal was more elaborate. No mention was made of the intent of the visit; it was both improper and unnecessary to do so. After a few hours the visitors returned home. They did not take back with them the excess food, as they might on another occasion.

Days or weeks later the visit was returned, following the same pattern, if the girl's parents were favorably disposed toward the yet undeclared match. This visit did not signify acceptance, merely interest. But if the reciprocal visit did not materialize within a reasonable time it was indication of rejection. This might mean that the girl's parents were antagonistic to the implied proposal, or merely that they wanted to postpone the marriage of their daughter somewhat longer. If the initiators guessed that the latter was the explanation they might make a second visit at a later time, or even a third. Failure to return a third visit indicated that the proposal was hopeless.

Assuming that the reciprocal visits had taken place, the next step was the all-important one of the actual proposal and presentation of presents. The food presented during the earlier visits was not looked upon as a gift. The boy's parents and relatives accumulated as impressive an array of presents as possible. In recent times horses were the preferred gift; if several were presented no other goods were necessary. Earlier the gifts were numerous and varied, selected from the whole range of valued objects: furs, skins, robes, beads, bows, arrows, quivers, canoes, baskets—but not food. As messenger, a close male relative was chosen to take the presents to the girl's home. He arranged to arrive at dusk; he hurriedly deposited the presents, often leaving them outside and departing without entering the house. The girl's relatives spent the evening surveying and analyzing the presents, eager to determine whether the value represented indicated a profoundly serious proposal and adequate recognition of the girl's merits. Conclusions were drawn, of course, in the light of the wealth of the donors. There was great excitement, too, in the prospect of possessing new and different valuables. Seldom was the final judgment unfavorable.

The messenger returned the following morning. To him was delivered the decision. If negative, he collected the goods and returned with them; otherwise he merely carried back word of acceptance.

In the latter case all was excitement at the girl's home and she was the center of attention, dressed in new and elaborate garments, and bedecked with many strings of beads and other items of ornament. Parents and relatives were busy accumulating many articles of value from among their possessions. These covered the same general range as the presents recently received, excluding horses. The presents received had meanwhile been distributed among the relatives but these of course were never included in the goods now being gathered for return. The total accumulated was judged sufficient when the value, including the girl's garments and ornaments, was roughly equivalent to or a little short of that represented by the presents they had received. The amount was seldom or never in excess of the latter.

About midday the party departed for the boy's home, the home which was temporarily to become that of his wife, the girl. The boy's mother met the party at the door and took the girl by the hand, leading her to a corner of the room where the groom's bed was located. Here the girl sat down, her right leg folded under her, left knee raised supporting her left elbow. Her head rested on her left hand with which it was partially hidden. She faced the wall. In this position she remained for the rest of the day. She did not leave her place except momentarily for the ensuing four days, nor did she look upon the activities of the house during that time.

The wedding party now consisted not only of the visitors and the boy's parents but also many relatives of the boy who had gathered

during the morning, and close friends. The boy, however, was not
present; he was "out hunting."

The presents which had been brought by the visitors were distributed by the groom's parents, to whom they had been presented,
among the boy's relatives. Close relatives were favored; the man
who acted as messenger received the most. If friends were present
they received small gifts. Amid much gaiety a meal was prepared
and eaten. Sometimes the guests departed late the same evening
but if sufficient food were available the close relatives, at least,
stayed for several days. When the bride's party departed, small
gifts of food were received.

During the wedding feast a small quantity of food was placed before the bride in her secluded corner, and at each meal thereafter
for the four days the same was done. She ate very little but this
was due to shyness rather than to any taboo. Late each evening the
groom returned home and joined his bride. Although he slept with
her from the first night he did not eat with her or with the rest of
the family. He spoke very few words to the bride, these supposedly
of a consoling nature: "How are you feeling? You must eat your
food. Don't be frightened and don't be lonesome. We'll move to
your house before long." The bride spoke to her husband and to her
mother-in-law, when necessary, in whispers. The couple was not
subjected to undue attention or joking remarks by others in the
household.

After the initial period the girl joined in the activities of the
household and ate with the others. She was expected to do her share
of the work; in fact, the more she did the better impression she
made. She was not yet at ease with her relatives-in-law and her
husband still remained away throughout the day. Therefore it was
to her advantage to keep busily engaged in routine work. It is said
that a reaction occurred when she returned to her parents' home—
she did no work at all.

The period most variable in length was this initial patrilocal
residence; it varied from five or ten days to a year. The factors
involved were the success of adjustment made by the girl, her
homesickness, and the relative economic positions of the two families. The latter was of considerable importance. If the family of
the groom were poor they could ill afford to provide food for two
persons who were not yet producing their share. At the same time
the wealthier parents of the girl did not care to have her live in
relative poverty.

When it was decided that the patrilocal residence should be ended

the groom's relatives brought small presents for the couple to take
to the girl's people. The girl was provided with a fine new dress,
the equally valuable one she had received from her parents being
left for one of her husband's relatives. The boy, too, was given
new clothing and presents to carry. The wife retained her dress
but the husband gave his garments to his relatives-in-law along
with the other gifts. In turn, he received new apparel from his af-
final relatives. The change of residence was made without other
ceremony. The couple was unaccompanied on the trip from the old
home to the new.

Stable matrilocal residence was now established. The couple remained here until they chose or were able to build a separate house.
The change was never made until a child was born, often not until
two or three children had arrived. Meanwhile they became an important part of the household. They were expected to carry a reasonable share of the economic load and their opinions were sought
on matters relating to the common welfare. Older men of the group
helped the young husband to learn the intricacies of men's work,
the best areas and times for hunting, and subtleties of group relationships and other matters needed to complete his education.
Occasionally visits were made to the groom's parents for a few
days at a time. Upon each such visit gifts of food were carried in
both directions. The parents and relatives, unaccompanied by the
couple, exchanged visits from time to time and continued reciprocal gift giving in a modest way.

When a separate residence was finally established it was customary to choose a location near the groom's parents, but this was
not mandatory and considerable variation existed. In intertribal
marriages final residence was more uniformly patrilocal.

Variability of subjective behavior is underemphasized in the
above type description. For example, it must not be assumed that
parents always avoided mention of the proposed marriage in the
premarital visits. Such reference was obliquely or humorously
phrased; thus the cultural pattern was not abused. The ideal bride
stared at the floor or wall for the first five days of her marriage,
and did not speak above a whisper, but brides in the flesh were
frequently more curious, impatient, rebellious, or hysterical. I
do not mean that these aberrations occurred more often than in
many another culture; I merely wish to correct any false notion
of invariability for which the type description might be responsible.

Any proper marriage required the formal exchange of presents
by the respective parents. The very poor could measure up to
this standard simply by exchanging presents of slight value and in

meager quantity. Even so, this was embarrassing to some and seemed hardly worth while to others. Consequently the children of poverty-stricken parents sometimes began living together with little or no ceremony. This did not mean that children born to the couple were illegitimate. If the parents were still united at the time of birth the union was a bona fide one and the child legitimate. Rather than neglect the formalities, however, most poor parents enlisted the aid of relatives and managed a passable ceremony. Parents that were poor but avaricious could get much more for a daughter known to be industrious than it was necessary to give in return.

For orphans the formula was changed from parent to guardian, the latter being the head of the house in which the boy lived. If he had lost only one parent the surviving one made the arrangements, gave and received the presents. Otherwise the same role was assumed by the guardian, but the ceremonies were relatively simpler.

Upon the rare occasions when an unmarried boy and girl slept together, deliberately allowed themselves to be discovered, and declared the reason to be that they were determined to be married, the parents hastily exchanged presents, usually of little value, in order that the marriage might be legal and proper. The girl's parents were glad to accept anything offered. The case differed from that in which the affair was clandestine, for the parents had hope of breaking off the latter without the girl becoming pregnant but despaired of such success in the former situation. This was the closest approach to elopement that existed in the old culture.

When an unmarried girl became pregnant as a result of a clandestine affair, her parents attempted to ascertain the identity of the father. If successful the two were forced to live together and were recognized as man and wife. But no presents were exchanged if the child were already born or if the girl's pregnancy were known to the community. The child was known as illegitimate and was taunted with the fact by his playmates. Even as an adult he might be reminded of the fact in the course of a quarrel or by an enemy. If the unwed girl refused to tell the name of the father, which was not unusual, or if she was unable to do so, the parents assumed responsibility for the rearing of the child, at least temporarily. When married, later, the girl might take over the care of the child, but permission of the husband was necessary and this was not always forthcoming. According to cultural standards marriage between individuals of any known degree of blood relationship was considered undesirable, but no punishment was suffered by offenders except social disapproval and laughter. Examples of in-

cestuous unions were not uncommon and there was one notable case
of brother-sister marriage two or three generations ago. Several
children were born to the union. Persons guilty of incestuous relations or unions were taunted by a name felt to be the most in-
sulting possible: "Paiute-like."

Extratribal marriages were very rare except with slaves captured from the Pit River country. More frequent than other inter-
marriages with freemen were those with the Klamath. The rarity
was not due to a specific prohibition; nevertheless no one today
can remember more than a few instances. Perhaps a partial explanation is the fact that once a woman married into another tribe
she was isolated from her relatives. But if Modoc men married
women from elsewhere the girl came to live with her husband's
tribe. Village and community exogamy, however, was considered
desirable although not obligatory. Perhaps three-fourths of marriages were to individuals of other localities.

Second marriages were contracted in a very different way from
first matings. If a widower wished to marry a girl not previously
married he approached her parents in person. He explained what
gifts he was able and willing to present and emphasized his recognition of the obligations of marriage. The parents gave him their
answer immediately or soon thereafter. If the proposal were accepted he returned at the appointed time bringing the presents.
These were distributed, as usual, to the relatives that gathered
for the occasion and an informal feast concluded the formalities.
The food for the feast was provided by the groom, who customarily
received from his parents-in-law certain presents, typically clothing or economically useful articles which were often bows and arrows. The man remained at the girl's home and the relationship
of husband and wife was established. At any time after the birth of
a child the couple might, if able, establish a separate home.

When both the man and woman concerned had been married previously the procedure followed still a different pattern. The man
visited the woman at her family home at night, arriving late and
leaving before dawn. Other members of the household, supposedly
asleep, pretended not to know of his presence unless the woman
gave the alarm when he arrived. In that event he simply left without a word and no one criticized him. A man did not venture to
visit a woman unless he was quite certain from previous events
that she would accept him. If she did so he returned several nights,
after which she went to live with him in his own or his parents'
home.

The preceding assumes that the individuals were not bound by

either the levirate or the sororate. Both of these institutions functioned extensively in the culture. The levirate was mandatory for
both the man and the woman unless abrogated by mutual agreement.
The penalties or rather the devices for retribution differed for the
two sexes however. If the widow married without her brother-in-
law's permission, physical revenge was taken by the man's relatives. But if the man shirked the duty of marrying his deceased
brother's wife she or her relatives hired a shaman to bring about
his death. The physical retribution for the woman was likewise
death, in theory. In practice such extreme action was rarely taken.
The man and woman concerned might even remain friends. The
point is that mutual agreement was assumed to exist unless one
or the other were sufficiently emotional about the matter to take
extreme action. The prerogative of pressing a claim under the
levirate on the man's side extended only to brothers. A younger
brother did not have prior right over an older one but an unmarried
brother's claim took precedence over that of a married one. Duty
was reckoned similarly. In the absence of brothers a cousin or
nephew might propose marriage but he was not obligated to do so
and the widow was free to refuse.

The widow was expected to wait until the end of the mourning period, about a year, before remarrying. In the absence of any statement from her brother- or parents-in-law the assumption was that
the former would become her husband. Chastity during this period
was required; her relatives-in-law watched her actions carefully.
The prospective husband was likewise expected to avoid associations with other women. Both remained in the family home.

The sororate operated in much the same way; it was likewise
binding upon both the widower and the deceased woman's unmarried
sisters unless specifically set aside. But in this case abrogation
could be arranged between the man and his parents-in-law. If observed, the man was privileged to choose any one of the available
sisters.

If a woman subject to either the levirate or the sororate married
another without permission, the husband might suffer instead of the
woman if the rightful claimant still wanted the woman as his wife;
but if the intruder agreed to step aside gracefully and the woman
accepted her proper spouse the breach might be overlooked.

The levirate and sororate continued to function until relatively
recently but with progressively decreasing emphasis placed upon
the obligatory aspect. The rigid applications described above refer
to the prebreakdown period.

Minor liberties and joking were permitted between a man and his wife's unmarried sisters and his brother's wives, but this was scarcely more than a courtesy between relatives. If fell far short of the institutionalized joking relationship. Polygyny was an accepted practice but the great majority of marriages were monogamous. At any one time four or five families out of a hundred might include more than one wife. Marriage to two women was not a more common form than marriage to three or four. The maximum number in remembered cases was six. Assuming numerical equality of the sexes it is safe to say that eight or ten men out of a hundred were wifeless. The unmarried individuals were not the same, however, throughout a lifetime, owing to frequent remarriages. Even so, it is said that however unindustrious and unattractive a woman might be she would always be married at least once, whereas the same could not be said about such a man. Rich men had plural wives more often than poor men but it was not necessary to have wealth in order to obtain and support more than one wife. A worthy woman always carried her share of the economic burden. In the summer camps it was customary for co-wives to have separate houses, especially when each had children. The children stayed with the mother, who had her own quota of meat from the village supply and her own store of roots which she had independently gathered. But these food supplies were kept equitable; no wife ate while another went hungry. The husband ate with one or another wife as he chose. Only in winter, when normally all lived together, did the question of principal position in the household arise. Formally there was no such position; certainly the first wife possessed no prerogatives automatically. From time to time the husband favored one and then another. The most recently acquired wife benefited from that fact. Co-wives were sometimes sisters but sororal polygyny was not a recognized pattern. It was the emphasis on the sororate which led to the relative frequency of this type of marriage. Co-wives were characteristically quarrelsome, the principal subjects of contention being the husband's favors and the children's altercations. Hair pulling was common. Serious injuries were sometimes inflicted but deaths are not known to have resulted. Quarreling women were lashed on the back with a willow withe by the husband if words failed to deter them.

Domestic strife was not limited to co-wives. The same causes led to bickerings and fighting between husband and wife. Petty annoyances resulting from differences in personal habits were infrequent in the type of life lived by the Modoc, and it was proper that those which did develop be overlooked. But laziness, favoritism to certain children, and adultery or the threat of it were potent sources of conflict.

If soon after her first marriage, during matrilocal residence, a girl attempted to visit, or succeeded in secretly visiting, other men it was customary for her parents to attempt to reform her, rather than for her husband to try. The girl was whipped by her parents and warned that repetition of the act would result in her parents-in-law seeking mortal revenge against them, her parents. Although the threat was untrue it was sometimes effective. If repeated efforts to break the girl of her adulterous habits failed she was told to go to her parents-in-law's home and never return. If the latter accepted her, as was customary, she was carefully watched and severely punished by her husband if she further transgressed. A flagrant adulteress was spoken of as "one who runs around like a dog" and might be taunted with the name in public.

An injured husband did not discard a wife because guilty of adultery. Indeed, there was no way for him to do so since only the woman was privileged to desert her husband, not the reverse. However, he might make life so unpleasant for her that she would leave of her own accord. But if the woman accepted the normal whipping for her act, she might remain and most husbands then overlooked the incident unless it were repeated. A husband might, however, take action against the guilty man if he were certain of the latter's identity. If he killed the adulterer he was within his rights but the dead man's family might seek revenge via shamanistic channels. The husband usually satisfied himself by inflicting injury short of death. It was not customary to demand reparation or to destroy the guilty man's property. When a man was known to have committed adultery the wife might leave him if she so desired and return to her parents. She seldom did so; never, it is said, if she had children. During matrilocal residence the man might be asked to leave if guilty of flagrant or repeated transgressions.

Gossip was the usual source of information which led to accusations. Sometimes a man, suspicious of his wife because she talked and acted in too familiar a fashion with other men, might pretend to go on a prolonged hunting expedition but actually remain nearby and watch the area from a hilltop. During the night he would return unexpectedly to the home.

When domestic strife due to causes less serious than adultery, or to mere suspicion of adultery, reached a critical point, the same general patterns prevailed. During independent or patrilocal residence a woman might leave her husband for any provocation and return to her parents. The immediate reason was usually harsh physical treatment, typically whipping over the back and legs. At the same time the man might order her to leave but she need not do so if willing to tolerate such treatment. Some women fought back, often effectively, but the usual practice was to leave for a few days. The woman might not return of her own accord but she knew that a husband customarily, and without embarrassment, appeared at the home of his parents-in-law after a few days and begged his wife to return. Her parents encouraged her to do so unless she already had had to flee his wrath several times. She was under no social compulsion to return. If she refused to do so she remained his wife, in the eyes of the community, for about a year and might not remarry within that time. If she nevertheless did remarry, her rightful husband might take her from the other man by force and punish or kill the usurper without fear of public condemnation. A woman dared to remarry at an earlier date only when she felt that her husband had no further interest in her. If she were right the marriage would be undisturbed by her recent husband and accepted by the community. A man, on the other hand, might remarry as soon as he cared to after being deserted by his wife. His case was not comparable to hers because he might marry even though his wife were still at home, polygyny being accepted. Indeed, a man's recourse when his wife became intolerable was to marry another woman and provide a separate hut for the ill-favored one. (Often the arrangement was reversed before many months had passed.) However, if a man remarried during his wife's absence he was expected to request her return immediately if he looked upon her as a co-wife. If he said nothing she was free and might remarry as soon as she liked.

Polygyny was also the answer for a man who desired children but whose wife had proved barren. Barrenness was not a recognized basis for divorce.

Marital difficulties occasionally but infrequently led to suicide by the woman. The methods were hanging or the swallowing of poison prepared from wild parsnips. No suicides by men, for any reason, are remembered.

Despite the pitfalls, many original marriages lasted throughout life. Often men did not remarry after the death of a first wife. Women more often remarried. The difference was due to polygyny rather than a difference of attitude on the part of the two sexes. Women were not more dependent than men.

The extensive operation of the levirate and sororate provided for the care of most orphaned children. In other cases young children were usually cared for by relatives of the deceased mother. Older children were permitted to choose where they wished to live: at the home of the maternal or paternal relatives. Upon divorce the mother retained custody of young children; older children were taken by either parent or some by each, determined by mutual agreement or by the attitudes of the step-parents. Often the actual rearing of the children fell to grandparents.

Love songs were known but played an insignificant role. They were traditional in character, not individual, and were sung more for amusement and jocularity than for serious love making. They were sung by both sexes but by older rather than younger persons. Love potions were known only as a practice of other tribes.

Other negative traits include parent-in-law taboos, child betrothals, and the circle dance. No particular time of year was favored for marriages. Parents-in-law were not consulted when a co-wife was taken. A woman never requested her husband to lighten her burdens by means of a co-wife.

ILLUSTRATIVE DATA

"Young girls were warned by their mothers or grandmothers of the dangers of careless relationships with men. The warnings were not specific; we were merely told to be careful. When a woman was mistreated by a man it would be held up to us as an example.

"I was ten or twelve years old when I received these warnings. I never stayed all night away from home. I was always afraid of strangers and even relatives. Home was always more comfortable."–Jennie Clinton.

"I can remember three men who married their mother's sister's daughters. And I knew of one who married his mother's sister. Nothing was done about these cases."–Peter Sconchin.

"When an unmarried girl bore a child the people used to say: 'That girl's mother and father wanted too many presents for that girl's marriage. That's why she didn't get married. That's why this happened.' "–Usee George.

"If a woman had children she would not leave her husband no matter how badly she was treated. She was afraid, I guess, that she could not keep her children. Some of them might stay with their father. She wouldn't commit suicide either, if she had children."–Usee George.

"Women sometimes hanged themselves when they were jealous. Or they ate wild parsnip. But the Paiute used that poison much more than the Modoc. Captain Jack's first wife killed herself by hanging with a buckskin rope from a tree. She was jealous about a man."—Usee George.

"A woman that had been philandering with her sister's husband killed herself with wild parsnip poison. Her sister had been uncivil to her. She wouldn't speak except to ridicule her. So the girl killed herself because she wasn't treated right. She was sixteen or seventeen years old. She ran away to a Paiute camp and ate wild parsnip. She did wrong in going with that man but that was not why she killed herself."—Anderson Faithful.

"My mother's brother left his wife because she bore no children, even after they had been married three years. First he consulted my father. 'My wife is a good women,' he said, 'but I am a young man and I have no children. I am like an old man. I want to see a child before I die. Everybody laughs at me. They ask, "What are you, an old man?"' My father agreed that he should leave his wife. But she went back to him three times before he finally got rid of her and married again.

[The above does not correspond to old practices. It indicates the rapid growth of individuality of action with the breakdown of the old culture.]

"I never saw a man interfere when his wife was fighting with other women. But I have seen women trying to stop men from fighting.

"A busy woman was never engaged in fighting. If she kept busy she didn't get into trouble. Women were more industrious in the old days than they are now."—Jennie Clinton.

KINSHIP TERMINOLOGY

The pattern of Modoc kinship reckoning was the same as that of the Klamath, as described by Leslie Spier *(Klamath Ethnography)*. The terminology varied in numerous phonetic details but not in any significant aspect of designation or classification. During the first years of reservation life the Modoc gradually abandoned the native terminology. They substituted the system of their white neighbors even before English speech was well mastered. This shift is understandable in terms of the functional weakness of the native system and the predilection of the Modoc for discarding cultural practices—even fundamental ones—when they no longer "worked."

⫼ BIRTH AND INFANCY

The restrictions and requirements to which the pregnant woman was subjected combined physiologically sound concepts with those of magical character. The practices were divided into two categories: those affecting the welfare of the mother and those relating to the health and character of the child.

Taboos designed to protect the mother related principally to activities rather than diet. One food prohibition, that against eating fish, was thought to keep her from developing an illness of which coughing was the principal symptom. A light diet was considered beneficial; the child would be delivered more easily. Water, preferably warm, was not restricted in quantity. Most important were the prohibitions relating to behavior at a doorway. The pregnant woman dared not stand at the doorway and look out, or hesitate while passing through. Starting out and returning, or stepping backward through the passage, were assiduously avoided. The former caused the infant to behave similarly during delivery; the latter caused an inversion of the fetus. Similar reasoning dictated that the pregnant woman avoid eating intestines or other types of food that might become "twisted" in her stomach. The infant's umbilical cord would do likewise. If the woman wore a belt, it was adjusted loosely so that stricture in the womb would not occur.

Other beliefs governing the woman's behavior were based upon assumed physiological needs. She did not engage in strenuous exercise. The ordinary duties of the household were carried on until the occurrence of labor but none of the heavy tasks that ordinarily she might perform was now safe, especially during the later months. She slept on her side, and slept alone when enlargement

became marked. Pregnancy was assumed to exist with the cessation
of the menses. Thereafter she avoided intercourse if she wanted to
be sure not to have twins. Coitus during pregnancy was the sole
explanation for twins. However, multiple births were not considered animal-like or in any other way undesirable except for the
possible difficulties of parturition and the problems of nursing.
Not many women considered these adequate reasons for avoiding
intercourse.

Sweat bathing and river bathing were avoided during the last two
months of pregnancy. Quarreling and fighting were considered
harmful to the woman because emotional or physical strain was involved, not because the child's character would be affected. Associates were more tolerant of the woman's idiosyncrasies than at
other times and altercations were consequently few.

The pregnant woman was subjected to a number of food taboos
designed to protect the unborn child. The flesh of several species
of birds was abjured so that the child might not be lazy, weak, or
ugly, qualities attributed to the birds in question. If meat of the
young porcupine were eaten the child would be slow of growth. The
flesh of animals that had been killed by choking or drowning was
taboo lest the child be unable to breathe when born. Animals taken
by impounding might not be eaten; the tightening rope was symbolic.
If spoiling food were eaten the infant might suffer skin troubles.

Merely to look upon certain things was equally harmful. Crippled,
cross-eyed, swollen, or ugly persons and animals were sights to
be avoided if the child were to be protected from having a similar
appearance. Specifically avoided sights included hairless or mangy
coyotes, the snake, and the frog. The frog's appearance and warts
were equated. The sight of a dead and desiccated weasel led to a
similar appearance and death for the fetus. The results were not
more serious if the woman laughed or commented upon the object.
The harm was done through vision alone. Any startling or frightening experience might have its effect upon the child. Hence the pregnant woman seldom left the house without a companion at her side.
As she walked she kept her head high and proceeded directly to her
destination.

The sight of human death was certainly to be avoided but when
it occurred within the kin group the woman was hardly able to avoid
visual contact and she was expected to attend the cremation. To
counteract the effects that the child would otherwise suffer, she
cut a few small strips from a blanket or robe of the deceased.
These were kept until after the birth of the child, when they were
dropped in the water used to steam the infant's body.

The dangerousness of visual experiences was greatest during the early months of pregnancy. After the "formative" period of five or six months had passed there was much less chance that the child would be affected.

Throughout pregnancy the woman slept under one blanket only so that the fetus might have but one placental wrapping, "not two or three which would make delivery difficult."

The father-to-be was unrestricted except in a very minor way. It was well for him to be cautious in the hunt and not to snare animals if they could be obtained by other methods.

A procedure conceptually related to those above was practiced by women when they desired to become pregnant. Shells were finely pulverized, mixed with warm water, and swallowed. This was done on the fifth day of menstruation at dawn while facing toward the east. The shell material was obtained in various ways. The shell beads received from the Pit River people were favored if a male child were desired. The inner layer of an ocean shell was used to induce conception of a girl. Some thought a shell turned up from an old mound by the boring of a mole was the only efficacious type. The decoction was prepared by an experienced woman, one who had been successful in previous attempts. The mixture was allowed to stand overnight before use.

No attempt was made to determine the sex of a child before birth. It was thought, however, that the mother could detect the presence of twins by the strength and extent of fetal movements.

Whenever possible midwives were used to supervise parturition. These women were semiprofessionals who had served often and thus demonstrated their abilities. They were paid moderate fees for their services but no financial discussion preceded delivery. They were selected and their services solicited by the woman's mother or some other woman of the household. Two practitioners were employed if available. In the absence of one or both the services were provided by a competent female relative or two. In an extremity the husband might serve. There was no prejudice against his assisting except that a woman, especially a midwife, was naturally more competent. Even though his services were not needed the husband might be present if he desired. Women from other households were usually present and gave whatever incidental assistance was needed. Women came out of curiosity if for no other reason.

Delivery took place either in the main house or in a supplementary hut, the latter being preferred. As soon as the woman gave evidence of labor a place was made ready for her. All that was

required was a warm and comfortable place to lie, with a blanket
for the infant and absorbent materials near at hand. Stones of
proper shape were heated in the fire so that they might be ready for
placing on the woman's abdomen and alongside her bed if needed.

The woman was not expected to remain silent during labor; there
was no taboo against crying out. She was given nothing to hold in
her mouth. During the latter stages of labor she knelt on the bedding provided. No mechanical support was employed. One midwife
stood behind and held her under the armpits, lifting her up and
down with a slow and regular motion. This action was occasionally
alternated with a downward massaging of the abdomen. When one
midwife was exhausted her place was taken by the other. When the
patient announced that delivery was imminent the midwife continued
to support her as before but ceased lifting. The other midwife sat
in front of the woman, a buckskin or fur blanket on her lap, and
her hands in readiness to receive the infant.

When delivery was complete the child was held on the blanket
and the umbilical cord was cut about a finger's length from the navel. The stub was wrapped fairly tightly with a section of fresh
intestine from a bird or small mammal. Then a mixture of macerated herbs and deer grease or tallow was rubbed over it to prevent swelling. A fawnskin band four to six inches wide was wrapped
around the infant's abdomen. Whether the body was washed before
the band was applied depended upon the habits of the midwife; practice differed. If washed, there was a further choice to be made
between warm or cold water. Washing was done with the child
resting upon the midwife's lap. Her hands were dipped in water
and rubbed over the body. As a minimum the body was cleaned
without water by rubbing the fingers over it. Oil was not used at
this time.

If the child did not breathe promptly the mouth was opened by
forcing the lower jaw down with the finger. This was necessary
more often when a cold bath was not used. In any event the mouth
was cleaned out with the finger before the child was put aside in
its cradle. Fawnskin or rabbit fur were preferred materials for
protecting the infant in the cradle. These were blankets; the body
was not wrapped.

Massage or pressure was used to effect rapid ejection of the placenta. Sometimes a drastic method was used: the woman stood up
and exerted pressure upon the abdomen by pushing against the end
of a pole which leaned diagonally from the ground. In extreme
cases the midwife attempted to remove the placenta manually. The
afterbirth was gathered on a reed mat, wrapped with the reeds,

and set safely aside. As soon as the mother was able to do so, she buried the material outside the camp, deep enough so that it could not be disturbed by animals. Two divergent beliefs were held regarding the consequences of an animal obtaining the placenta: either the infant would die or no other children could be borne. Sometimes a woman who had suffered severely during delivery would intentionally, but secretly, give the placenta to a dog so that she might have no further children. If the fact were discovered the woman might be severely criticized by her husband and his parents but no punitive action was taken.

The placenta was never burned, nor was it necessary to bury it in the woods or in any other specific location. No one but the mother was permitted to dispose of it.

The mother rested on the bed where delivery had occurred. To make her more comfortable hot stones were placed alongside her body and at her feet. Sometimes flat heated stones were placed in a shallow depression, then covered with tule mats or brush. The woman lay on this heated bed, well covered with robes. The sweating thus induced was considered beneficial. To protect against retention of any of the blood of parturition, flat heated stones were placed on the abdomen and held in place by a band of buckskin. Except in winter the heated bed was used for only a day or two. In frigid weather or in cases where complications had occurred, this might be continued for five days. Usually the mother left the bed from time to time after a day had passed, and left finally in two to five days. Factors affecting the period of inactivity included ease or difficulty of delivery, first or later confinement, and individual attitudes. The woman who arose soon was believed to bear subsequent children more easily. The abdomen was kept wrapped with buckskin even after the bed was left.

Midwives did not tarry beyond the first day unless complications occurred. Protracted labor was often attributed to internal inversion, sometimes upon visible evidence. The midwife's method of correcting the condition was to cause the woman to be held aloft by the feet. While assistants, men or women, held the patient in this position the midwife massaged her abdomen. Another procedure was to place the woman on a blanket, several persons grasped the edges of the blanket, lifted the woman and twirled her around several times. If these techniques failed a shaman was called. Internal version was never attempted either by midwife or shaman.

When the midwife diagnosed delayed delivery as merely due to "failure of the muscles to relax" the woman was given copious drafts of warm water. This was considered beneficial in any event and was continued for several days after delivery. Danger of hemorrhages was thought to be lessened thereby.

When a shaman was called he used the ordinary curing procedure in which sucking was not employed. His diagnosis included the physical condition as well as the factors responsible. He might declare that the fetus had grown to the mother's womb, that the position was inverted, or that the umbilical cord was twisted. The cause was given as the breaking of a pregnancy taboo. In treating the patient he called spirits such as Buzzard that were "not afraid of unpleasant odors." Significantly, the midwives continued to work during the shaman's activities. It was the husband who called the shaman (or the invoker) when he was needed. The husband was subject to no restrictive taboos at this time but hunting and traveling were avoided for five days after the child's birth.

Nursing was begun on the day of birth if possible. The first of the mother's milk was invariably released on the coals of the fire; this was thought to insure an adequate supply. Also, this milk was thought to be unfit for the child. If necessary, the nipples were opened with a tiny quill or a stiff whisker hair from a dog. The breasts were massaged but were neither oiled nor steamed.

The infant was given a steam bath on the second day, "so that he may be light in weight and easy to carry." The child was placed, while in his cradle, on the top of a large basket containing water and hot rocks. He was left there so long as the steam continued to rise, a brief period in any event. Water-lily seeds were floated on the water because they are so very light in weight. The mother attended to the bathing if she were able. A careless mother might neglect the matter altogether.

The navel stump was expected to slough off on the fifth day. When it became detached it was placed in a small buckskin bag prepared for the purpose. This container, often decorated with beadwork, was tied to the cradle on the right side near the child's shoulder. It remained here throughout the period of use. It was not removed when the cradle was disposed of by burning.

Beginning soon after birth and continuing for two or three weeks the facial areas and limbs were oiled and massaged to give them the appearance considered most attractive. Large eyes, a thin straight nose, and straight limbs were especially desired. The mother or other relatives might do this. As with the steam bath, the mother's interest largely determined the amount of attention given. Beginning not later than the fifth day, the child was bathed regularly, as often as every morning and evening or as seldom as once in three or four days. Water was sprinkled on the body and rubbed with the hand. This was done regardless of the season. Cold water was used for older infants to induce good sleeping habits, strength, and good health. Oil continued to be used but it was no substitute for bathing. An ointment consisting of a macerated tuberous root *(lopaqs)* was placed in the armpits and between the legs to prevent chafing.

Fish, shellfish, and meat were taboo to both the mother and father during the child's first five days of life. Neglect of the taboo caused illness to the parents, not the child. There was no restriction on the quantity of roots, seeds, or berries that might be eaten. On the sixth day both mother and father took sweat baths and resumed normal activities, but if the child were born during summer traveling the parents might delay movement for as little as two or three days.

After the birth of a child it was considered impolite to inquire directly as to its sex. Instead, one asked, "What is it?" If a boy, the answer was, "It belongs to the home"; if a girl, "It will go away"; reference was to the initial postmarital residence.

If snow or rain fell immediately after the birth of a first child it was attributed to the mother, who was thus characterized as "unlucky" or "one of bad omens." Although no fear was associated with the birth of twins it was thought that one of them would surely die, whether they were identical or fraternal. In the latter case the sex did not indicate the ill-fated one. A stillborn child was cremated and mourned in the same manner as any other child. No special taboos were involved.

Contraception and abortion were seldom attempted. A vague notion was current that some women knew of a contraceptive medicine. Knowledge concerning abortion was more specific. The technique employed was pressure on the end of a projecting log or other object, but it was rarely called into use. Infanticide was more common. Unmarried mothers not uncommonly delivered their children in isolation and secrecy and immediately disposed of them. This was more or less anticipated by the community, but not condoned. However, if no measures were taken by relatives to prevent the act the community was not concerned.

If the mother died at childbirth, or during a child's nursing period, or if she proved incapable of nursing, a relative was sought to serve as wet nurse. No alternatives such as the use of broth or tea were attempted. The mother or wet nurse kept the child at the breast until about two years of age, the usual time for discarding the cradle. It was not unusual, however, for a tolerant mother to allow a child to nurse until four years of age or occasionally even older. These older children were teased by their playmates, but not thus deterred. If a child were born while another was still nursing the latter was not automatically weaned. The two might be nursed together for some time. Children were allowed the breast whenever they appeared hungry.

The milk diet was supplemented with other food after four to six months. A gruel of finely ground roots (epos, *Carum* sp.) and pieces of soft fat were used; also, meat, fish, or roots prechewed by the mother. A piece of tough meat was given the teething infant to chew on.

The cradle was of openwork, twined-basketry construction; willow withes or tule were the materials employed. Willow was preferred for its greater durability but tule was easier to weave and was more comfortable when few blankets were used, as in summer. The shape was ovoid and the construction was identical to that used for the woven moccasin, including the method of binding. The shape was achieved by spreading or contracting of warps, as necessary; secondary warps were not employed. The loops for lacing were merely modifications of the wefts at the sides. A buckskin thong was used for lacing.

The child was placed in a cradle within a few hours after birth. The delay was due to the necessity of weaving the cradle after the child was born. If done before, the infant might be stillborn. The first cradle was usually of tule, woven hurriedly and with no great care by one of the women present. Later the mother prepared a better specimen for the child, usually of willow. This was used until outgrown or damaged. The child used the cradle until walking age, variously estimated at one and a half to two years plus. The cradle was not then immediately discarded; it was kept for use, when the child was ill, until completely outgrown. Then it was burned, never being saved for another infant.

In recent years ("since the coming of the whites") the Modoc used the Plateau-type board cradle for infants older than one or two months. This was borrowed from the Klamath with slight modifications. The board was triangular, pointed at the bottom, the other two angles slightly rounded. The handle was a triangular projection at the top or a small hole in the upper middle of the board. Holes were made along the edge of the board by burning; lacing loops were threaded through these. A piece of buckskin or rabbit skin was laid over the board, the child placed on this, the edges of the skin folded over, and two bands laced over the infant to hold it in place. The lower band extended from the feet to the groin; the upper covered the abdomen and chest. It was only necessary to remove the lower latchet in order to change the diaper material. Shredded sagebrush bark or tule were used for this purpose. The child was held in a semisitting position by means of a bundle of tule which was not a part of the cradle but was inserted under the child's buttocks. The tule was woven into a rectangular mat which was folded to size and crushed to shape. A willow hoop extended over the head of the cradle board as in most Plateau forms. From this were hung objects for the amusement of the child but its primary purpose was protection in case of a fall. The pointed bottom, a specialized feature, permitted the board to be thrust in the ground to stand upright while the mother was engaged in such activities as root digging. The mother carried the board by means of a shoulder tumpline. The cradleboard was made by the child's father. The material used was cedar. Several children might use the same one successively.

The basketry cradle continued in use for young infants. It was carried on the left arm, with the child's head to the left. The latchet string was over the child's right side, the side near the mother. If ever carried on the back a forehead tumpline was used. Cradles for boys and girls were identical in both basketry and board types.

The child was kept in a cradle, of either type, throughout the day except for brief periods when it was removed and allowed freedom of activity. These "rest" periods were necessarily more frequent in summer than in winter. In the home during the daytime the cradle rested on the floor near the mother. Even the board cradle was laid on its back. At night the child was removed and taken to bed with the mother.

When it was necessary to carry older children the ordinary forehead tumpline was employed. The child sat in the loop at the mother's back and grasped her shoulders or body. If the mother were carrying a burden basket the child might be supported in that, if empty, or on top, if filled.

Children received names, entirely without ceremony, during the first months of their lives. These were conferred by the father or mother or any other near relative, particularly the grandparents. The names were meaningful, usually descriptive of some peculiarity of the child. Ancestral names or those of living relatives were not taken, but names were sometimes duplicated because of parallel traits and the limitations of the pattern. A shaman

sometimes conferred a name following a cure, similarly meaningful, usually with reference to the illness. Individuals, young or
old, were often called by the place names of their nativity, as nick-
names. These were especially useful when the personal name could
not be remembered or when mourning taboos forbade mention of
the name.

12 CHILDHOOD

Parents expected an additional child every two to four years. Two years were considered the minimum time spacing between births. The infant mortality rate was relatively high; recorded data indicate that not more than two out of three survived the first few years. Consequently fraternities were not especially large; ten children were considered a very large family, perhaps the maximum. The mode was closer to five.

Children were never offered for adoption in order to reduce the size of a family. Adoption was limited to relatives and to cases where the child was an orphan or was neglected or deserted by a widower father. Adoption was not formal but the child was entitled to all the rights of a blood offspring, including inheritance. Slave children were well treated but did not enjoy the status of the adopted child.

Deep parental affection for children was shown in many ways. When the first child was born it was not unusual for the parents to alternate in sitting up with the infant throughout the night. Being well aware of the high infant mortality they feared the child would become ill and not receive prompt enough attention. Even though the child slept well the vigil might be kept for the first weeks at least. In winter one of the objects was to keep the fire burning so that there would be no danger of illness from exposure. The first and last children are said to have been the favorites of most parents. Fathers gave more objective evidences of love to children than did mothers; they had more time to do so. Frequently they fondled the youngsters, holding them, hugging them, and performing amusing antics. Mothers seldom or never did likewise. Fathers

105

often cared for the children in the absence of the mother, even though others were available for the task. A father might sit for hours at a time beside an ailing son or daughter. The physical care of the older and apparently healthy child was often neglected, however. It was recognized that some of the skin diseases suffered by children were the result of allowing them to become too dirty. An ointment was applied to the skin, but little attention was given to correction of the cause. Children were never summoned for meals. This was not a mark of neglect but rather of recognition of the child's individuality and prerogatives. It was assumed that he would come at the proper hour if hungry. At any hour he was privileged to come to the house for any food available without preparation.

Older children were expected to supervise the activities of the younger ones. Even a child of cradle age was often tended or carried by a brother or sister only a few years older. The object was to free the mother for other efforts rather than to acquaint the child with adult responsibilities. Few formal tasks were assigned to the young child. Carrying wood and water was an incidental activity which a child was asked to do if older persons were otherwise occupied. Formal training in economic activities such as hunting and basketmaking was not begun before adolescence. For example, it was rare for a young boy to accompany his father on a hunting expedition. Girls more often went with their mothers to seed-gathering or berry-picking grounds. They carried small baskets but these were principally for amusement since they seldom gathered many seeds or berries before they wandered away for play. They were not recalled to the task.

Children were permitted to watch adults at work as much as they cared to, and boys did, for example, learn to make respectable bows and arrows of small size; girls made passable baskets in miniature. When these were shown to parents praise was abundant and children were encouraged to persevere. The praise stemmed from true pride in the child's achievement; it was not a mechanism for stimulation. As phrased by one informant, "My parents were proud of me; and the prouder they were of me the more I wanted to work hard and the better I felt. So I was never lazy."

The small game killed by boys was never eaten by them, but only by adults. The first deer killed was left lying where it fell. Parents or other adults brought it to camp and it was dressed and eaten but the boy was given no share. Thereafter, however, he could eat flesh of game of any kind that he felled. There was no ritualization of this event.

Boys and girls were occasionally required to bathe in cold lakes or streams, even in winter, in order that they might become strong and brave. A child might be aroused in the middle of the night, without previous warning, and be taken or sent to a nearby body of water. Upon return home the child was permitted to warm himself by the fire. Emphasis upon this kind of training was very slight, a mere shadow of that found among tribes to the north.

The appearance of the first permanent tooth was used as a measure of age but no further significance was attributed to the phenomenon. When a milk tooth became loose it was pulled out with the fingers. At dusk the child threw the tooth away, toward the west, while facing the setting sun.

The activities and games of children are well portrayed in the reminiscent narratives of two informants, Peter Sconchin and Jennie Clinton. First, Sconchin:

ILLUSTRATIVE DATA

"When I was a child the first thing I did in the morning was to go out and play. I played around Tule Lake where the tules and grass grow thick on the north shore. Many of us boys played there together. We used to go out in the high tules, about seven of us. There three of us sat down and closed our eyes while the other three went off to hide. We covered our eyes with our hands but the seventh boy watched to see that no one stood up or opened his eyes. This boy didn't play. After a while we got up to look for the other boys. When we found them we went hiding and the others had to look for us.

"After we played this game for a while we went swimming in the lake. We had races to see who could swim farthest under water, or stay under longest. I played this game often when I was young.

"Every boy had bows and arrows that his father had made for him. The bows were made of young juniper. We used to go out in the tall grass of the lake and look for chub fish. When the chubs moved around the grass waved. Then we knew where to go; we pushed the grass aside and shot at the chubs with our arrows.

"I killed frogs, too, with small arrows that my father made for me. I also killed lots of watersnakes. I was afraid of them but I shot at them just the same.

"I used to go with the bigger boys to hunt chipmunks. I headed

off the chipmunks while the bigger boys shot at them. At times I
spent all day chasing chipmunks that ran from brush to brush.

"When wild rye was ripe the bigger boys would try to hit the
stalks with their arrows. We used to see how many of them we
could hit.

"After a while I played with rye-grass arrows. We used strips
of bark as feathers. A big boy would sharpen the stalk to make a
point. We played at dodging these rye-grass arrows. If you were
hit by one it broke the skin. When you saw an arrow coming, you
turned aside. If two or more arrows came you twisted around and
jumped sideways.

"With several other boys I played a game of dodging a tule ball.
We made up two sides. If I failed to dodge successfully I was out
and a boy from the other side took my place. When I was hit it
didn't hurt. But when I was hit behind the ear with it, it hurt.

"When we were about ten we got a long pole and tied a large
ball to the end loosely, with tules. Then we gave a strong thrust
to the pole, so that the ball left the pole. It was pretty hard to
dodge that mud ball. Only a good quick boy could do that. About
five or six boys played on each side, alternating as with the tule
ball game.

"We also played at driving the other side away with long poles
with mud balls on the ends. The poles were very flexible and had
a good snap to them.

"We used to get a section of hard willow about a foot long, hollow
on the inside. We made a ramrod of another stick. Then we split a
stalk of tule, took out the pith, and twisted it tight and slender and
about six inches long. We then stuffed it in the hollow willow pipe
and gave a quick push with the ramrod. The twisted tule shot out
like a bullet. We saw who could shoot farthest with it. We could
only shoot eight or ten feet but it shot hard.

"Little boys used a similar hollow willow. They put juniper berries in them and blew on one end with their mouths. The berries
went pretty far.

"We also played with a slingshot about three feet long. The pocket
was about three inches wide and six inches long and made of buckskin. The strings were buckskin also. At the end of one of the
strings was a small loop for the index finger. This side was never
let go. A rock was put in the pocket and the other end drawn up
and held in the same right hand. The sling was twirled a couple of
times around the shoulder, and the rock let fly by letting go of the
loose end. It would travel pretty far. We killed birds, squirrels,
chipmunks, rabbits, and even ducks with this sling.

"In the springtime we ran races by hopping on one leg. We bet weasel hides on our races.

"Most of the time boys ran ordinary races every evening, and wrestled. I did this when I was old enough to wrestle. I wrestled until I was a man. I was a good wrestler.

"We used to play at dodging sling shots but when they hit they nearly broke your skull. They left bad bruises. We used to stand a long way off. When the boys shooting them came closer we would run off. They weren't easy to dodge.

"In winter I went hunting cottontails with my sling. But if I had a bow with me I would shoot them with that. If I only had a rock I would try to kill the rabbit with that. We saved the skins until we had enough to make a rabbitskin blanket.

"When I came back to lie down before going to sleep, I used to hear my father's mother tell stories of the mythological times.

"When we moved I had to walk. All young boys walked. While on the way I always wondered what sort of a place we would stop. I was always in a big hurry to get to our next place as quickly as possible. I couldn't wait."–Peter Sconchin.

"We used to play a game in which we held hands and danced around in a ring. We also played at trying to outdo one another in jumping while in a crouching position. And we would see who could jump farthest on one leg. That was certainly amusing: when a girl fell down we laughed and said that she did that because we were winning over her in the races.

"We climbed the mountains wherever we lived. It was difficult climbing. We had good times thus. We would say, 'Let's see who can go up first and get down first. The winner will be respected and will be a great person.' I used to fall down often when I tried to win. When I fell while going down the others shouted at me, 'Now that rolling down doesn't count!' I shouted back at them because I was angry.

"We used to try to make little baskets faster than each other. We would say, 'If someone is only half finished when the others are all finished we'll look down on that one as the poorest kind of person.' How tickled our parents were when they saw our little baskets!

"We never gambled when we were small. We had no bad habit of trying to win things from one another.

"Once we were sent to gather duck eggs, mudhen eggs, and any other eggs we could find in swampy places. We carried little burden baskets on our backs in which we put the eggs. The first girl to bring the eggs back got a little wristlet of beads or a small necklace. People who had many beads used them to get the children to do these things."–Jennie Clinton.

In addition to the toys and games mentioned in the narratives, girls made dolls of tule and constructed houses of mud. Boys threw willow javelins at a sagebrush target. A moving target consisting of a disc of sagebrush about two inches in diameter was shot at with unfeathered arrows of rye grass, the point sharpened by burning. The disc was rolled along a smoothed section of ground. Balls of grass or tule were rolled along a similar playing area with the object of hitting a sagebrush target. Sides were chosen by the numerous children that played together at these games. A wooden ball was fashioned by further shaping a bolus cut from the trunk of a tree. This was used for tossing from one player to another. Boys and girls shared some games and were permitted to play together whenever they cared to do so but most often they chose the company of their own sex.

The lack of pressure upon children to perform useful labor or to gain technical skills was mentioned above. However, from earliest infancy children were conscientiously trained in ethics, behavior, and tradition. Myths and anecdotes were told to them directly, or to the family group with the children as the significant auditors. Advice was frequently given respecting relations with other children and proper attitudes toward adults. They were admonished not to fight with other children so that the parents might not have trouble. Respect and obedience to adults were strongly emphasized. Lying was not tolerated. Older children were forbidden to punish younger ones left in their care.

"A child that talked back to its elders got a good whipping. Children were very obedient to all adults, whether they were relatives or strangers.

"If a boy were 'mean' his parents would try to whip it out of him. If he were caught lying they would give him double punishment. If a girl were mean she would be whipped in the same way. It's no wonder that children were good when they saw other children being lashed.

"Sometimes children were punished by being given very little to eat.

"At other times a child was put in a sweat house for punishment. The entrance was closed and the child couldn't get out. It certainly was hot when they did that to me! I had been disobedient and I thought I was going to die in that sweat house.

"Parents were insistent that they be obeyed. But children were not as bad as they are now.

"We were told, 'These mountains, these rivers hear what you say and if you are mean they will punish you.' As little children we used to hear the old people talk about what the earth did to them."– Jennie Clinton.

Young children were scolded or lightly punished–the pulling of an ear or switching on the legs–when they disobeyed, falsified, or caused damage in the home. But children above six or seven years of age were expected to know the rules of proper behavior. They were no longer punished for minor transgressions but were more severely handled for serious infractions. Severe fighting with other children was the most frequent action calling for punishment. Whipping with a heavy willow withe over the back and legs was the usual penalty. Either the mother or the father did the whipping, commonly the latter. Other relatives were not privileged to do so although grandparents did not hesitate to give advice.

The more serious altercations between children and the consequences of such are discussed in the following remarks of Peter Sconchin. This informant's tendency to dramatize and exaggerate must be taken into account in judging his comments.

"Both boys and girls fought with the fists, but not like the whites. The fists, clenched, struck with a downward motion, rather than from the shoulder. They mostly pulled the hair and tried to throw the opponent down. They held the hair and kicked. They struck with rocks and sticks.

"Three girls, one larger than I, once whipped three of us boys. The big girl threw me down and hit me with a stick. We all ran away as soon as we could.

"Brothers fought with one another when small. Parents stopped such fights and talked at length to them, saying it was very bad to fight. If a boy was always fighting and couldn't be stopped his father told him to leave home and go to those with whom he could get along. The boy usually went to his father's brother's home or he could go to any relative's home that would have him.

"If a boy ran away they let him go. He had to find relatives, or even strangers, with whom to stay. Relatives asked the boy why he had run away. Then they decided whether to take him or not. They might send him away but they would never take him back. Where he stayed the boy had to help with the light work. After a while the father and mother might visit the boy and if he talked convincingly they would take him back. He had to promise not to fight.

"In whipping a hard willow switch was used over the back and legs until the boy said, 'I will be a good boy.' While the boy was being whipped other boys came to jeer and make fun of him. After

a boy was whipped he was very mad. He went out to hide where he
couldn't be seen. There he cried and felt bad. Other boys were
afraid to taunt him then because that might start a fight.

"Sometimes a big boy came while a small boy was being whipped
and said, 'Don't whip that boy any more; he'll be a good boy.' If the
one being punished said that he would be a good boy and not do anything more bad the parent might say, 'All right, I'll not whip you
any more if you will keep your word.'

"Sometimes a boy didn't go out after being punished. His mother
might give him something to eat and say, 'Now you be a good boy.'
His father might sit beside him and say, 'Now don't do that any
more.' He told him what he should do and what he should not do.
The boy would say, 'All right, I'll do that.'

"If a boy was young he had to be cared for, and he had to be
whipped until he said, 'I'll be a good boy.' If he wouldn't say it he
was whipped until he did.

"Sometimes a boy killed his brother in a fight. My father said
that his brother once killed a younger brother. Nothing was done
to him. If a boy was considered good he wasn't whipped or sent
away even if he killed a brother [since it must have been uninten-
tional]. But if he should be whipped, either his father or mother
did it. He was whipped until he was like dead on the floor.

"A boy's punishment was a family concern. Other people had
nothing to do with it. Sometimes relatives or friends talked to the
parents about a bad boy or talked to the boy to make him good."–
Peter Sconchin.

13 DEATH AND MOURNING

Cremation was the only method of disposal of the dead recognized by the Modoc. Rich and poor, shamans and laymen, freemen and slaves, homicides and suicides, and the stillborn were cremated. The only exceptions were the disapproved and secret burials of aborted fetuses, and infanticides. Those killed in war were brought home for cremation if possible; otherwise the corpse was burned near the battleground unless circumstances made this quite impossible. Similarly, hunters or travelers who died far from home were returned for cremation. Only when physical circumstances left no alternative was a corpse abandoned. Naturally the person not well regarded would be judged impossible to return under conditions less forbidding than would be the case for the prominent or well loved man.

Preferably the corpse was taken to the regular cremation place of the paternal relatives, the spot where a person's father had been cremated or expected to be. If circumstances made it highly desirable to utilize a crematory nearer the site of death, permission to do so was requested of the paternal relatives.

When a corpse had to be carried a long distance it was customary to partially cremate the body before transporting it. Then only the bones had to be carried. Transportation for a short distance was accomplished by a strong man using a pack strap with one end around the thighs, the other around the chest of the corpse. The dead were never transported by canoe.

Sometimes a dying man spoke to the members of his family, asking them not to grieve and giving them his last words of advice. But he always talked in a normal way and did not offer prophecies

113

or make confessions. Only in delirium did he speak the name of the shaman guilty of his death.

Cremation was carried out as soon after death as was feasible. Under ordinary circumstances this did not exceed twelve to eighteen hours. Burning was never done at night, however. A person who died in the afternoon was cremated early the next morning, but a morning death was followed by disposal soon after noon.

In the meantime the corpse was not removed from the death bed, nor was the bed moved. If a shaman had been in attendance he departed as soon as it was evident that death was imminent. He announced this fact, received his fee, and left. Death was assumed to have occurred when breathing ceased. As soon as the body temperature became markedly lower, preparation of the corpse for disposal was begun. The body and face were washed and the hair was combed and braided in the ordinary way. The washing and other preparations were carried out where the corpse lay. The face was not painted; nothing was put on the hair. The fists were unclenched. The eyelids had been pulled closed at the time of death. New clothing was ready if the death had been anticipated. If not, or if poverty had made such preparations impossible, the man's best clothing was placed on the body. The old clothing was laid aside to be burned on the pyre. In addition to the new clothing—also in the absence of it—many ornaments and decorations were added, particularly necklaces and other beadwork. Specially prepared dress differed from the ordinary only in its newness and elaborate ornamentation. After the corpse was washed and dressed the arms were folded on the chest and the task was complete. This work was performed by one of the female relatives not numbered among the chief mourners. She was not compensated.

A marked distinction was made between chief mourners and all other relatives. A chief mourner was one who had lost a spouse or a child. The loss of a parent or sibling did not render one a chief mourner, but certain practices, such as cutting a child's hair upon the death of a parent, set these individuals apart from the lesser mourners.

When the chief mourner was a man he left the house immediately for the first phase of his crisis quest, or to weep in secret. He did not necessarily return until the hour of the cremation, even though a night intervened. If the mourner were a shaman he did not return for the funeral. Instead he continued his mourner's quest for several days. A shaman avoided all cremations out of fear of illness to himself. He explained that this was due to the spirits' dislike of the sight of burning. However, a shaman's corpse was cremated in the same manner as that of a layman. A female chief mourner remained in the house and talked and wept simultaneously. She spoke of her lonesomeness and of the cause of death, naming the doctor responsible for the loss if she thought she knew his identity. "Now my husband is dead. That evil doctor killed him. I don't know why. Now I'm all alone. . . ." News of the death spread rapidly and relatives and friends gathered. These talked quietly with one another, and wept, but they did not cry out in the manner of the chief female mourner. The latter continued to express her grief in this way, recalling the deeds of the deceased one and other such matters as they occurred to her. A complete fast was begun by chief mourners immediately after the death, to continue until after the cremation or, in individual cases, for three or four days. The others present were subject to no food taboos; they ate at the usual mealtimes except during the cremation proper. When the corpse had to be kept overnight a number of relatives and friends remained at the house, some staying awake at all times.

The pyre was prepared before the corpse was taken from the house. The builders, usually women, arrived at the crematory at dawn if the death had occurred on the preceding day. Crematories were located on rocky eminences near the various villages. In the selection of a site consideration was given to convenience coupled with isolation, fuel supply, and the presence of broken stone suitable for covering the ashes. The first task of the pyre builders was to clear an area for use. Stones were carried aside or rearranged to provide a level spot. It was desirable to bare the ground but this was seldom possible owing to the extensive deposits of ashes. No pit was dug unless it was feared that cremation could not be continued until the corpse was completely reduced to ashes. Under threat of time or scarcity of fuel—usually at a makeshift crematory—a shallow trench was dug and the fuel piled on this. Later, when the fuel had burned out, any bones remaining could be covered in the trench where they lay by using ashes and stones. The pyre built at a regular village crematory was rectangular, about four by eight feet, and at least three or four feet high. It was considered necessary to use much more fuel for a male corpse than for a female. Any available brush or timber was used, usually pine, juniper, and sagebrush. Large logs were placed at the base, with lighter material on top. When their work was completed the builders returned to the house. All but the chief mourners participated in a morning meal. If a male mourner had spent the night outside he returned at this time.

With completion of the meal, the corpse was prepared for the

bearers. White buckskin was used as a wrapping if available, for
either an adult or a child. An infant was not placed in the cradle;
this was carried separately. In the absence of a white skin wrapping, tanned buckskin or matting might be used, but never a fur
robe. This first covering was wrapped loosely around the extended
corpse. Then a carrying blanket of tanned buckskin was placed underneath and each of the four pallbearers grasped a corner. The
bearers were preferably men; if necessary, however, two men and
two women might serve; the men carried the forward end. An infant
was carried in the arms of one man. The bearers were friends or
distant relatives. The corpse was carried from the house, through
the doorway, head foremost.

The pallbearers preceded the rest of the company but there was
no formal procession. At the crematory the bearers deposited the
corpse on the pyre and folded the corners of the carrying robe over
the body. The head faced the west, the direction of the supernatural
world. The old clothing and all of the personal possessions of the
deceased person were placed alongside the pyre. These had been
carried by other members of the party. Sometimes a slave was
brought, too, and killed here with an arrow or a blow from a club,
and his body placed beside his master. If this were anticipated a
larger pyre would have been built. Often the additional fuel proved
superfluous, because anyone present might save the slave from
death, and take possession of him, by substituting beads of reasonably comparable value. This was usually but not invariably
done. As a substitute, in postwhite times, one or two horses of
the deceased man were killed, quartered, and thrown on the pyre.
Still later, the skin only was burned and the meat eaten.

The property, ostensibly brought for burning, was likewise subject to appropriation. Either beads or services might be given in
compensation. If a man took a quiver of arrows from the pile, for
example, he might at the same time throw a few beads on the pyre,
or he might pick up a long straight pole and thus indicate that he
would serve as fire tender. Pyre builders and pallbearers were
expected to take what they liked from the pile of property. It was
not improper for a man or woman to appropriate an article without
giving any beads or services, but the recipient thereby obligated
himself to reciprocate in some manner at a later time. Similarly,
if a person gave services or offerings of beads but did not take
any property, the chief mourners were expected to do likewise
when the donor lost a close relative. No other obligation was incurred.

The appropriation of a slave preceded the lighting of the fire;

the taking of other property, and the flinging away of beads, took place during the burning. New fire was made with a drill for the kindling of the fuel. A fire tender usually performed this task but a relative might do so if he desired. Four tenders kept the fuel piled compactly around the body, using long poles for the purpose. The pyre builders replenished the fuel as was necessary.

Both mourners and spectators sat in small groups around the fire, the former closer than the latter. Children were present despite the fact that adults urged them to remain away. No one stood up except the fire tenders, and they did so only while working. No ritualist was in charge; no speeches, prayers, or songs of any kind were uttered. Even conversation was meager and hushed. Men occasionally filled their pipes and smoked for a while. The weeping of the chief mourners was audible over the crackling of the flames, but friends attempted to soothe them and urged them not to exhaust their strength by great sorrow. From time to time beads were thrown on the pyre. The strings holding the beads were always broken before they were cast away. Other goods, as well as beads, were burned, especially at the height of the fire. A relative or friend sometimes tore the garments from his back and threw them on the pyre. When it became obvious that no further property of the deceased was to be claimed the remainder was burned. Seldom was anything of value left to be thus discarded.

All present, whether relatives or merely friends, remained until cremation was complete and the fire burned out. This required a half day or more. The ashes of bones and fuel were smoothed over and broken stones were placed on top, not to mark the site but rather to obliterate it. The ashes of the bones were never gathered or in any way saved. Friends who had homes nearby returned to them. Near relatives and friends that had come from some distance often remained overnight with the mourners. They prepared food for themselves but the chief mourners did not eat. This was not a funeral feast; there was no such observance.

After the cremation the badges of mourning were assumed. These included the smearing of pine pitch on the skin and hair, the use of charcoal for blackening, the cutting of the hair, and the wearing of a few simple insignia.

A woman's hair was invariably cut upon the death of a husband, occasionally for a child, but not for parents, brothers, or sisters. The cutting was done by the mother-in-law or the aunt-in-law of the mourner; it was cut quite short. A man's hair was sometimes cut in mourning for a wife, seldom for a child, and never for parents or siblings. The man performed the operation himself, hacking the hair off at shoulder length. Thereafter he regularly combed his hair but did not rebraid it for the duration of mourning. A child's hair was cut upon the loss of a parent but not for brothers or sisters. When the father died the mother performed the shearing; when the mother died the paternal grandmother or paternal aunt did so. The hair removed was destroyed by burning.

Pitch was smeared upon the remaining hair and upon the face by women and rarely by men. If a basket hat were worn it was also covered with pitch. When pitch was used by men it was removed after ten days, as also was the facial pitch worn by women. But after the death of a husband a woman kept pitch on her hair for about a year. She carried a supply in a buckskin bag. The last application was allowed to wear away or was removed with grease and a porcupine quill comb. Sometimes pitch was also applied to the hands during the first part of mourning. Over the pitch it was customary to rub charcoal to blacken the skin and to render the resin less sticky. The latter object might also be achieved with rotten bark.

Black buckskin bands were worn on the wrists but not on arms or legs. These were removed after ten days but women wore belts of serviceberry brush for a prolonged period. Ornaments and facial painting were avoided for a minimum of ten days, usually longer.

The chief mourner might leave immediately after the cremation for a quest of several days duration. Men did this far more often than women. The quest was undertaken only upon the loss of a child or spouse, not after the death of parents.

If the death occurred in summer, the house, being a temporary structure, was burned immediately. Prior to setting the fire by scattering embers about, all furnishings were removed. The homeless ones were given places to sleep in the shelters of friends or relatives for the brief period required to build a new structure.

Even a winter house might be burned after the death of an occupant, but this was not often done. The death of a visitor, even a close relative, was not followed by destroying the house. Burning was less common after the death of women than men, and rarer still upon the death of children. After burning had been decided upon the firing was often postponed until spring. Even then the house might be partially dismantled and the large timbers saved. A number of specific factors were involved in these decisions. During patrilocal residence, when a woman lost her husband, the heads of the household, her parents-in-law, lost their son. There were three chief mourners. The widow normally returned to her parents' home for the duration of mourning. The parents destroyed their house as soon as possible. If, however, the wife died there was but one chief mourner, the husband, and the house did not belong to him. It was not likely to be burned. Under matrilocal residence, the death of a husband left one principal mourner, the wife. The house did not belong to the deceased man and the owners, parents of the girl, were not inclined to vacate it. If the wife died there were three chief mourners, including the house owners, but the widower had no title to the house and dwellings were less often burned upon the death of a woman than of a man. It might be allowed to stand. With independent residence the house was burned without delay if the husband died since the wife and children had to go elsewhere to live anyway, but if the wife died during the winter, occupancy of the house was characteristically maintained until the following spring or longer, if the man did not remarry in the meantime. The man would not bring a sister of his widow, or any other new wife, to the house in which the death had occurred. When a child died during the matrilocal or patrilocal residence of the parents the house was never burned. During independent residence the parents decided one way or the other, usually for saving the house, at least until spring.

The reason for destroying a house and the reason for burning or giving away the property of the deceased may be considered together since they derived from a single cause, the desire to eliminate any reminder of the dead person, and thus to ease mourning. There was no fear of supernatural power of a harmful sort being associated with the possessions or habitat of the deceased, or of his ghost remaining about in consequence. It is true that unpleasant dreams involving the dead man were expected if these precautions were not taken, but it was simply association with his things that induced the dreams, not his ghostly presence. When he appeared in a dream he was merely a man—the individual as he had been in life—not a ghost. This was true despite the fact that a well developed concept of ghosts was present in the culture; the concept functioned in a different sphere, the shamanistic. If the inexplicable phenomenon of death had been responsible for the burning of property, no distinctions would have been made in terms of sex, house ownership, and degree of relationship, nor would the personal property of the deceased have been appropriated rather than burned, to be used by the recipients without any magical procedures to divest it of harm-producing essence. The horses of the dead man were used immediately. His bow was used after rewrapping the hand grip to suit the new owner. Clothing was worn after being washed. The fact is inescapable that, from the psychological point of view, property was destroyed simply to avoid painful reminders of the deceased. Degree of intimacy with the dead person and consequent potency of the reminders determined the character of decisions as to disposal, tempered by vested interest as in the case of a house owner. When the economic factor weighed heavier than the emotion of loss, a house, for example, was saved until spring or not burned at all.

It hardly need be added that keepsakes of the dead were unknown, or that a name taboo was observed. For a period varying from two years to a generation the name of a deceased person was not used by his immediate relatives or employed by others in speaking to them. The person was referred to by circumlocutions of various kinds such as the place of his nativity: "he of such-and-such a place"; or place of death: "the deceased of such-and-such a place"; or as "the one I lost."

It might be felt that the wearing of marks of mourning was inimical to the avowed object of putting the deceased out of mind. But these were formal practices, in no way personal in their significance. They were passive in character; worn constantly they lost their power of association. Indeed, they served largely to remind others that the wearer could not properly engage in hilarity or receive the advances of suitors.

Here may be recalled the offerings of beads and property at the time of cremation. These were not for the use of the person in a subsequent life; they were merely a mark of respect for the deceased. Even when a slave was burned a few beads were thrown on the fire. The Modoc emphasis upon wealth made the sacrifice of property a mark of high honor to the deceased and made of the donor a fellow sufferer with the chief mourners.

Death was feared as an emotional crisis but it held no horror as a mysterious phenomenon. This contention of informants is borne out by the evidence already presented, and also by the mourning observances which included a crisis quest but no purification ceremonies, either for the chief mourners or for those who handled the corpse. Mourning taboos were few in number and followed formal patterns of the culture. Fish—an unimportant food—was not eaten for the duration of mourning, a period of a year or more. It will be remembered that this taboo applied also to the parents of a new-born child. The penalty for violation was the same in both instances, a coughing illness. For the ten days of intensive mourning both men and women used a scratching implement. This was a flat wooden piece about a half inch by three inches in size, charred and then scraped; or a bone piece of about the same size. It was hung from the right wrist with a short piece of string. Use of the fingernails for scratching resulted in sores, it was thought. Again the pattern is found in another crisis, puberty. Properly speaking there were no food gathering taboos associated with death. All but the chief mourners continued these activities uninterruptedly. The mourners did not do so, but that was because for them all ordinary activities were suspended and formalized mourning substituted. At the end of intensive mourning these pursuits were resumed. Sweat baths were taken at the termination of mourning observances, as in any crisis ritual. They were not used to counteract contamination.

As indicated earlier, mourning was divided into two parts, an intensive period of ten days followed by modified mourning for a year or longer. The initial period was further divided into two five-day terms. The first of these was devoted to the quest, if that were undertaken. The second five days were spent largely in the sweat house. If the quest were omitted the total period might be telescoped to five days with alternating periods of weeping and sweating. Weeping was semiformalized. In the mornings and evenings particularly, the mourner wailed loudly; if he were in the village others heard him and wept also, but did not go to join him. During the midday hours the mourner wept less loudly and less formally. The complete fast was broken on the second or third day. Vegetal foods, seeds, and fruits were eaten during the remaining days, meat and fish being avoided. During the sweating period the mourner might spend his whole time at the sudatory, using it as a sleeping place at night, or he might merely visit there several times a day. Usually the mourner remained at the sweat house throughout the days but spent the nights in his dwelling house. Steam baths were taken only occasionally through the day even though the mourner did not leave the lodge. The remainder of the time he sat in the warm lodge and mourned, sometimes weeping or sleeping but never praying or singing. Mourning songs were unknown. The sweat house used was always a new one built for the purpose. It was large enough for two people but was ordinarily used by one person only. A man and woman mourning the loss of a child might use the lodge jointly, either at the same time or alternately. Sweating followed the usual pattern. The body was not massaged or in any way specially treated; steaming was of the usual intensity and duration. No medicines were drunk. Special bedding or eating utensils were unnecessary.

After the ten days the ordinary routines were resumed and all foods except fish might be eaten. Rules of the second period of mourning were only moderately restrictive. Boisterous behavior, loud laughing, and singing were improper, and playful relationships with those of the opposite sex were prohibited. That was all. In individual cases, however, a person of his own accord prolonged some phases of the initial period, especially semi-isolation, in order to show the profundity of his grief. It was assumed, too, that the length to which secondary mourning was carried, sometimes as long as two years, was a reflection of great consciousness of loss. The objective mark of end of mourning was remarriage. It was recognized that women generally remarried much sooner than men. The differential is properly interpreted as a function of polygyny and consequent shortage of women.

Men and women who characteristically devoted much time to gambling were especially inconvenienced by the prohibition in secondary mourning against hilarious activity. Literally interpreted this ruled out gambling until mourning was ended. Some persons abided by the restriction but prominent and successful gamblers seldom did so. Their friends, when losing, would beg them to enter the game and help them recoup their losses. Such entreaties were seldom ignored, especially when, as was customary, a horse or other valuable piece of property was offered to the mourner as an inducement. The person who gambled while yet in mourning was apt to be reckless, winning much or losing all. But his luck was thought to be more favorable than unfavorable because he had not gambled for some time. Anyone who forewent gambling for some time supposedly had better than average luck when he resumed.

The only property of value remaining after a funeral was slaves or horses. Normally these were inherited by the sons, particularly the eldest son. The exact distribution desired was often indicated by a man before his death. If there were no sons the wife was the most likely recipient. If the sons were young their mother received any available slaves but horses were given to her only to hold until the sons were old enough to have them. Brothers and sisters did not inherit, nor did other relatives. Women did not ordinarily own horses but they might have slaves to pass on to their children upon death.

Upon rare occasions the aged father of a deceased man committed suicide at his son's cremation. He might attempt to jump on the pyre and when restrained cut his throat with an obsidian knife, or hang himself. Mothers were also known to do this. The reason was combined grief and loss of a familiar home and economic security.

There were no anniversary ceremonies or other subsequent honors for the deceased.

14 GAMES AND GAMBLING

The social and ceremonial significance of games and gambling in Modoc life was very great, as comments throughout the preceding pages have indicated. All social occasions were enlivened by the playing of games, which is to say, gambling. In Modoc speech one word *(ca ʿqla)* signified both games, of the nonathletic variety, and gambling. The skilled and successful gambler was a man of high status both socially and economically. Very considerable quantities of goods changed hands in the course of gambling. To the extent that chance determined winnings, no fortunes could be made. The stakes were sometimes quite high in a single game, but within the tribe one game followed another throughout the year and the leveling effect was felt, if not today, then tomorrow. No man could win heavily in one or a few games, take his winnings and retire from future play. Only the consistently unlucky man was privileged to withdraw from play for a prolonged period of time.

However, some men did win more consistently than they lost because the gambling games involved more than the factor of chance; a large element of skill was present. All of the games utilized marked pieces that the player arranged, then kept hidden, until his opponent offered a guess as to the arrangement, whereupon they were shown. However, the guesser was permitted unlimited preliminary guesses, without being committed to such guesses until he accompanied one with a subtle formal signal. Likewise, until such a signal was given, the opponent was privileged to shift the position of the pieces at will. The result was a contest between two men, who studied one another's eyes and suggestive face and body movements, as preliminary guesses or the arrangements of

123

the pieces were varied to suit all possible combinations. The one who interpreted his opponent's actions the more accurately and moved the more swiftly to make the signal, or to accomplish a rearrangement, was certain to be the winner in the long run. Consequently, the skillful gambler was usually in a comfortable economic position.

Less talented players were able to boost their winnings by betting with the more successful gamblers. The games played by men involved teams varying in number from a minimum of two to an indefinite maximum of fifteen or eighteen, with five to ten as the usual range. One man was the organizer and leader. The others were those who bet with him and who served as singers. The leader, sometimes with a partner, carried out the actual play so long as he was satisfied with the degree of his success against the opposing team. He might retain the active role throughout a short game—one of two or three hour's duration—but games often lasted for many hours, or even many days, with recesses. The duration of a game was largely the result of the frequency of shifts in the fortunes of the respective sides. In the course of a lengthy game the leader often successively utilized all the members of his team as active players. Therefore, rather conflicting factors were involved in the making up of a team. The poorer players sought places on the teams of consistently successful leaders, whereas such a leader tried to enlist men whose accomplishments approached his own since he might have to relinquish the play to them.

Tribal wealth, in the sense of the aggregate possessions of individual members, depended not inconsiderably on gambling fortunes. Intertribal gatherings were invariably the occasion for intensive gambling and in these games the opposing teams were always from different tribes. Furthermore, the stakes were highest and the competition fiercest in these contests. At the same time, these intertribal games emphasized individual betting more than the encounters at home. In the latter, the goods wagered by teammates were pooled and the two leaders had to agree upon the essential equality of the aggregates. At the end of the game the leader of the winning team presented each of his men with goods of roughly double the value of the bet. In the intertribal games, however, all bets were individual and had to be covered individually. Thus, the member of a winning team received his original bet plus the specific goods with which it had been matched.

The intertribal contest was called the basket game *(p'a ˇlaga ɑ· ˊqla)* and was never played intratribally, not even between subdivisions of the tribe. The game was initiated by a challenge from

one man to another. These two became the respective leaders and
the acceptance of the challenge was followed by the recruiting of
team members and the gathering of goods for betting—activities
which took considerable time, sometimes hours. Games were
played either day or night, hence the teams assembled as soon as
the preparations were complete. The site was any comfortable and
convenient level spot but was usually a regularly utilized location
within the village but a hundred feet or more from the nearest
house. The teams formed parallel lines several feet apart, with
the leaders in the middle positions. A blanket, buckskin robe, or
mat was placed between the lines. If it were dark, a fire was built
between the rows, the blanket to one side. Each man squatted on
his right leg, left knee raised. Women were allowed to watch, if
not menstruating, but they stood some distance behind the rows.
They never participated in the play.

When the rows were formed the bets were offered. A man would
throw an object upon the blanket. This might be anything of value:
an article of clothing, a robe, a weapon, or a tool. When a horse
or a canoe was offered the gambler merely identified the wager by
description or name. Any man on the opposing team was privileged
to match the bet. Teammates deferred to the first man offering
a match but if he were not successful others would make proposals.
Usually the matching was accomplished with a minimum of bick-
ering. The match might involve a single object or a combination
of items. When agreement was reached another man, on either
team, would offer a bet. Participants were not required to make
wagers, nor was there any limitation on the number of separate
bets that might be made. Play was initiated when no further of-
fers were made. The time occupied by the arranging of the wagers
was sometimes brief, sometimes hours. The goods accumulated
varied from a meager amount to the equivalent of a small fortune.

The play required gaming pieces, a covering plaque, and counters. The pieces were of wood, cylindrical, and four in number,
constituting two pairs. Each pair consisted of one relatively large
piece, plainly finished, and a smaller one wrapped the full length
with buckskin. The plaque was circular, spirally woven with chev-
ron design ornamentation and deer dew hoofs fastened to the top
center to serve as rattles. The plaque was kept flexible by periodic dampening, and raised sides were formed by bending it over
a stick. The resulting semibasket shape gave the name to the game
and permitted the plaque to be used to cover the gambling pieces
while they were being manipulated, the uncreased sides providing
openings for the player's wrists. The ten counters were sections

of willow or serviceberry withes, sometimes painted red, and pointed on one end for thrusting into the ground.

The team which accepted the challenge was given the favored first position, that of holding the pieces. The game opened when the leader and his teammates started a favorite gambling song to the accompaniment of beating on a raised pole or log which was placed before them. The leader displayed his gambling pieces–each man used his own–then placed them under the plaque and started his manipulations. When he was satisfied with the arrangement he removed his hands, swung his arms back and forth with a shoulder motion, elbows flexed and loudly ejaculated *''tcu· ', tcu· ', tcu· ' ''* repetitively while his teammates continued their singing. From time to time the song would be changed. Sometimes a particular song was used for a particular opponent. All of the songs were specific for this game and the repertory was quite large. Since this was an intertribal game the songs of the two sides sometimes differed considerably in pattern and also, of course, in the language of their words. Likewise, subtle aspects of the game itself and the paraphernalia differed on the two sides, even between the Modoc and the Klamath. Each tribe followed its own traditions and respected the right of the opponent to do likewise.

The leader of the inactive side intently studied the actions of his opposite and, from time to time, made formal gestures indicating one or another possible arrangement of the gambling pieces. These guesses were made with the right hand, the fingers extended to indicate the positions of the small pieces, and might be accompanied by a shouted word indicative of the placement. At the same time the left hand was held near the right shoulder, palm open. Between guesses the hands were rubbed together, and clapped. All guesses, both by gesture and by name, were merely preliminary and exploratory until the left hand was clapped against the chest on the right. Until the latter signal was made the opposing player disregarded the gestures except as danger signals. If he feared the guesser's next indication would be correct he hastily rearranged the pieces, as was his privilege. The greatest danger to him came at the point when the guesser had tried all possible arrangements except the correct one. It was an accomplished gambler who could keep from letting his opponent know, by some reaction, that he had reached the point at which the next guess would be correct. Seeing this the player, of course, immediately indicated an effective guess and won the point, or points.

When an effective guess was correct with respect to both pairs, the opponent immediately stopped chanting, his partners stopped singing, the plaque was removed and the gambling pieces retrieved, and two counters were pulled from the ground, tossed to the other side, and play was resumed with the roles reversed. When the guess was correct for one pair only, this pair was removed and one counter was given to the opponents. Play was then resumed and continued until a correct guess for the remaining pair reversed the sides.

When the guess was wrong for either one or both pairs, the plaque was not immediately removed. Instead, the leader threw back his head and whistled and his teammates shouted their glee. When he raised the plaque he grasped one or two of the pieces and struck them hard in a crosswise manner against the other pieces. The play resumed without a change of sides. When the guess was wrong for both pairs the game nevertheless advanced a step, with an advantage to the guesser's side, because one pair of gaming pieces was removed, thus improving the odds for a correct guess on the next round. This removal may have been optional, perhaps upon agreement before the game, or with certain tribes.

Although holding the pieces was the favored role, the guesser's side had the advantage of being able to make effective a split-second decision since the movement of the hand by only an inch or two, or the voicing of a single word, was all that was necessary to make final a guess. The opponent, on the other hand, could only change the position of the pieces by moving his arms from a raised position and placing his hands under the plaque. Another complexity of the game reversed these positions. The player holding the pieces was permitted to arrange them in an unorthodox arrangement which would not count one way or the other when an effective guess was made but would allow him to experiment with the guesser's reactions and patterns, with possible advantage in subsequent plays. Also, while such a play was perfectly legitimate, it tended to annoy certain guessers and consequently to put them at a disadvantage.

The game was concluded when one side had won the ten counters of its opponent. The possible arrangements of the gaming pieces and the hand signals for indicating the various positions were as follows:

1. Four pieces parallel, small pieces at opposite extremes; palm upward, forefinger extended, others flexed.

2. Four pieces parallel, both small pieces inside; palm upward, middle and ring fingers extended, others flexed.

3. Four pieces parallel, one small piece between two large ones, the other at either extreme; thumb raised.

4. Four pieces parallel, both small pieces to the right or to the left of both large pieces; unorthodox: no play.

5. Three pieces, in any arrangement, parallel or crossed; unorthodox: no play.

6. Two pieces, crossed; unorthodox: no play.

7. Two pieces (after two had been removed) small piece to the right, as viewed by the guesser; thumb pointing to the right, fingers flexed.

8. Two pieces (after two had been removed) small piece to the left, as viewed by guesser; thumb pointing to the left, fingers flexed.

Cheating was possible, and was not uncommon. The guesser and his team were constantly alert for infractions of the accepted rules for handling the gambling pieces and altercations resulted from suspected or actual violations. These conflicts seldom, however, broke up the game, even when physical encounters took place. The injured side was eventually soothed, either by the opponents surrendering counters for the contested play or merely through the overt expression of their hostility.

The technique of cheating most frequently involved the placing of one piece on top of another so that the upper piece could be pulled to one side or the other with the edge of the plaque when the latter was removed. Any failure to lift the plaque vertically, as was proper, was certain to lead to a challenge.

For this intertribal game players sometimes painted their faces with designs traditionally associated with the game.

The major intratribal gambling mechanism was the hand game *(na´iyaDia)*. It resembled the basket game in all psychological and procedural respects except for certain technical differences. Bets were pooled, as has been mentioned, and the quantity of goods wagered on a single game was generally considerably less than in the intertribal version. As would be expected of the Modoc, cheating was rampant, even more so than in the games with other tribes, and the devices for cheating were numerous. The gaming pieces called "bones" were cylindrical sections of willow, mountain mahogany, deer bone, or deer horn. They were used in pairs, one plain, the other marked with a center wrapping of buckskin or a painted band of black. The size was such as to permit them to be hidden in the closed hand. Cheating was accomplished by momentarily slipping off the buckskin band, by substituting a different piece which had been hidden on one's person for that purpose, by using a piece which had the black center marking painted on one side only, or by speedily and dextrously changing the positions of the pieces after the guess was made. Cheating led to bitter altercations, as in the intertribal games, but the successful cheater was envied and respected, albeit ambivalently.

Women were permitted to participate but the teams were predominantly of men. The physical arrangements were similar to the basket game and ten counters were used in recent times, a reduction from twelve of earlier days. The pieces were held by a pair of players, on opposite sides of the center. The active players were rotated so that all might take part in the course of the game. Guessing was done by the leader, a role he might transfer to one of his teammates at will, however. Each active player shifted his pair of pieces from hand to hand, with much swinging of the arms from side to side, and periodically opened his hands to show the arrangement, sometimes one piece in each hand, sometimes both in one, hoping to confuse his opponents by demonstrating that they could not follow his speedy interchanges. After much display of this sort, each of the two players crossed his arms and held his fists tightly closed near the shoulders. The guesser now proceeded with his trial guesses, followed by a definitive guess indicated by the exclamation *"He⁀' "!* The players holding the pieces had then to display them immediately and to surrender counters, if the guess were partially or wholly correct, as in the basket game. However, the players holding the pieces were free to resume manipulations at any time before the guesser's exclamation was uttered. Unlike the basket game, the players often kept their eyes averted from the guesser during most of their manipulations.

The symbols used in guessing were designed to indicate the positions of the unmarked pieces. The various possible combinations and the associated designations are listed below. All gestures by the guesser were made with his right arm.

1. Two players, both hold unmarked pieces in their right hands; guesser makes sweeping motion to his left (the player's right).

2. Two players, both hold unmarked pieces in left hands; guesser's gesture to his right.

3. Two players, unmarked pieces in hands nearest center of line; guesser's arm lowered medially, fingers spread.

4. Two players, unmarked pieces in hands nearest ends of the line; guesser's arm raised medially, palm down, fingers spread, or thumb and forefinger extended, others flexed.

5. One player, unmarked piece in right hand; guesser gestures to his left.

6. One player, unmarked piece in left hand; guesser gestures to his right.

A woman's gambling game, using dice made from beaver teeth,

porcupine teeth, or wood, was borrowed from the Paiute when
the coming of reservation times ended the warfare between the
two tribes. The game differed in a number of respects from the
Klamath version and, being a recent innovation, exhibited variations in technique and scoring even among the Modoc. The typical form involved the use of a flat stone on which the dice were
thrown with a slight sweeping motion and removed by scooping
them with the right hand into the left palm held below the edge of
the stone. In recent times a basketry mat was used instead of a
stone. Two women only played but others might bet. A run of losses
sometimes led a woman to ask another to throw the dice for her.
The initiator made the first throw of the game, then the dice passed
from side to side when the player failed to make a point. Ten counters were used as in the basket game. Men sometimes watched the
women but they never played the game.

The four dice were marked as two pairs, one with zigzag decoration, the other with parallel hachures, on the face sides. The opposite sides were left blank. The scoring of the possible combinations was as follows:

1. Four marked sides (two pairs) up, two counters.
2. Four unmarked sides up, two counters.
3. One pair of marked sides up, one counter.
4. One pair of unmarked sides up, plus two unlike marked sides,
one counter.
5. All other combinations, no score.

Gambling was a prominent feature of certain athletic games, the
principal ones being a ball-kicking game played by men and the
double-ball shinny game which was exclusive to women. Bets were
individually arranged before the start of the game. Both of these
contests were engaged in during the spring season only. They were
primarily intratribal games but were played against other tribes
when the opportunity arose.

The ball-kicking game was played on an open, flat field. The
actual playing area was marked by stakes or a willow arch at either
end, the goal lines. The length of the field varied considerably,
from a hundred feet to several hundred. The ball, which was of
buckskin filled with deer hair or grass, was several inches in
diameter, a maximum of perhaps eight. At the start of play it
was placed in a shallow depression at the middle of the field. Two
men, one from each team, stood on opposite sides of the ball with
their hands on one another's shoulders. At a signal each one tried
to throw the other off balance so that he could kick the ball to his
teammates. The latter, numbering five or six to the side, stood

in strategic positions of their choice. The team receiving the ball attempted to move it toward their goal line by kicking. There were very few formal rules to the game but carrying the ball was forbidden. It might, however, be picked up for kicking. The players, wearing only breechcloths and, optionally, moccasins, contrived in numerous devious ways to win the game. In the absence of rules about fouls the play was very rough, with kicking, hair pulling, and other forceful tactics characteristic. Sometimes the games were of short duration, occasionally they lasted for hours. The team which succeeded in putting the ball through the willow arch or the paired posts–an opening six or eight feet wide–won the game.

The double ball of the women's shinny game was really double sticks. Two sections of a willow trunk, about one inch in diameter and five or six inches long, were notched at the middle for a thong of hide. This thong was six to eight inches long between the sticks, thus forming a double "ball," the thong of which could be picked up or scooped up with the end of the straight pole which served as the player's staff. The latter was of willow, four or five feet long, depending upon the woman's height. She grasped the staff at one end with the right hand and held it with the left at about the middle. The field was similar to that of the men's ball game, the playing area being approximately one hundred feet long. A simple stake marked the goal line at either end. The players, four to six to a team, arranged themselves at the middle of the field in facing lines four to six feet apart. The ball was thrown into the air, between the lines, and the opposing players nearest the point of descent tried to catch the thong and throw the ball back toward their respective goal lines. Once the ball was in play, the various players distributed themselves over the field, with one guarding each goal line. The ball could not be carried. It had to be picked up and thrown by means of the staff. When the ball crossed one or the other goal line the game was over.

A great deal of shouting accompanied the two ball games but songs were not sung. The women's game was rough but did not match the men's contest in this respect.

Simple distance running races were popular, both within the tribe and intertribally. The course was sometimes five or six miles long. These foot races took place mostly during the spring season and were accompanied by moderate betting.

Individual betting also characterized the playing of the hoop and arrow game. In the Modoc version the hoop was made of bundles of tule, wrapped with tule, also. The diameter was approximately two feet. The hoop was rolled down a field perhaps a hundred feet

in length. Two players contested at each roll. They lined up their
arrows with the course of the hoop and shot in rapid succession.
The object was to pierce the hoop on both the near and far sides,
with the same arrow, as it rolled toward the end of the field. The
first man to succeed was the winner. No other kind of a hit counted.
Children played the same game but on a reduced scale and without
gambling.

A ball and lance game was also the occasion for a certain amount
of betting. The ball was a bundle of tule about a foot in diameter.
It was thrown to a point about thirty feet away while a lance consisting of a pointed willow pole, about six feet long, was thrown
at it. The first man to achieve ten hits won the game.

A similar game utilized a bundle of tule about eight inches long.
It was thrown quite far into the air and arrows were shot at it.
Both men and boys played. There was no wagering.

The ball and pin game was popular as a nongambling pastime.
The ball was made in the shape of a top, an inch or two high. A
string attached the ball to a thorn or porcupine quill. The ball was
jerked upward and an attempt was made to catch it with the quill
or pin as it rose. Caught at the point of attachment of the string,
ten points were won. A strike at any other point counted one point
only. Bets were not made on the outcome but the winner in a match
was privileged to thump his opponent sharply on the fingers, nose,
or back.

A considerable number of string figures were known, most of
which were moving figures. One symbolized a fish hawk diving for
its prey; another represented two women searching, without success, for a man. The making of these figures "killed the moon,"
that is to say, hurried the month along–obviously a winter pastime.

A buzzer device–a kind of bull-roarer–was made by attaching
the knee bone of a deer to the end of a string. The buzzing sound
it made when swung around, above the head, was half seriously
thought to bring snow and consequently better conditions for deer
hunting. It was used only by men. Children were not permitted to
use it as a toy.

No tug-of-war or push-of-war game was known but men amused
themselves by sitting with the soles of their feet touching and pulling on a short pole, the object being to raise one's opponent rather
than be raised. Poles were also arranged laterally under flexed
knees and inside flexed elbows.

A few games of children will be described briefly here to supplement the anecdotal accounts in the chapter on Childhood.

Several games involved play in the water. Water-splashing teams were formed—boys on one side, girls on the other. The side which caused the other to retreat was the winner. Underwater races with boys teamed against girls were popular. The side having the larger number in advance at the end of the race was the victor. Boys also contested with girls, on a team basis, for staying under water the longer. Walking into the water to one's height, then continuing by treading water, was another kind of race.

Boys were matched with girls in a bouncing contest which required one to jump up and down while grasping the calves of the legs.

There were contests for holding the breath and an ingenious technique for timing. A long stick was marked with equidistant transverse bands. The contestant said *"dps, dps, dps,"* and so on without taking a breath. With each word he touched another marker on the pole. The contestant proceeding furthest won. This device was also used for timing underwater swimming. (This is reminiscent of the "one thousand, two thousand," and so on counting of seconds in contemporary practice.)

A boy's game involved an attempt to maintain one's position on a small hillock while kicking. The boy was surrounded by a ring of others who, first one and then another, kicked toward him. He kicked back and tried to keep from falling during the rapid shifts which he had to make and the occasional contact of foot and foot.

Both boys and girls played at spinning tops made of pine or fir bark or carved from the jaw bone of a deer. The tops were disc shaped, thickest at the center, and the wooden ones were supplied with a pin of serviceberry wood or willow. They were spun on rock or wood, using the two hands, never string.

Finally, Modoc children, inevitably, had a game in which each team tried to laugh longest and hardest.

15 WARFARE AND SLAVERY

The warring exploits of the Modoc, in aboriginal times, were infrequent and brief but bloody. The war parties were small—a few score men. The Pit River Indians and the Shasta were traditional enemies and no excuse other than this enmity was needed in justification for an engagement. After the coming of the horse, and particularly in postwhite times, the Paiute were included in this category. Relationships between the Modoc and the Klamath were seldom genuinely friendly but they frequently were allied in battles, particularly against the Pit River tribes, and they never openly fought one another, at least in recent times. The Modoc and Klamath were the aggressors in the engagements with Pit River groups, and the conflicts occurred on Pit River soil. The defenders as well as the aggressors reckoned the Klamath and Modoc to be the superior fighting men. Indeed, Pit River defense was always headlong flight if such were possible. Not so with the Shasta. The Modoc respected and feared the fighting units of this tribe and hailed any victory over them as a great achievement. However, engagements with the Shasta were infrequent. Even against the Pit River tribes the Modoc seldom moved more often than once a year. Each such venture typically involved a single battle lasting only one or two days.

This is not to say that raids were uncommon. The Modoc were the takers of Pit River slaves in the very considerable trade which saw the Klamath serving as middlemen in the movement of such slaves to the markets on the Columbia River. It was this commercial partnership which maintained the uneasy peace between the Modoc and the Klamath and which made the two tribes allies in oc-

134

casional open encounters with their common enemies. Ordinarily, however, the Modoc were alone in their battles with the Pit River tribes and always they were alone in the raids for slaves. The latter were planned and performed with the prime objective of obtaining slaves without the hazards of open conflict.

The circumstances which led to open fighting were mainly three: the discovery of an enemy party in Modoc territory; retaliation for territorial encroachment, the stealing of property, or harassment; and the wish to take slaves. The first of these, discovery of an enemy party, invariably led to fighting but it was unplanned and the nature of the engagement—relative strength of the forces, character and duration of the fighting—varied greatly as a consequence. The remaining causes led to planned ventures, the nature of which will now be examined.

The Modoc fighting unit consisted of ten to a hundred men. The latter number was reached only when the forces of one tribal village or division were augmented by those from another, or by Klamath men. The Modoc, by choice, only fought the Shasta in company with the Klamath but the latter occasionally fought this enemy alone. The Klamath, in turn, did not customarily attack the Pit River tribes except as assistants to the Modoc. Small fighting units characteristically consisted of volunteers from a single Modoc village. The parties tended to become larger as two or more villages joined forces, or two or more divisions. There was no pattern for the association of villages or divisions in the formation of a war party except for the inevitable geographical factor, neighboring groups tending most often to be united. When an attack was to be made by the forces of more than one group, they always combined to form one unit under a single war chief. When a war party from a single village suffered initial defeat, reinforcements from other villages were sometimes solicited.

Because war parties returned to home territory in a day or two—three at the most—it was not necessary for women to accompany the men to provide food and shelter. The men carried concentrated foods such as dried meat and roots. If they were out but a single night they selected a protected location as a camp for the hours of darkness but they did not sleep. If circumstances kept them away longer they made out as best they could. Women did not stay at home because they would be an impediment to the men or bring them ill luck but because of fear that they would see their husbands killed. It was said that women whose husbands possessed armor were not afraid and did, in fact, sometimes accompany the fighters. These women did not engage in the fighting, except to try to steal property. They also guarded women and children taken as slaves.

Shamans regularly accompanied war parties. Indeed, their presence was considered more or less essential to success. They employed various devices and rituals, some of which have been described in the chapter on Shamanistic Practice. When the war party had to wait out the night in enemy territory, the shamans were particularly busy with ritual activities designed to bring success on the morrow and to keep the impatient waiting men occupied and alert. The latter objective was unacknowledged but nevertheless of first importance. Shamans also fought alongside their fellow tribesmen in the battles and they cared for the fallen to the extent that the intrusive-object concept was considered applicable to the injury.

The leader of each engagement was one of the regularly recognized war chiefs of the tribe. Ordinarily such men acquired their positions through demonstrations of prowess in warfare but they never formally held the office until installed by action of the division or the tribe. After receiving the position a man held it throughout life unless he abdicated, as was commonly done by older men, or was removed by the people for actions detrimental to the welfare of the tribe or for obvious loss of the qualities of leadership. The civil leaders of the tribe exerted great influence in the raising of men to the level of war chiefs but Leaders did not themselves go to war. It was considered improper for them to do so because their sphere of competence was in the field of civil affairs, and because of strong feeling that the action or fate of a war party should not be allowed to jeopardize the lives of noncombatants and the stability of activities on the home front. A corollary was the complete freedom of any man to accept or reject an invitation to join a war party. Most men did ordinarily reject such calls. The bulk of the population always remained at home during the ventures at war and were very little affected by what was taking place in the field. This was true whether the engagement was one involving a few men only—a village effort—or many, as when it was a tribal activity. Indeed, all warring activities were really tribal in character. The fighters from a single village, on the march, were recognized as representing the tribe. Their activities were in the name of the tribe and their enemies proceeded against them in terms of their being Modoc warriors. Conversely, intratribal warfare did not exist. The Modoc could not recall a single example of conflict between village and village or division and division. Literally, there was no such thing as a Modoc warrior, in the

sense of one being either a regular and recognized fighting man,
or of participation in war as a professional activity. Every war
party was made up anew and the composition was never the same
on two separate ventures. Indeed, the personnel was often different
to the last man in one engagement and in another.

The last-mentioned facts point up the role of the war chief. He
had no fixed following and no authority to conscript. Therefore,
the few most able war chiefs were regularly found at the head of
fighting units. Lesser war chiefs only infrequently were in the lead
and in such instances the parties numbered relatively few men.
Their role on larger exploits was that of serving as secondary of-
ficers.

The initiation of a particular venture was basically in the hands
of the people. War chiefs were sometimes quite energetic in the
seeking of a following for an attack individually conceived and
planned. However, the following was not forthcoming unless the
war chief could present convincing arguments for the desirability
of such an action and reasonable assurance of success. True, the
proposed aggressions were against traditional enemies but other
questions were always raised. Do we feel like fighting at this time?
Have we had enough repose since our last battle? (Even when the
proposed venture was ostensibly retaliatory the period customarily
intervening was several months or a year.) Are our weapons in
order? Are we certain we know the location of the enemy? Is this
the right season? (Attacks were seldom made during the winter
or other inclement weather.) Will our ceremonial activities or economic pursuits be interrupted or adversely affected? Can we afford to lose any more of our men at this time? Will there be a good
chance for the taking of slaves and booty, or may we encounter
the men apart from the women and the villages? (A victory without
the taking of slaves and property was an empty one, no matter how
soundly the hated enemy was trounced.) Is it not time to seek a
prolonged period of peace and, perhaps, even a truce with the
enemy?

This last question introduces another circumstance under which
questions of war or peace were decided. As indicated, it was the
privilege of a war chief to attempt to organize a war party and,
if successful, to carry through. The civil leaders did not have
the same prerogative, as individuals, be the issue either war or
peace. However, it was their duty to bring to the people as a whole,
through the assembly, all questions of local or tribal welfare where
there was any question as to the disposition of feeling. In principle,
a Leader could make use of the assembly in an attempt to thwart

the efforts of a war chief to organize a war party. However, this
was seldom or never done, not only because of the dangers in such
a conflict of civil and military leadership, but because the reaction of the people to the war chief's solicitations inevitably exposed the village or tribal consensus.

In the assembly the war chief was merely one of the citizens
present, albeit one whose views on war carried great weight. The
Leader, on the other hand, presided over the meeting and was expected to make long speeches with the object of presenting the is-
sues and guiding the actions of the people. He was therefore in a
powerful position with respect to any question of war or peace and,
more often than not, favored peace. The mechanism of the assembly and the nonaggressive position taken by most Leaders unquestionably were responsible for the fact that most of the days
of the Modoc year were peaceful, despite their bent toward war.
The Leaders characteristically had the support of the women of
the tribe, the majority of whom spoke out vociferously for peace
whenever the question was discussed.

The following is typical of the more pedestrian speeches made
by a Leader under these circumstances: "Now I speak to all of you.
I ask for your close attention. I have given deep thought to the
problem before us. I have not been able to sleep at night because
it has troubled me sorely. The thought I bring to you is this: We
are, after all, one people—just people. But we kill one another.
That is not good and I think we should stop, this time and for all
time. I want us to become friends with those people who have been
our enemies, those people we talk about fighting and killing. That
is why I have called you together. I want us to discuss ways and
means to stop the fighting because it is bad. I do not want talk about
when and how we shall go to war. I suggest that we send a peace
commission to those people. We have slaves from that tribe. We
can select a good woman, a slave who has a Modoc husband, and
we can send them to talk peace. They can say that we want to end
war, we want to visit peacefully, and that we will take presents
to them—dried roots and meat. We can trade with them so that both
of us will have a better living. We can even say that we'll send our
young people to marry their young people. That way we shall always be friends. Think carefully of my words. It will be good if
you do as I say. Now speak your minds."

These speeches were quite unrealistic if intended literally, but
such was not the case. An intelligent and experienced Leader would
never assume that his words could bring the Modoc to stop warring
with the Pit River tribes. Indeed, he would not want it to be so.

The cultural economy was firmly based on the taking and selling of slaves, and the tribal ethos involved concepts of Modoc nationalism, cultural superiority, and the glory of war, all so firmly held as to make the notions of intertribal peace and mutual respect wholly unrealistic. The speeches are thus revealed for what, in fact, they were; that is, rhetorical devices for dissuading the people from dissipating their energies too much in indiscriminate warfare, from entering upon engagements foredoomed, and specifically, from carrying forward the particular venture under current discussion. With respect to the last, a talented Leader was often successful.

The Modoc believed that in times past they had initiated peace talks with Pit River tribes and had even carried them through to successful conclusions, but such accounts have a folkloristic aura and specific documentation is not forthcoming. An uneasy and temporary peace may sometimes have been achieved.

The exhortations for peace, in the assembly, never silenced those who favored war. Their speeches followed a pattern, exemplified by the following: "Our enemies have killed Modocs. They did that long ago; they are still doing it. We must avenge those who have died. They were killed by people who are nothing, people who are stupid and weak and only fit to be slaves. Yet they kill our people and they sneak into our country and steal our possessions. We are tired of their depredations and their insolence and we should show them how we feel. We should fight. We should bring back many slaves. We should teach them to run when they see a Modoc. We are a brave fighting people. What are we waiting for?"

Once war had been decided upon, by action at the assembly or through the successful recruiting of a war party by a recognized war chief, the venture was carried out with little delay. With the great variations in the size of the war party, differences in leadership, and the long periods separating engagements, the patterns of conduct naturally varied greatly. This was true of preliminary activities and tactics, and even of weapons employed. The basic cultural pattern provided for the organization and planning of the venture under the direction of the war chief. This was accomplished in an informal manner, while en route to enemy territory, if the party were small. Exploits of larger scope required a gathering of all participants prior to departure, at which time lieutenants were chosen, the route of travel was agreed upon, tactics were discussed, and, sometimes, a dance of incitement was held. The dance involved imitation of fighting, women's songs which were scornful of the enemy, ritual performances by shamans, and

related activities. However, these predeparture performances
were weakly structured and were not considered essential to success. One of the shamanistic rituals employed at this time involved
the purported swallowing of arrow points. The shaman's assistant
held the arrow points in his hands or in a basket and rattled them
by shaking up and down. One by one he dropped them into the shaman's open mouth. To his audience, the shaman declared that his
spirits would soon arrive and retrieve the arrowheads. He then
sang two or three songs, after which the spirits supposedly were
heard to speak, announcing their presence and saying that the arrowheads would soon reappear. The audience then heard clicking
sounds, apparently originating at various places under the shaman's long cloak. With each click an arrowhead dropped to the
ground.

The fighting men departed, by preference, early in the morning. Women followed them for some distance, singing a song that
symbolically called for great success and the return with a scalp.
The men did not look back. They marched forward in mass formation, their destination ten to thirty or more miles distant. At the
appropriate point in the journey, scouts were sent forward. When
a full day's travel was required to reach the locale of the enemy,
the scouts went out at night while the others remained at a base
camp. They selected advantageous locations and remained until the
morning light and, possibly, smoke from the fires of the enemy,
gave them the information they sought. This intelligence was carried back to their war chief, who then revised his plans and ordered an attack as soon as possible. During the approach no particular formation was maintained. It was the responsibility of each
man to keep under cover insofar as possible. The war chief directed the advance as long as was feasible but often circumstances
soon put him out of touch with most of his men. Once the enemy
village—or root-digging camp, a favored situation for attack—was
reached, every man was on his own, including the war chief. (The
latter's role had been played in recruitment, organization, and
planning. He was now just another fighting man.) Every effort was
made to surprise the villagers in their homes. This was seldom
successful because of the dispersion of the individual attackers,
the unavoidable noise of approach, and the fact that ideally a guard
was on the lookout during the early hours of the summer mornings. In any event, fighting did not, by design, take place in the
village. As soon as the alarm was spread all able-bodied men
grasped their bows and arrows and ran at top speed to a previously
chosen point of concealment some distance from the village. In

the meantime the women and children dispersed to whatever places
of hiding they could find but the attackers captured any they could
reach that were eligible as slaves—women of young or middle age
and children beyond infancy. Profound insight into the ethos of
Modoc warfare is provided by the behavior of men who were successful in taking slaves at this juncture. They remained behind,
guarding their captives, and gave no assistance to their fellow
tribesmen in the battle which followed!

The retreat chosen by those attacked was one which, ideally,
provided protection for individuals—trees, large rocks, hillocks—
but at the same time was generally open so that the enemy would
have to approach with a degree of exposure which would permit
reaching them with their arrows. A battle was often won or lost
in terms of the amount of time the villagers had to find places of
concealment and to make ready their defense. The attackers often
gave them ample time through tarrying at the village in the attempt
to take slaves or to pilfer. In the attempt to shorten the interval it
was the duty of men who did not possess armor to rush ahead first;
those wearing armor could not move so fast. The attackers spread
out over a wide front, typically an eighth of a mile or so for thirty
or forty men, irregularly spaced, so that the enemy would not have
the advantage of concentrating their fire. The company was divided
into groups of two or three fighters each. In such a unit one man
kept a 360-degree lookout while the other aimed and released his
arrow. The roles were alternated with each shot, or as dictated
by the exigencies of the moment. If one man ran out of arrows he
shared his partner's supply. If one were wounded the other took
his arrows. If the wound were slight the man stayed on, serving
as a lookout or assistant. If seriously wounded, the fighter was
carried to the rear by his partner. These partnerships were based
upon circumstances and shifted from time to time with the ma-
neuvers of the battle. They were not planned in advance and friend-
ships were not a consideration. The attackers protected themselves as best they could, taking advantage of any available cover,
but their object was to reach the position of the enemy, to kill as
many as possible, to rout the remainder, and to take a scalp or
two. To achieve this they had to move forward and this was done
as rapidly as possible along the whole front. The advance was continued to ultimate victory whenever possible. Loss of men did not
lead to retreat unless the survivors were seriously outnumbered.
Contrary to the feelings of many American Indian tribes, loss of
men from the fighting force was not considered disgraceful by the
Modoc. Indeed, the killing of the leader himself, the war chief,

did not deter his men from continuing the battle–another atypical attitude.

Characteristically, a battle lasted one or two hours. Victory was achieved when one side was put to full flight. The fighters remained on the field of encounter to take booty and scalps. The scalping of a man yet living was, according to the Modoc, a Shasta custom to which they never stooped. If the man to be scalped were still alive the Modoc dispatched him by choking or by a blow with a rock before taking his scalp. Modoc custom decreed that only one scalp be taken back by the returning war party but custom did not always keep more than one fallen enemy from being scalped or keep even more than one scalp from being taken home. Any mutilation of the fallen foe other than scalping was not condoned by the Modoc.

In the rare event of defeat, the Modoc war party returned home as swiftly as possible, leaving their dead on the field. They were sometimes pursued for a short distance but not beyond their own tribal borders.

When the Modoc were victors they remained in the vicinity to dispose of the corpses of their dead by cremation. Before or after this rite, the village of the defeated, now abandoned, was visited for the taking of loot and the surrounding country was searched for women or children who might be returned as slaves. These activities were not allowed to occupy many hours because of the ever-present danger that the routed villagers might succeed in obtaining reinforcements. Also, it was a principle of Modoc warfare that the return to home territory be accomplished as quickly as possible.

It was a Modoc boast that they never retreated from the enemy without fighting, regardless of the odds. The Pit River tribes, on the other hand, were reputed to run whenever they could. This was an exaggeration but there undoubtedly were instances of Pit River villagers being sufficiently forewarned of an attack to be able to leave only empty houses for the attackers to discover. In such an event the Modoc party took all property of any value and returned home. (The houses of a village were never burned.) This constituted victory in the eyes of the aggressors.

The victorious party returned, therefore, with a modicum of property and no lives lost, or with property and possibly slaves, and usually a scalp, but minus some of their tribesmen who had set out with them. In a typical battle the losses on both sides were unusually heavy considering the small number of men involved and the short duration of the engagement. As accurately as can be estimated, 5 or 10 per cent of those engaged in such a battle were killed. As already mentioned, the Modoc killed injured fighters abandoned by the enemy and they also used some poisoned arrows in the fighting. Each Modoc fighter reputedly carried forty or fifty arrows and took pride in never running out of these missiles, as their enemies frequently were supposed to have done. The Modoc never tried to retrieve spent arrows, as did their adversaries.

The tribesmen at home knew whether their forces had been successful or not in battle when the returning party approached home because the scalp was displayed immediately. In the village it was fastened to the top of a seven-foot pole which was fixed in the ground. There was, however, no immediate celebration. Two or three days were allowed for the news to reach other villages. If the party had been a large one, with participants from several villages, they stopped at the first large town within Modoc territory and waited for relatives and friends from other localities to arrive. The victory dance was celebrated here, never in the several villages.

The dance was conducted on a smooth piece of ground outside the settled part of the town. A circular enclosure was made by piling brush in a wall-like arrangement with an opening left at one point. Additional brush and wood were gathered for burning. The fireplace was prepared in the center of the enclosure. A good dancer—one who knew many songs—was informally chosen as leader. The dance was performed on five successive days, always with the same procedure and the same leader. The fifth day did not differ from the others; there was no feasting even then. Dancing occurred either during the daylight hours, or at night, or both. The dancers proceeded, in line, clockwise near the edge of the enclosure. The leader, carrying the scalp on the long pole, started a song and led the procession for the three or four circuits that the song lasted. He signaled the start and finish of the song, and that unit of the dance, with a loud call, "*kololololu,*" repeated five times, accompanied by all the dancers. A series of such dances, separated by short intervals, continued for about three hours. The leader initiated the songs until he exhausted his repertory, then he called on others to start the singing. The dance form was a simple walking step with knees variably flexed to give a springing up-and-down motion, while the body swayed from side to side. Men and women occupied alternate positions in the line. Slaves that had been taken were required to join in the dance, performing in the same way as the others, except that they did not sing. Shamans were present, and danced, but merely as participants. Children were not permitted to be present. Ordinary clothing was worn by the dancers. In objective appraisal the Modoc scalp dance was remarkably dull, being merely an endlessly repetitive performance with no special features and no distinctive role for the fighting men, their captured slaves, the shamans, or even the war chief. At the end of the five days the scalp was unceremoniously thrown into the fire by the man who took it or by one of the women. The various participants then returned to their homes. No rite of purification was required of the recent fighters.

The majority of the slaves captured by the Modoc undoubtedly were taken in small-scale raids which cannot be called warfare in any proper sense of the term. Hand-to-hand fighting occurred in these raids but never in warfare, where one or the other side always retreated before reaching the point of man-to-man combat. No weapons were carried for close encounter.

The armor of the Modoc was made of elk rawhide. Sometimes only a vestlike garment was worn but the preferred, coatlike covering reached from shoulders to ankles, sometimes doubled in front. The pieces were sewed with sinew; the sides were fastened by tying. Alternatively, two pieces were used, forming a poncho-like garment tied at the sides. Fighters wearing the larger garments were unable to run. Wooden-rod armor was also known but was considered inferior to that made from elk hide. Only a few men wore armor. Most fighters disliked being so much restricted in their movements. Instead, they wore only breechcloth and moccasins, never hats or headdresses.

The war chief gained glory if he returned victorious but his only material gain was the loot which he personally had succeeded in taking. Each fighter retained that which he had individually procured; this included slaves. There was no evidence that war chiefs obtained more slaves than ordinary fighters. Indeed, the contrary seems to have been the case. This is consistent with the fact that the war chief could not loiter at the village, at the time of initial encounter, in order to capture slaves. The only slaves possessed by civil leaders were those they chose to purchase since they did not participate in war or slave raids. Those purchased were, ostensibly at least, for resale although some were kept for a long time and served the master in the various ways appropriate to his office and its responsibilities.

Most slaves were soon sold to the Klamath who, in turn, traded them farther northward. Occasionally the Modoc owner himself took a slave directly to the Warm Springs country or even to the Dalles market on the Columbia River. The few slaves which were kept by the Modoc were those to whom the owners became attached. Female slaves were sometimes made concubines. When a male slave, taken as a boy, reached marriageable age he became essentially free if he married a Modoc girl, but some stigma remained throughout his life. Slaves that were kept for prolonged periods were assigned hard work but were quite well treated. However, no protest was raised when a master killed a slave in anger. Retained slaves were permitted to participate in ceremonies and enjoyed complete freedom of movement within the village and beyond. There is no question but that any able-bodied slave could have escaped if he cared to do so but there was no place for him to go. His own people would not take him back.

Modoc tradition held that the taking of slaves had always been a tribal practice.

16 HOUSES

A Modoc village exhibited a considerable variety of house forms. The winter accommodations included a semisubterranean, earth-covered lodge which was entered through a hatchway at the top; an elongated, mat-covered house with steep, sloping walls and a flat roof, with entrance at ground level on one end; and a dome-shaped, mat-covered hut used principally as a utility house but also to a limited extent as a dwelling. The typical summer house was the domed structure just mentioned. In addition, circular windbreaks of sagebrush were used, especially when traveling. The domed house is said to be the oldest type, with a more extensive use in winter than is the case more recently. It may indeed have antedated the earth-covered lodge, or may merely have enjoyed wider usage. It is certain that acquisition of the steel axe greatly stimulated the construction of earth houses and the elongated mat house.

The houses of a village were not arranged according to any re-strictive pattern. In general houses were quite far apart, several hundreds of feet. If the village were located on a stream, the tend-ency was for the houses to form an irregular row. In the absence of a watercourse the buildings were randomly distributed, limited only by topographical considerations. The individual house was generally oriented to the east, that is, the steps or doorway faced that direction. However, houses might have doorways facing north or south, as well, since the eastward-facing habit was not due to a preference or to ritual emphasis on that direction, but came about because east is the opposite of west. The land of the dead lay to the west and fearful influences emanated from that direction. Those who slept in the west portion of the house lay with feet to wall, reversing the preferred position. Otherwise they would suffer frightening dreams in which the dead would appear; they would be impelled to eat snakes and to walk into fires. From such dreams serious illnesses resulted. In a normal eastward-facing house the most desirable quarters were those nearest the door, the least desirable those furthest from it, incidentally thus reversing the preferences of the Indians of the Northwest Coast.

Houses were jointly owned by all adult occupants. This accords with the practice of all adults contributing labor toward the original construction. Only to a limited extent was labor provided by others, and then under reciprocal arrangements or anticipations thereof. One exception was the influential man for whom others might work for the purpose of ingratiating themselves with him.

The earth-covered house was a structure of considerable architectural refinement and functional adequacy. Substantial in construction, spacious and warm, it provided the protection so desirable during the cold winter months. The building of such a house required about a month of steady labor from all of the adults who were to occupy it; it was the major creative project in which the Modoc engaged. Some family groups lacked the ambition and resources for a venture of such magnitude, contenting themselves instead with one of the inferior structures better adapted to summer use, but the majority of winter houses were of the semisubterranean, earth-covered type.

The earth house was comfortable at all times except during the relatively rare periods of protracted rainfall. Drainage was adequate and water did not collect on the floor, but the whole structure became damp and the interior humidity excessive. This was counteracted to some extent by temporarily enlarging the roof opening to increase the circulation. A tentlike arrangement of mats kept out most of the rain. A larger and more or less continuous fire was kept for its drying effect and also to aid circulation. During the ordinary winter of light snowfall and low temperatures, the fire was kept only during a brief period in the early morning and early evening. It was allowed to die out at bedtime and a tule mat was loosely laid over the roof opening, supported by a few light cross sticks of willow. The temperature remained high enough for comfort, even without bed covering, for most of the night. Only toward morning were covering robes necessary to supplement the protection of the ordinary clothing which was worn at night as during the day.

A considerable excavation was necessary as the first step in construction. The average depth was about four feet. Sometimes

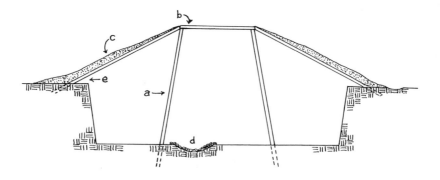

Earth-covered house, side view. Profile at main roof supporting posts. (a) Main post; (b) long stringer and plate; (c) rafters, sheathing, and earth covering; (d) fire pit; (e) shelf area

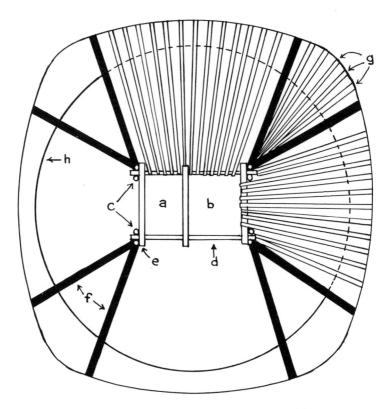

Framing pattern of roof of earth-covered house. (a) Smoke hole; (b) hatchway; (c) main post; (d) long stringer and plate; (e) short stringer and plate; (f) corner braces; (g) rafters; (h) outline of excavation

this was increased to five, and only rarely was it reduced to the two or three feet typical for the neighboring Klamath. The plan was ordinarily round, occasionally elliptical, and rarely approached rectangularity. The diameter varied within a range of sixteen to forty feet, with the mode at about twenty-two feet. The smallest size was adequate for one or two families while the largest accommodated six or eight families. The earth was broken up with the common root-digging stick or specially prepared sticks of similar type with points fire-hardened. Digging tools of horn were used also. The loosened earth was scooped with the hands into carrying baskets or tule trays and carried just beyond the proposed edge of the pit. Digging proceeded from the center outwards. When completed the pit was encircled by the excavated earth which would soon be used for covering the lodge.

The wall and floor of the pit were carefully smoothed during excavation; care was taken not to dig irregularly because depressions which had to be filled produced an unstable wall or floor. The slope of the wall was slightly less than vertical.

In the meantime logs had been gathered for the framework. The heaviest structural pieces were preferably of pine but juniper and cottonwood were available closer at hand and were commonly used. Smaller poles were oftener of pine since many could be carried at one time and a few long trips would suffice. The largest logs were the four used for the main supports. For the average house these were ten to fourteen feet long and eight to twelve inches in diameter. Each was carried on the shoulders of two or more men. Smaller timbers were carried horizontally on the back by means of a tump line supported by the forehead. Generally, women dug the pit while men gathered timbers. However, each might assist the other under stress of circumstance.

Holes two feet deep were dug in the floor of the pit to receive the main posts. Adequate depth was important because these timbers were not set vertical but were raked about ten degrees so that the floor rectangle formed by their bases was larger than the roof rectangle. Structural stability was thus somewhat lessened in order to achieve a desired architectural result, a greater free space in the center of the room. Engineering considerations alone would have dictated a slope in the opposite direction. The consequent weakness was reduced by thrust timbers placed between the tops of pairs of posts, and strong tying of stretcher plates. In the houses of the smallest size, the bases of the supporting posts were placed at the angle of the floor and wall, but in larger structures the postholes were situated six feet or more from the walls, thus provid-

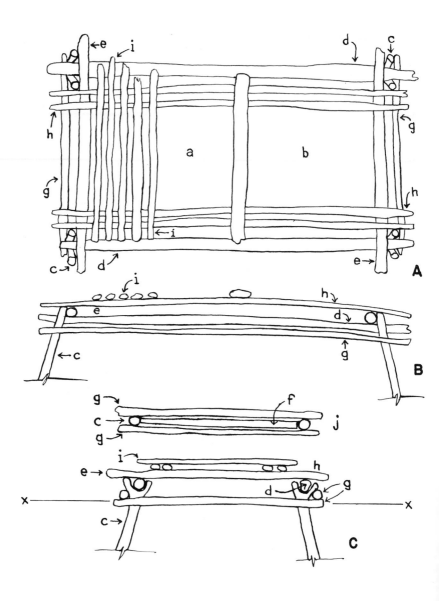

Framework at hatchway of earth-covered house. (A) Top view. (B) Side view. (C) End view. (a) Smoke hole; (b) hatchway; (c) main post; (d) long stringer and plate; (e) short stringer and plate; (f) thrust beam; (g) tie rod; (h) rooftop joists; (i) rooftop sheathing; (j) section at x–x ing space for beds to be arranged around the room between posts and walls. The arrangement of the framing at the main post tops, with thrust beams, plates, and auxiliary ties, is shown in the accompanying figure. The main post bases were set to form a rectangle with sides of proportions of one or one and a half to two. These proportions were carried to the top, the resultant frame having sides of differing length. The dimensions in an average house were about five feet by eight or ten feet. The stringers forming the long sides were set in natural crotches in the main post tops, or in deeply cut notches. The short stringers rested on the long ones, outside of the post crotch projections. Thrust beams were inserted between the posts, below the stringers, and held in place by the rods adjacent to them and outside of the posts and by tying. Where stringers intersected they were securely tied, and these in turn were likewise secured to the main posts. The material used for these and the many other critical tying requirements was stout cordage of swamp grass.

The next step was the placing of the corner braces. One or two radiated from each corner of the roof top frame, the number depending on the size of the house. These were essentially rafters but were extra heavy and had their bases secured in shallow holes. The holes were several feet beyond the edge of the pit, which permitted the true rafters to be placed on nearly straight base lines. The roof therefore became a structure with a rectangular plan at the top and a rounded rectangle at the base, set over a round or elliptical pit. Such a roof may be approximately described as a flat-topped hip roof or even as a mansard roof.

The rafters were poles of medium diameter or, preferably, roughly split planks. Juniper and cottonwood, and sometimes pine and cedar were the woods used. Splitting was accomplished with the horn wedge and wooden mallet. The rafters were placed as close together as the available material permitted. In a well constructed house the intervening spaces were but a few inches wide. A poor and short-lived roof could be built with rafters a foot apart. The main post stringers served also as plates; rafters rested on these plates and were tied to them. Except at the corners the rafters formed right angles with the plate as viewed from above. The bases merely rested on the ground, the weight of the covering material held them in place.

The top portion of the roof was completed next. This was nearly flat, consisting of a criblike arrangement of plates, joists, and sheathing. Parallel with the long stringers or plates, and resting on the short ones, were placed the roof top joists. These were two

or three in number on each side, placed close together. These
joists supported the roof sheathing which consisted of roughly split
planks laid side by side over one end. The other end was left open
as a combined smoke hole and hatchway. On large houses the two
were separated by a section of sheathing. Later the sheathing was
covered with a tule mat.

The sloping roof sides were covered with three layers of material. Fastened directly upon the rafters were one to three layers
of tule matting. Mats of swamp grass were sometimes used as an
inferior substitute. Where the rafters were close together, the
matting functioned as a sort of sheathing but where they were widely
spaced it was essentially an inner lining. In both cases the matting
served to keep dirt and moisture from entering the room. The
mats were laid in courses overlapping about eight inches. Their
natural resiliency permitted shaping them to the contours of the
structure. They were tied to one another and to the rafters with
cordage of swamp grass or sagebrush bark. In applying the courses
the women, whose duty this was, worked from top to bottom so
that it would be unnecessary to walk on the newly laid matting.

If only one thickness of matting were used this layer might be
supplemented by a coating of loose swamp grass or tule. Indeed,
in some construction loose grass was used exclusively, but this
required plank rafters very closely set.

The second layer consisted of strengthening material. Preferably planking or bark was used; the poorest material was sagebrush. Planking was rough-split and irregular in size. Bark pieces
were as large as obtainable; pine was most satisfactory. These
materials were laid up so as to be self-supporting as far as possible. Bark, especially, was arranged in alternating horizontal
and vertical layers so that the one might support and strengthen
the other. Sagebrush was used only in poorly built houses or those
with closely spaced rafters. The branches of sage were interlocked
as much as possible, and sometimes laid in successive courses.
It served more as a reinforcing material to hold the earth covering than as sheathing.

The final coating of earth was applied from top to bottom so as
better to control the thickness. It was easier to smooth downward
than upward. Men and women carried the earth in the same recep-
tacles as those used when excavating it. The thickness of the covering depended upon the proportion of pit size to roof size; all excavated material was used. The layer varied from a few inches to
a foot in depth. At the base of the slope a gutter was dug if natural
drainage of the site was inadequate.

The slope of the roof varied from thirty to forty or more degrees, depending upon the size of house, depth of pit, and length of center poles. Also, the slope was steeper on the hips of the roof than on the sides, because of the elongated top opening. To reach the hatchway, usually placed to the east, one ascended by a pathway up the steep end. This often called for steps as a convenience if not a necessity. These were integral with the roof structure, consisting of a rung type ladder laid on the bark sheathing during construction. The rungs were held by natural forks of branch stubs, supplemented by notches, in the uprights which were commonly of juniper. Tying was not generally required since the slope and earth held the rungs in place. Toe spaces were cut in the earth covering, above each rung.

Tunnel-type entrances were not unknown, but were distinctly atypical and probably recent. They are said to have been a sign of opulence.

The flat top portion of the roof was not covered with earth, but merely with matting. This made for flexibility, since the sizes of smoke hole and hatchway could be modified to suit circumstances of weather and social activity. The sheathed portion was covered with a mat of tule which shed the rain well but was brittle when dry. The hatchway was protected by a more flexible mat of swamp grass. In a well finished house one end of this mat was made permanently fast so that it might be rolled closed or open. It was supported by removable willow withes. In the coldest weather the smoke hole was covered similarly.

The house ladder was of the rung type similar in construction to that used for steps, except that all rungs were securely tied. The base was fixed in the pit floor and the top rested against the stringer on the east side of the hatchway, to which it was fastened. The side poles projected several feet above the roof level. The angle of the ladder was nearly vertical. The notched-log type of ladder was never used. One faced the ladder when climbing or descending. Young children clung to the backs of elders. Etiquette demanded that house occupants avert their eyes when a person of the other sex used the ladder.

The fireplace was in the center of the room near the foot of the ladder. The fire was not used for cooking, except by those too indolent to build a separate cookhouse, and hence was small and seldom necessary except in early morning and evening. The fire developed a natural pit, sometimes requiring filling in with rocks to aid the draft. The central portion of the room, which accommodated the ladder and the fire, was bare and set off from the re-

mainder by a rectangular arrangement of four prone logs held in
place by pegs in the ground. Except in the smallest houses, this
area was about the same size as the flat portion of the roof above it.
The remaining floor area was covered with swamp grass to an
original thickness of several inches. This packed down with use
but retained considerable insulating value. Less satisfactory material included rye grass and bunch grass. Over the grass were
placed twined mats of swamp grass. These were preferably carried up the walls as well, and onto the shelf area between the base
of the roof and the original ground level. The mats were tied together with sagebrush cord and were staked in place with branch
crotches of serviceberry. The main shaft was used as the stake
which was driven into the ground adjacent to the mat. The diverg-
ing branch stub, projecting downward, caught the edge of the mat
and held it fast. Good housekeepers occasionally replaced the grass
padding, for which purpose a supply of the material was kept in a
storage hut.

Over the flooring mats were placed the sleeping mats of twined
tule or robes of fur. These were kept rolled against the wall except when in actual use. Occupants slept with their heads to the
wall except on the east side, behind the ladder, where the position
was reversed. This area was not used for sleeping unless necessary. Occupant families had designated parts of the room in which
to sleep but no partitions of any kind were used. General storage,
such as firewood, was in the space behind the ladder. Bedding
rolls were used for temporary storage of personal items; the shelf
above the head of the bed served for more permanent storage.

Children were forbidden to play on the house roofs from fear of
damage. After each snowfall paddles and planks were used to remove the snow. The life of an earth-covered house was short,
about three years maximum. Many required rebuilding after one
season. Pits were reused after being cleared of debris but timbers
generally had to be replaced, because of rotting, and new mats
made. Discarded timbers were later used as fuel. Houses were
frequently destroyed owing to deaths occurring within.

The mat-covered house was primarily a winter dwelling smaller
in size and simpler in construction than the earth house. As such
it played an important role, being used by small family groups,
those of limited resources, and whenever erection time was a lim-
iting factor. However, it served also as a summer residence where
relative permanency and substantial accommodations were required.

When constructed for winter use the mat house was provided with a shallow excavation of twelve to eighteen inches; it was banked with earth for a foot or two above the ground; and a relatively thick covering of mats was applied. Otherwise, the winter and summer versions were the same.

The mat house differed from the earth house in the shallowness or absence of the pit, the absence of a bark or plank layer, the lack of earth covering, the more elongated rectangular shape, and the entrance at one end. Also, it was relatively smaller and more specialized in use of floor area, particularly the corners on either side of the door which served as storage areas.

The width was usually twelve or fourteen feet, the length perhaps twice that at maximum. The elongation was possible with the same foundation arrangement as the earth house because the weight of covering material was so small a factor. Straighter sides resulted from this elongation and the absence of a pit. As the ground plan lengthened, the flat portion of the roof was correspondingly lengthened. The main house posts were four in number and were erected vertically. Although much lighter in weight, they were framed at the top much as in the earth house, except that thrust beams were unnecessary. The corner braces carried out the lines of the stringers and plates as viewed in plan, creating right-angled areas in the corners of the room around which the walls curved.

Rafters were light and relatively widely spaced. The mat covering consisted of at least two layers. The inner, waterproof layer was of sewed tule; the outer cover was of swamp grass in thick, twined construction. The latter provided insulation and the swamp grass was less susceptible to damage than the tule, which broke easily when dry or frozen. Superior construction employed three layers, with the middle layer, of swamp grass matting, running at right angles to the other layers. The same construction was sometimes used when the available mats were worn and weak. Several materials were available for tying the mats to the framework, including swamp grass cordage and string of sagebrush bark or Indian hemp.

Framing and covering materials at the roof top were stripped of bark as a fire preventive measure. A space about three-feet long was left open at the middle as a smoke hole. The remaining flat area was covered with tule matting. Sometimes a mat or plank was arranged as a movable wind screen at the smoke hole.

Where the side matting touched the ground pieces of pine or cedar bark were often used. If intended merely as a protection for the matting these pieces were placed on end, side by side. If the bark were to be covered with earth, as was customary in winter, the pieces were laid on their sides to obtain a better bearing against the rafters.

A single doorway was provided at one end, that facing the water or perhaps the east. It is said that the direction of the prevailing winds was not considered. The opening was at ground level. It was protected by a swamp-grass mat overlapping on the outside and hung from the top by swamp-grass cordage or buckskin thongs. The opening was small; occupants stooped when passing through. The slope of the end walls was fifty degrees or more; that of the side walls slightly less. The maximum inside height was seven to nine or ten feet.

The floor plan was similar to that of the earth house, but areas

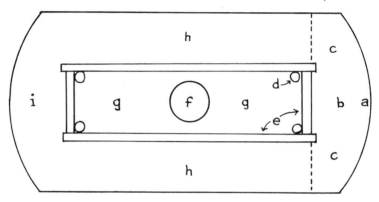

Floor plan of mat-covered house. (a) Door; (b) entry; (c) storage area; (d) roof post; (e) retaining logs; (f) fire pit; (g) fireplace area, bare ground; (h) sleeping area, mat-covered; (i) sleeping or storage area

were distinctively named, as shown in the accompanying figure, and some cooking, especially of meat, was done on the central fire. Most foods, however, were prepared in a separate cook-house. No poles or shelves were provided for drying or for storage. The room corners, particularly those adjacent to the door, were used for storage. If this space were insufficient, the opposite end of the room was used if not necessarily utilized as sleeping quarters.

A single mat house might be occupied by two or three families. The time required for construction was less than half that for an earth house of the same size.

A third type of dwelling was the dome-shaped house. This was a simple structure with a framework of bent willow poles and a covering of matting. The willows were set in the ground to form a circular enclosure about ten feet in diameter. Those on opposite quadrants were bent over and tied in pairs to form a series of parallel arches decreasing in height in both directions from the middle. Those of the other quadrants were arranged likewise, and tied to the original set at the intersections. Willow-bark cordage was commonly used for tying. The maximum height of the dome thus constructed was about seven feet. Over this mats were laid, two or three courses sufficing. The uppermost course had to be stretched considerably at the bottom to make an approximate fit at the top. A smoke hole opening about two-feet square was provided at the top center. The door, a small rectangular opening, was placed in any quarter other than the west. It was covered by a mat hung as in the mat house.

The domed dwelling house was essentially a temporary summer structure and served most of the housing needs of that season. However, it was also used to a limited extent as a winter home for elderly persons. The latter sometimes found it difficult to climb the ladders of the earth houses. Furthermore, there was a tendency to provide separate housing for the aged. For this use the domed dwelling was made warmer by additional layers of matting and by banking earth around the outside edge. Food was carried to the occupants by their relatives, and wood provided for the fire which burned continuously except at night.

One other type of summer shelter was used, a simple circular windbreak of sagebrush. Bushes were forced together so that their branches interlocked to produce a wall about four-feet high. The diameter varied from five or six feet, for one or two persons, to ten feet or more, for several occupants. A small segment was left open as an entry; the top was never covered.

The brush windbreak was the characteristic shelter for temporary use in spring and fall when protection from cold winds was desirable. In summer, however, even this was dispensed with, travelers preferring to sleep in the open. Sometimes, in cool weather, a man would shape a sleeping space to fit his body in loose earth or sand, then warm it with hot rocks, before lying down. After the rocks were removed grass was spread in the depression. Or more simply, a man merely lay down near his camp fire, which he replenished if roused by the cold.

Utility houses were built for several purposes. All earth houses and most mat houses were supplied with separate cooking huts situated adjacent to the dwelling house in a position near the door or steps. These structures were used exclusively for cooking; no other activity was properly conducted there. A second important type of utility hut was that used for the storage of bulky materials, other than food, such as floor grass, mat-making grass and rushes, extra mats, firewood, metates, and the like. In addition to being storage places these were the work rooms of the women. Mat making, sewing, spinning, and other such sedentary activities were carried on here. Finally, there were the menstrual huts in which women were isolated at times of menstrual flow and childbirth. Sometimes the storage and work huts were used for the purpose.

All utility houses were identical in structural details to the domed dwelling house.

When an earth house or mat house was completed an informal celebration was held. The occupants invited neighbors, particularly relatives, to join them in a feast. This was thought to insure against accidental destruction of the house.

No special ceremonial or assembly houses were built. A ceremony such as the shamanistic initiation had to be conducted in an earth house if it were to be impressive, but the house used was simply that of the shaman himself. No one else's house would be borrowed for the purpose.

Dwelling-house furnishings were meager. Space was at a premium; a house was built no larger than necessary to provide sleeping accommodations. Bedding mats and robes were essential. When rolled against the wall, in the daytime, these served as back rests. Pillows were rare; those used were flat wooden blocks over which were draped robes or pieces of matting. Clothing, small tools used by men, personal possessions, and gaming implements were stowed here and there, wherever space and considerations of security permitted. Another article kept at hand was the broom which consisted of the wing of a large fowl, or two or three of these bound together. With this the floor matting was swept each day.

The responsibility of caring for the fire was delegated to a particular woman of the house. An attempt was made to keep a fire alight at all times either in the dwelling house or the cooking house. Then a firebrand could be carried from one place to the other when necessary and new fire would not have to be made. At night the fire was banked with ashes and often kept until morning. If it died, fire was sought from a neighbor. Only rarely was the firedrill used in a permanent camp.

House groups usually consisted of related families but not infrequently other alignments were made. Groupings were fairly stable throughout a single year but each new autumn saw considerable shifting. Each family brought to the winter residence its accumulation of dried foods. This was stored in separate units and each woman, when cooking, properly took food from her own supply. However, the cooked food was distributed evenly among all house occupants, including guests. At the end of the season the remaining stores were drawn upon without respect to original ownership. The various women of a household rotated the task of cooking, although not with any fixed order. In a large household two women usually shared the task of preparing a meal, often using separate cooking huts. In winter two meals a day were served. The morning meal, served at daybreak, consisted typically of boiled roots and seeds. The second meal, which included meat as well as other available foods, was eaten late in the afternoon. In summer, when morning and evening meals were further apart, a midday meal was customary, except at times when snacks were taken throughout the day.

Each man and wife occupied a fixed portion of the house. The arrangements were casually made in the fall and continued throughout the winter. Various factors were involved in the disposition, but these were mostly personal, not formal, in character. Children usually slept with their parents although grandparents were favored, when present, by the older children. Permanent house members slept adjacent to the wall; guests had to occupy more central areas in a crowded house.

With respect to house composition, the village of Steo´kas, on the northwest side of Clear Lake was typical. It consisted of one large earth house, five mat houses; population, thirty-three; *circa* 1880. Earth house: south side, Mary Chiloquin's paternal grandfather, his wife and two children; west side, father of above man; northwest quarter, Mary's "uncle" (?); northeast quarter, a man and his wife; east side, storage; total, eight. First mat house: south, Dr. George, two wives, one daughter; west, a man; northwest, a son of George; northeast, the mother of one of George's wives; total, seven. Second mat house: south, Bobu´mpkas, his wife, one son; north, two daughters; total, five. Third mat house: south, Celia Lynch's father, a wife, two daughters and one son; north, another wife; total, six. Fourth mat house: south, Chief George and his wife; north, a daughter; total, three. Fifth mat house: south, Dr. Charley and his wife; north, two sons; total, four.

17 SWEAT HOUSES AND SWEATING

The Modoc built sweat lodges of two distinct types. One was an earth-covered structure of unique design. The other was the so-called Plains type, a dome-shaped lodge of bent willow poles covered with matting or robes. The latter type was used throughout the Plateau to the north.

The native name for the domed lodge *(spu ˊklɑs)* is translatable only as sudatory; that for the earth-covered type is the same, plus a qualifying adjective and translates literally as earth sudatory. The common distinction in English parlance is summer lodge (domed) as contrasted to winter lodge, but either is used at any season.

The domed structure was identical in construction to the domed utility house, except that the door was sometimes omitted and no smoke hole was provided. When lacking a door, the lodge was entered by raising the matting at any point. A single thickness of matting sufficed in summer but in winter three layers were often used. In quite temporary structures a blanket or robe was thrown over the frame instead of matting, which had to be tied. The height of the dome was four or five feet, the diameter six or eight feet, such a size accommodating about four persons.

The earth-covered sudatory was built over a shallow excavation of trapezoidal plan. The width at the front was about double that at the back and the greatest dimension was front to back. The pit sloped uniformly from ground level at the front to twenty inches or more at the back. Two sturdy posts were planted at the front corners, perhaps seven feet apart. The tops of these, across which a heavy plate was fixed, were about five feet or six feet high. Other

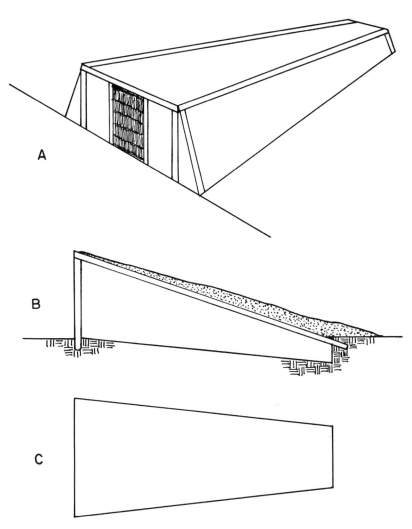

Diagram of earth-covered sweat house. (A) Front view. (B) Side view. (C) Floor plan

timbers were sloped from the back corners to the post tops. On this framework were erected a vertical front wall, with a central doorway, and steeply sloping side walls. These walls were constructed and covered exactly as those of the earth-covered dwelling. The roof was closely sheathed with planks; this was covered with matting or grass; and finally a heavy earth coating was added. The resultant structure resembled an earth hummock with a ver-

tical section cut away. The doorway was covered with a swamp-
grass mat hung from the top.

In both types of sweat lodge the floor was covered with grass
which was frequently replaced. Fires were never built within.
Rocks were heated on an outside fire and rolled inside. A pit, usually centrally located, was provided for the rocks in the domed
structure. In the earth lodge the rocks were conveniently rolled
down the inclined floor to the narrow back portion. The rocks provided a certain amount of heat but the effect of this was invariably
intensified by sprinkling them with water. The required amount of
water was brought in a basketry container and set beside the rocks,
from which position it could be sprinkled by flicking with the hands.
Anyone was permitted to do this, but there was no contesting to
drive others out by overly increasing the steam. Occupants sat
or squatted on the grass-covered floor, or lay down if so inclined.
Reclining was also protection against unusually high temperatures
since it was relatively cooler near the floor. During the five-day
sweating vigil accompanying mourning men lay down and slept for
hours at a time.

Except during such occasions as mourning the sweat house was
not visited daily. The average man spent several hours there once
every several days. This contrasts strongly with the brief daily
visits of the Klamath and other Plateau peoples. No attempt was
made to bring the temperature of the sweat house to more than a
moderately high level. Not only is this explicitly stated, but the
customary hour or two spent in the lodge at one sitting would have
been impossible with the temperatures characteristic of the Plateau houses. In other words, temperatures sought were in accord
with those of other California tribes, and differed sharply from
those of the Plateau where the domed sweat lodge was typical. Nor
was it customary to plunge into cold water upon emerging from
the lodge. The structure was located without regard to stream or
lake. Ordinarily one merely sat quietly outside to cool off. Sometimes water was sprinkled or rubbed on the body.

Several persons characteristically used the sweat house at one
time although there was no prohibition against individual utilization. Both sexes used the same sweat lodges, usually at different
times but occasionally together. Women spent as much time sweat
bathing as did men. All sweat houses were community property
regardless of by whom built. A person employed the sweat house
most convenient for him, or visited a house where he might expect
to meet friends. Only adults used the sudatory; children were forbidden to do so.

The prayers mentioned in a preceding chapter were the only ritualistic utterances in the sweat house. No sweat house songs existed and no singing was indulged in by the occupants. Conversation was carried on more or less freely.

18 DRESS

Considerable body protection was required in winter, but in summer the Modoc were contented with but meager covering. Propriety dictated that all those over puberty wear a loin covering at all times, but beyond this the individual was free to assume or discard clothing as he desired. The upper body was seldom covered except out of doors in the winter. Leggings and moccasins were worn for protection only. Hats were more consistently worn, both because they were considered decorative and as protection from sun in summer, cold in winter, and chafe of the forehead tumpline by which burdens were carried.

Children, it need hardly be added, wore nothing except under extreme conditions. Then moccasins, usually of tule, were assumed and a robe of some kind, perhaps a piece of an old one, was wrapped around the shoulders. Infants in cradles were protected, of course, with blankets.

Clothing was characterized by the extensive use, first of tule, and secondly of other fibrous materials, particularly swamp grass and sagebrush bark. Some form of every garment was executed in these materials. Fur was not neglected; it was used as extensively as the resources and technical skills of the Modoc permitted. Buckskin was only meagerly exploited.

A time came, however, when buckskin was the most important clothing material. Plains influence, reaching here at a relatively early date considering the remoteness, was responsible. The story is the familiar one of an unimpressive clothing complex being all but obliterated by the spectacular Plains interpretation. This was only possible, here and in many other areas, because of the improved economic conditions resulting from the acquisition of fire-arms, steel axes, steel needles, and the like.

The Modoc believe that they received the Plains clothing styles from the Paiute on the east. This is contrary to the common assumption that the interior Oregon valley was the route of cultural diffusion, which would require that the Modoc be directly indebted to the Klamath. The Modoc view, however, demands serious consideration in view of the many differences, some quite fundamental, which distinguish the two neighbors in the field of dress.

The standard loin-covering garment for both men and women was the apron. A single apron of generous proportions was worn in front by men. Two such garments, equal in size, were required by women, one to hang in front and the other in back. The apron shape was square in all cases. Various materials were used, buckskin being the most common. Skins with fur, worn with the hair side out, were popular in winter. Men preferred groundhog skins, women favored coyote skin. The fastening for the single buckskin apron was integral with the garment. Two narrow strips were cut from each side from the bottom to near the top, where they were left attached. These were carried around the waist and tied. The same method was used for other skins of sufficient size. Small skins which had to be sewed together were suspended from a separate skin belt. The apron shape was square even in the garments built up of small skins. In the absence of any more satisfactory material, women wore small tule mats as aprons, which were provided with cords for tying. These were also worn when engaged in work that might damage the finer materials. Other fibers might have been used for the apron, some far more suitable than tule, but custom dictated exclusive dependence on that all-purpose rush.

An alternative garment for women was the all-around skirt. In this case sagebrush bark was the preferred material. The fibers were shredded but not spun. Bundles were twined with Indian-hemp string. Other materials used were swamp grass and tule. The latter was considered poorest. The skirt was one piece, put on over the head and drawn tight at the waist with a cord which was then tied. The garment hung to the knees or just below.

Buckskin was used to make a skirt of different type. This was one rectangular piece, wrapped around the waist and tied on the right side. This skirt was longer than the fiber one. The opening along the right side was left unfastened so that the wearer might open the garment for working on the thigh as in spinning cordage. This skirt was straight along the bottom as were the aprons, not fringed.

Skirts were never worn by men, but either sex might wear the breechcloth. This was of buckskin or of fur with the hair worn outside. A belt of skin or Indian hemp was worn. The cloth was passed between the legs and over the belt both front and back. The cloth ends fell several inches below the belt. The breechcloth was never worn with apron or skirt. The distinctly un-Californian breechcloth was probably imported along with the Plains shirt with which it is so intimately associated in the Plateau and Plains. The Modoc think of it as a garment of older possession but it is considered to be "more dressy" than the apron or skirt, which implies a cultural association with the impressive Plains-type shirt.

Moccasins were of two types, one of skin specialized for summer use, and a winter style of woven fibers. Both men and women wore the same types although there were some preferences, as noted below. Children, too, shared the common styles on the rare occasions on which they wore footgear. Indeed, adults wore moccasins only when necessary to protect the feet from extreme cold or rough ground. In the house, around camp, and in canoes everyone went barefooted, even in winter.

The summer moccasin was made of skin. Deerskin both in full tanned form and semitanned with the hair adhering was used; men preferred the former, women the latter. For the semitanned shoe the skin taken from just above the hoof was preferred. The hair was usually inside; sometimes the reverse. Antelope buckskin made soft but less durable moccasins. Badger and bear fur were chosen when greatest durability was sought. These semitanned skins, with the fur inside, were even worn at times in winter.

The skin moccasin was fashioned to a simple one-piece, center-seam pattern. A rectangular piece of skin was rounded on one end, folded lengthwise, and sewed on the rounded portion to form the center seam and on the straight end to form the vertical heel seam. To the open portion might be sewed a short noninserted tongue and also, if desired, an ankle flap. A string was provided at the ankle for drawing tight and for wrapping around the ankle flap. The moccasin was then turned inside out, to put the seams inside. These were slightly projecting because the sewing was through pieces lying side by side. The heel pucker was cut to form a squarish trailer, of single or double thickness. In the lightweight summer moccasin the pointed toe was snipped off and sewed square before turning, but the heavy fur type retained the point without modification. Also, in this moccasin, the ankle flap was an integral part and the tongue was omitted. The accompanying figure illustrates the details of patterning. Seams were sewed with an awl and sinew

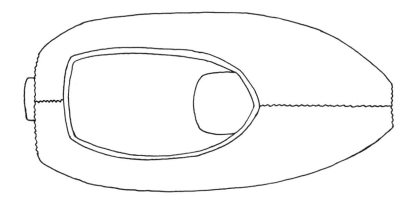

Moccasin pattern

or Indian-hemp thread. Heavy soles were added when moccasins became worn, never when new. Holes were not patched; an entire sole was applied. This was preferably of semitanned thick skin from the neck of a buck. True rawhide was not used. Inner soles of thinner deerskin with the hair were occasionally inserted without sewing. Padding or footwrapping was never practiced with the skin moccasin.

The winter moccasin or shoe was a crude article of fibers in openwork twine, but it was warm, comfortable, and in all respects satisfactory except for its short life. The tule moccasin was reckoned as good for ten to twenty days of ordinary continuous wear. Those made of sagebrush bark wore several times as long, thus correcting somewhat the basic shortcoming of fiber footgear. However, the sagebrush type required several times as long to weave as that of tule. Hence tule continued in favor and was the material most often used. A man wearing tule footgear for a hard hike over crusted snow carried along an extra pair or two if he expected to be gone several days. The fiber moccasin derived its warmth from the foot wrapping which was used with it, rather than from the shoe ifself. Shredded sagebrush bark, swamp grass, or fur was used to encase the foot. In mild weather the padding was placed on the bottom only. In coldest weather fur was used under the foot, sagebrush bark over the top.

The technique of weaving the tule moccasin was similar to that employed in mat making. The tule warps were about twenty inches long. The weft was introduced at the middle and weaving proceeded in each direction. At one end the warps were carried around to

form a shaped heel to extend quite high on the ankle. On the toe end
the warps extended several inches beyond the length of the foot. As
the toe position was approached, the twining was tightened somewhat to draw the warps closer together. Just beyond the foot length
the weaving was discontinued, leaving the loose projecting warps
to be bent back over the instep in the manner of a tongue, and held
in place by the sides of the moccasin which were folded over and
laced across the instep by a cord passing through loops formed
for the purpose by the weft as it changed directions at the edges
of the fabric.

Some fiber shoes were of the height of short boots. In addition
to the materials mentioned above, a shoe of moderately good wearing quality was woven of swamp grass. Nettle fiber and Indian hemp
were also used for warp as well as weft. Fiber footgear was always
hung up to dry after being worn on the snow or wet ground.

Leggings were regularly worn by both sexes, in summer as well
as winter. These were simple rectangular pieces of buckskin or
woven fiber or tule, of a size to reach from knee to ankle. They
were wrapped around the leg and tied by means of attached thongs,
arranged in three or four matching pairs. Another technique was to
provide a single row of thongs with matching holes opposite. The
legging overlapped the flap of the moccasin top and the ties were
on the outside of the leg. The fiber of which leggings were woven
was typically sagebrush bark. In tule leggings the warps at the
ankle end were left loose to provide greater flexibility. Simple
decoration was achieved on some leggings by the attachment of a
few beads, but painting was not practiced. Recently fur has been
used as legging material.

A basketry hat of twined tule was habitually worn by women. Men
wore a similar hat more rarely, usually as a protection from chafing the forehead when carrying a pack supported by the head strap.
It served the same purpose for women, but only incidentally. The
common male headgear was a cylindrical bark hat in summer and
a peaked fur hat in winter.

Both plain twining and diagonal twining, triple strand, were employed in the weaving of basketry hats. Women's hats were decorated with woven designs, but those of men were plain. Dyed porcupine quills were used as decoration. Both were of simple basket
shape, without brims and rather flat on top. They fitted the head
closely, extending to the middle of the forehead. Women wore their
hats in the rain as well as other times, since they were waterproof. They also served as emergency drinking cups. Men of the
Gumbatwas group are reported to have favored basketry hats more

than other Modoc men. The few hats imported from the Shasta and Pit River tribes were considered superior to those made by the Modoc. No material other than tule was utilized as the warp in hat weaving.

The bark hat was a cylinder of cottonwood or inner pine bark of proper diameter to fit the forehead. Those of cottonwood stood five to nine inches high, but the pine bark type which had to be built up of strips sewed together, was lower. The top was left open in summer. The occasional hat of this type worn in winter had the top pinched together and sewed, giving a wedge-shaped appearance. The vertical seam, which was overlapped, was worn in back. Simple designs in red paint were sometimes applied. Shamans often attached pendent feathers, claws, or other symbolic objects to the walls of the hat.

The winter headgear of men was a tailored fur article. It was cylindrical where it fitted the head, but rose to a peak at the top and back. This was achieved by a tear-shaped insert of fur placed in the open top in a sloping position. A less common type of fur hat utilized the scalp of an animal with only minor tailoring. These sometimes had front projections resembling a narrow visor; this resulted from the stiffness of the semitanned skin. Another variant was a long "stocking cap" type. The leg fur of a large animal was sewed to regain its original shape, the large end placed over the head and the excess length allowed to fall in back. This hat was considered amusing in appearance. The materials used for fur hats were numerous, including raccoon, groundhog, marten, otter, coyote, wildcat, fox, beaver, and badger. Bear and rabbit fur and duck skins were not used. With the fur hat, especially those of the finer materials, it was proper to wrap the hair braids with fur, preferably beaver. Hats of buckskin were also known.

The garments described above constituted full attire for summer weather or mild winter weather. For extreme winter weather a robe was added. These were always rectangular in form with one exception, noted below. These robes doubled in service as blankets, supplemented by a few blankets of larger size but of the same materials. Robes were of four types of construction: single skin; sewed skins; woven of fur or feather strips; and woven of tule or swamp grass. Single-skin robes were made of deer hide with the hair, elk skin with hair, and bear fur; but not antelope skin. The deerskin robe was the most serviceable of any type, being equally good for wet or dry weather since it had no seams as weak spots. A deerskin robe of special shape was used by men in hunting. The scalp was left attached to the body skin, and worn over the head. The body skin was squared as usual. This was not a disguise. Sewed robes were made of all suitable small skins, including raccoon, groundhog, badger, otter, beaver, coyote, and deer. The pieces used were squared before being sewed together. Infants' blankets were usually made in this manner, often of very small skins. Rabbitskin was used only for the twined-strip type of robe. One other material, mudhen skin, was used in the same way. The skins were cut spirally into strips and twined on a frame with weft of Indian hemp or sagebrush bark. The rabbitskin blanket was the warmest of any type, and double the value of a deerskin robe, but it would not be used in the rain and was rather fragile. Tule, swamp grass, and sagebrush bark were the materials, in order of importance, used in fiber robes. Tule was employed in the natural form and also in shredded form; the former was preferable for rain, the latter for warmth. Swamp grass was warm and sagebrush bark was durable but both required much more labor to weave than the tule garment. The technique was open twine tightly bound. Like the skin robes, they were rectangular.

All robes were worn in the same fashion—by both women and men, and occasionally children—except for the hooded hunting robe of men. Two thongs were provided at the top to be tied around the neck, and one or more belts were worn. Skin robes were wrapped around the sides of the body; one belt at the waist usually sufficed. Fiber robes covered the back but less of the sides, and a chest-level belt was often worn in addition to that at the waist, to control the stiffer material.

Mittens were not made. When a robe was worn the hands were kept warm, when inactive, by crossing the arms and wrapping the hands in the edges of the robe.

In the days after Plains influence was felt, clothing habits were extensively modified. The crudest, and perhaps first, of the new garments was a poncholike shirt worn by men, women, and children. It was simply a tanned deerskin, roughly squared, with a hole for the neck and side seams. No sleeves at all were provided. It was put on over the head. These garments were necessarily short, requiring breechcloths or aprons.

The double-skin garment also came into use. With it came long buckskin leggings for men. The breechcloth was worn with the man's shirt and leggings, but the woman's dress was ankle length and the aprons were discarded. Sleeves were separate pieces, completely tailored. On the dress they were sometimes of wrist length but oftener they extended only to the elbow. Shirt sleeves were long. Apparently the natural form of the skin was never ex-

ploited as it was in the Plains. The head was placed at the top, tail
down, but at both extremities the skins were cut to a pattern. A·
rounded or V-shaped neck was provided and the bottom was cut
square. Fringing came into use for the first time. Fringes were
applied as bands around the chest and at knee level on the dress.
The bottom of the shirt and the sleeve seams were fringed. The
sides of both shirt and dress were sewed; the garments were put
on over the head. Simple appliqué decoration was used around the
neck line and in vertical stripes on the body of the dress. Yellow-
dyed porcupine quills were sewed in corresponding double lines on
each side of the front from neck to waist or below. On the back
similar rows were placed on the mid-line of the garment. Men's
shirts were decorated with pigment as well as quills. Women continued to use knee-length leggings but the tule and fur types gave
way to buckskin.

These new styles were imitated in woven tules and grasses by
those lacking the requisite amount of buckskin. However, the old-
style garments were never completely eliminated until the adoption
of modern clothing. The moccasins worn today are of the Plains
one-piece, side-seam style.

Distinctive ceremonial dress was never developed or adopted
by the Modoc. The better clothing, with added decorations, sufficed for special occasions.

⑲ BODY CARE AND ADORNMENT

Several styles of hair dress were practiced although there was little differentiation between men and women. First, hair was worn loose. This was invariably true of children under the age of puberty. The more careless adults, as well, were often satisfied with this casual style, except for special occasions. It is doubtful that any person adhered exclusively to this pattern. It may represent a condition more prevalent in earlier times.

The second style of coiffure was one in which the hair was gathered in bundles or clubs. The hair was parted in the middle and arranged into two clubs at either side of the head by tying around with strips of fur. The loose ends of the bundles hung down in front of the shoulders. The favorite materials for tying were otter, weasel, and mink, in that order. Where the supply of the valued otter skin was limited the women of a family were the ones privileged to use it. This coiffure was used exclusively for ceremonial occasions by both men and women, in recent times. This strongly suggests that it is an older style than the braids mentioned below. In earlier days it may have been the dress for gala occasions while the hair was worn loose at other times.

Three-strand braiding to form one plait at either side of the head, falling in front of the shoulders, was the third type of hair dress common to both men and women. This was by far the most extensively used coiffure in recent times. The hair was always parted in the middle and the braids dropped from a position just forward of the ears. Shorter hair in back was allowed to fall unbraided. Other details varied. Ordinarily the ends of the braids were bound with buckskin thongs or fiber cords, but for social occasions strips of fur were used. Sometimes a considerable length of the hair was covered with such a wrapping, but pendent fur pieces were not used to increase the apparent length of the braid. For work, women and occasionally men tied the ends of the two plaits together and threw them back over the head. Alternatively, women double-folded, or even tripled, the individual braids and bound them at the sides of the head with buckskin thongs. This suggests the doubled clubs of other northern California tribes. The double plaits themselves can hardly be interpreted as other than a modification of earlier loose rolls in response to the popularity of braiding as learned from the Plains and Plateau.

The fourth style was most Plainslike of all. This was a three-plait arrangement, two temple braids and one back braid. Most of the hair was gathered into the back braid. The shorter temple braids were completely covered with fur or buckskin wrapping. The temple braids were even used at times with the side braids, by withholding a few strands from the main plait. Another variation, used by men while hunting, was a single back braid doubled up and tied at the nape of the neck. It should be noted that the single back plait for women was never adopted.

Only the hair of boys, mourners, and slaves was cut. An obsidian knife was used for the purpose. Boys' hair was cut to ear length and properly not allowed to grow below the shoulders. The hair of a newly acquired slave was cut to ear length as a means of identification and "so he wouldn't have to take care of it." The latter is shown to be a rationalization by the fact that the captive's hair was never recut. Female chief mourners had their hair cut quite short and smeared with pitch. Male chief mourners shortened their hair to shoulder level. The hair was never singed to shorten.

Deer-fat pomade was used by both sexes; bone marrow was preferred, from the leg bones. One application was considered adequate for several days. The hair was re-dressed infrequently, sometimes not oftener than semimonthly. Braided hair was not loosened while sweat bathing. Washing seldom was done except when swimming or bathing. No saponifying agent was used unless it was alkali dust. An aromatic plant was used as a hair perfume. The hair was never painted or dyed.

An ingenious hair brush was made of the tail of the porcupine. The quills were shortened and hardened by singeing. Bone and flesh were removed and replaced with tightly stuffed sagebrush bark. The skin was sewed together on a cord tied from one end to the other at the back of the arched brush. When in use it was held by the string with the fingers resting on the back.

The only hair comb was a compromise brush and comb made from the roots of a rye-grass plant. The root cluster was cleaned and cut evenly to a proper length. The base of the grass stems was cut and bound to form a handle. A woman's head scratcher was made of deer rib. It was a simple smoothed splinter of bone about a quarter inch in diameter and three inches long, with one end pointed and the other end notched to hold a string of sinew. The latter was attached to the woman's wrist or suspended from her neck, during the periods in which it was used, that is, puberty, mourning, and menstruation. Personal designs were applied to the scratchers; these were simple geometric motifs, nonsymbolic and freely chosen. They were applied in pigment or by burned incising.

Men plucked out facial hair after first smearing the face with dry ashes. The latter absorbed some of the oil of the skin and provided needed friction for the removal with apposed fingernails. Tweezers were not known, nor was any means of cutting used.

Eyebrows were never plucked or disturbed. "The Modoc were proud of their eyebrows!" Nor was the hair line modified in any way.

Facial painting was practiced for decorative and protective purposes, but symbolic and ritualistic aspects were meager. The latter were concerned with shamanism, puberty dancing, and war. The shaman painted the parting of his hair with red-oxide pigment mixed with oil. This was his only distinguishing mark so far as hair dress and painting were concerned. The pubescent girl had her face painted black during her ritual. Warriors assumed white face paint in simple lateral-striped patterns. The whole face was covered with white paint, including the forehead. The pigment, which was chalk, was mixed with saliva by chewing, then smeared on with the hands. Before drying, some was removed by scraping with all fingernails from the nose and mouth outward and downward. The neck was left bare but similar lateral bands were applied from the chest to the knees.

The above applies to the period preceding extensive trade with the Paiute. The latter had extensive quarries of red earthen pigment in their territory, a material which was exceedingly rare in the Modoc area—enough for the shaman's frugal use but little more. Chalk deposits, on the other hand, were plentiful in the region, and charcoal was easy to make. The result was that most all facial painting was done in these pigments. As soon as the Paiute red began to be imported the use of this color broadened. Warriors began to use it along with the traditional white. Gamblers used it more and more, until it came to be typical of them. Its utilization for purely decorative purposes grew to the point that it was even applied to the cheeks of infants, "to make them look pretty."

Decorative painting was permissible for any social occasion and was extensively used by young people during the courting age. Older men painted seldom except when gambling or fighting. Men covered the cheeks and forehead with white paint, sometimes the chin. Women painted the cheeks and chin with a single dot each, applied with the tip of the index finger. Sometimes lines of black were superimposed on the white by either sex. When red became plentiful it was used largely on the cheeks, without design, together with white on forehead and chin. Gamblers sometimes daubed white spots on their reddened cheeks.

Charcoal black was most often used for protective purposes; also earthen red. To insure against sunburn the whole face was covered; as protection against snow blindness the area around the eyes, including the lids, was thickly painted. Deer grease, without added pigment, was applied as an antisunburn measure, and also to relieve chapping of the legs resulting from exposure to water and mud. Rump fat or marrow was used similarly. Pitch was applied to the face as a treatment for chapping. Ashes were rubbed over the pitch to make it less sticky.

Pigments other than white were mixed with deer grease before applying. The dry paint was carried in a small buckskin pouch with draw string. The grease was kept separately and the two were mixed, in the palm of the hand, just before applying. Saliva or water were the only vehicles used with white chalk.

Charcoal black was derived from various woods but the most satisfactory material was the meat of the wild plum. The pits were placed in the embers of a fire and reduced to charcoal, the shells cracked, and the inside portion removed and used.

The meager local supply of red pigment was derived from small pebblelike pieces obtained in the vicinity of the southeastern arm of Tule Lake. These pieces assumed red color only after baking for an hour in a hot fire. After cooling they were placed in a buckskin pouch and pounded in a mortar. Occasionally it was ground without the bag, an uneconomical method. Sometimes the ground pigment was adulterated with white chalk, moistened, and formed into small balls, and rebaked.

Certain other pigments and dyes may be mentioned here although not used for face painting. A blue clay was pulverized, mixed with oil, and used for painting such articles as bows. A blue mud, perhaps the same material, was used for dying tules

by burying the rushes in it for several days. Depending upon the
time, various shades of blue and black were achieved. A green
juniper lichen served to dye porcupine quills bright yellow, when
they were steeped in a hot infusion for two or three days. A stone
mortar was used as a container which could be kept at the edge of
a fireplace. Alder root provided a red dye.

New-born infants were powdered with finely pulverized white
clay.

It should be added that special face-painting designs were adopted
in connection with the Ghost Dance.

Regular bathing was never required of children or practiced by
adults. However, children loved to play in the water and learned
to swim at an early age. Some instruction was supplied by adults.
Children competed in swimming races at play. The discarded skins
of water snakes were worn on the arm as a magical aid to swimming. The stroke was half way between a breast stroke and an underwater overhand or dog paddle, with the arms alternating in action. Swimming on the back was also known. Poor swimmers used
a bundled tule mat for buoyancy, which enabled them to cover considerable distances. Both rivers and lakes were used for sport
swimming.

Head flattening was popularly but not uniformly practiced. The
object was to produce an attractive appearance. High frontal flattening was sought particularly but the methods used produced a
combination of frontal and occipital deformation. A small elongated pad of folded buckskin or a bag filled with deer or antelope
hair was placed on the forehead and sometimes another on the oc-
ciput. These were held in place by a band of deer or antelope hide
tied at the back with sinew. When the board cradle came into use
the band was made fast to the board at the sides of the head. Thus
the board cradle produced occipital flattening whether a pad was
used or not, even when a cushioning material was employed. Head
binding was formerly begun a few days after birth; with the advent
of the board cradle, binding was often postponed until the cradle
was put into use, at the age of four to six weeks.

In typical Modoc fashion some parents neglected to deform the
heads of some or all of their children. These children were taunted
by the others who called them ugly and sometimes avoided their
company. Girls attempted to hide their unattractive normality by
wearing large basket hats but boys were not afforded even this protection.

Likewise, nose ornaments were considered desirable but many

persons failed to have their septa pierced for the purpose. Piercing of the child's nose was done by a parent, using a gooseberry thorn or horn awl. The age varied from four years to puberty. If the parents were disinclined or the child strenuously objected, the operation was omitted. When performed, the procedure was wholly informal. Kumookumts was credited with having established the custom but the operation was without ritual significance.

The aperture was kept open during the healing period by means of a charred and oiled wooden pin, which was removed and replaced from time to time. After healing, the hole was enlarged by inserting successively larger willow pins in the opening. The simplest permanent septum pin was a char-blackened, double-pointed wooden piece, or a bird bone of similar shape. Wooden pins which curved upward beyond the nostrils were considered most decorative. A more elaborate ornament consisted of a straight wooden pin with a small round shell piece attached to each end. A simple but impressive ornament was a single long dentalium shell. Two shorter shells might be worn with the smaller ends fixed in the septum. More elaborate was an ornament made of fish vertebrae. Several bones were drilled and were strung on a piece of moist buckskin. When the skin dried a stiff, apparently continuous, decorative rod was produced. A circular ornament was made by tightly stringing clamshell beads on an Indian-hemp cord.

Ear lobes were pierced in a like manner to permit the wearing of ornaments. Virtually all girls had the operation performed at the same age as that for septum piercing. The procedure was optional to boys and the incidence was consequently lower. Only the lobe was pierced, not the rim. Occasionally two or three perforations were made. Since the required hole was small, a string of Indian hemp was usually sufficient to keep the hole open during healing. In order to insert a section of such string, one end was charred to harden it and bring it to a point. Ear decorations were simple and small. A few clamshell beads or juniper-berry seeds were strung on Indian hemp and hung in a ring or two or three short pendants. Juniper seeds are very small and great care was required to make the holes for stringing. A small sharp-pointed awl of rabbit bone was employed. A single clamshell disc was also used as an earring. The most elaborate ear ornament was a bit of hummingbird skin with the feathers attached.

A slight amount of tattooing was indulged in by both men and women, but the practice was of recent introduction. No distinct local patterns were developed. Techniques used were likewise

heterogeneous, a result of recent acquisition from various neighbors with differing practices. Both obsidian blades and bone prick-
ers were used; porcupine quills were occasionally employed as
well; and all these were displaced by the steel needle. Charcoal
black was the only pigment inserted; plum-pit charcoal was considered best. Areas decorated were those favored by the northern
California neighbors, particularly the Shasta and Pit River tribes,
from whom the practices were borrowed. Women marked the chin
with vertical lines; one, two, or three in number. Either sex might
decorate the wrist, inside or out, with a pair of short lines running
with the arm. Men tattooed random lines on the chest. These were
the tendencies; none was restrictive. The ritual character of tattooing on the Lower Klamath river never penetrated to the Modoc.

The most valuable decorative beads were imported. At the top
of the list was the long, slender, tubular marine shell, dentalium,
which reached the Modoc only after a journey of six hundred miles
along trade routes from the Strait of Juan de Fuca, its place of
original gathering. It arrived via the Columbia River and interior
Oregon route, the Modoc receiving it directly from the Klamath;
and also via the Klamath River, with the Shasta and Pit River tribes
acting as the last intermediaries. Dentalia were used as nose ornaments, necklaces, and clothing ornamentation. They also served,
in the manner of hoarded jewels, as an item of wealth.

The money bead, however, was the marine clamshell disc. This
was also received in trade from the tribes of the lower Klamath.
Strings of standard length were recognized, but for decorative use
the beads were restrung as necklaces and wrist bracelets, but not
anklets. Another type of clamshell ornament was the polished half
shell, either uncut or cut into quarters, then rounded or squared.
These large and valuable pieces were drilled at the edge-the middle
of a side on the square pieces—and interspersed on a necklace of
round-shell beads, producing the ultimate in dear and ostentatious
jewelry.

Domestic-shell beads of distinctly poorer quality were fashioned
from fresh-water shells. Beads were also made of sections of duck
bone, cut with obsidian blades, and dyed. Hollow reeds were likewise treated; the best ones were received from the Shasta. Porcupine quills, dyed yellow, were cut into sections about an inch long
and used for necklaces. The quill sections were pendent from the
cord which encircled the neck; each quill was threaded on an individual string knotted at the bottom. Seed beads were mentioned
in connection with earrings; beads were not made from berries.

Bear and eagle claws were drilled and strung as necklaces, but neither beaver teeth nor elk teeth were thus utilized. Woodpecker bills were not used as beads but were sewed to clothing for decorative effect. There were no sex distinctions in the styles of bead wearing. Sinew, nettle, and Indian hemp were used for stringing.

20 SUBSISTENCE

The annual cycle of economic activities of the Modoc was highly formalized in terms of the resources of their habitat and the knowledge and skills of the people. Rigid adherence to the schedule was necessary not only for the sake of social conformity but also for physical survival.

The winter houses at the permanent villages were dismantled as soon as the snow had melted in the vicinity; this was usually in March. All of the timbers were carefully cleaned and the covering materials were stored in piles in a protected place. The framing timbers were left in place in the houses which would be reoccupied the following winter. However, the house pits were essentially open to the sky and this exposure insured a dry and sanitary house when rebuilt. At the same time, small mat-covered houses were constructed for the elderly and crippled persons who had to stay in the village throughout the summer. The far-ranging economic pursuits of the active population precluded taking along those who could travel slowly or only with help. At the same time, this meant more travel for the younger people because they had to make return trips throughout the summer to bring food to those left behind and to care for their other needs.

The first travels were to locations for the early spring fishing. Sometimes a whole village moved to a single spot. More commonly, two or more fishing camps were established, usually not far from one another. The sites for these camps were semipermanent, characteristically reoccupied summer after summer. There was good reason for this, the sites having been chosen originally because of the economic productivity of the locale. The same was true of the summer villages which would be established at other locations later in the season. The houses built at each site were domed, mat-covered structures. These were designed so that they could be erected quickly, but the finished structure was a comfortable house—no mere hut. Each summer village or camp was occupied as long as possible. The occupants moved only when the specific economic season gave way to another or when the local resources were exhausted, as in root digging, and the remaining patches were too far distant.

The season of the spring fishery lasted three weeks or a month, during which time the men devoted all their energies to catching suckers. The women divided their time between the cleaning, cooking, and drying of fish, and the gathering of roots of the desert parsley and other early but lesser species. These roots were not available until near the end of the spring sucker run, which was fortunate because the women were amply busy handling the fish. Aided by the men, they had to bring great quantities of pine saplings from the hills to be used as fish drying racks. The Modoc did not use racks of the frame type. Instead, the small trees were trimmed of unneeded limbs and foliage and planted in the ground at the village. The remaining limbs served to hold the drying fish. A fishing camp took on the appearance of houses set in a thicket of trees.

At the end of the sucker run the villages were moved to the digging grounds for epos, the root crop which played the largest role in Modoc economy. At the same time, trout were beginning to appear. The choicest village sites for this season were those on streams or rivers where the men could secure trout and the women would be within reach of the epos. The latter consideration was paramount, however, because of the critical nature of the crop and because trout would be available until August. This season was also a period of intensive gathering of the eggs of waterfowl.

Another move was necessary when the camas ripened in late June or early July. Camas was highly valued but rather scarce in Modoc territory. Consequently, this season saw the most widespread dispersion of the population and frequent movement from camp to camp was necessary. The men continued to fish whenever trout-bearing waters were at hand, and they also hunted waterfowl and small game.

Late July marked the transition from the digging of camas to the search for the so-called white camas, a different genus. Also, some hunting of antelope on the plains and mountain sheep in the lava beds occurred at this time. The gathering of numerous minor varieties of edible roots received the attention of women during this season, as did the gathering of water-lily seeds. The latter opened the seed-collecting activities which continued through September and took the Modoc groups to all parts of their territory. In late August and throughout September the men were busy with the second run of suckers while the women harvested and dried the numerous lowland berry crops. Hunting activities started toward the end of this period when the camps were removed to remote locations and higher elevations. The men pursued the deer and elk; the women gathered huckleberries and other high-elevation fruits.

The hunting season, thus inaugurated, involved intensive activity by all men until the snows came in December. During this time, usually in October, the groups returned to their winter village sites where the hunting was continued with the village as a base. The main work at the village was the rebuilding and refurbishing of the winter houses. Those who found the existing framework of their houses in bad repair or their house pits caved in often chose to build new structures. The rebuilding of an average house required about two weeks' time while the construction of a new home consumed four to six weeks. The women assisted in the work on the houses. They also worked intensively on the repairing and making of bedding, blankets, and robes. Materials had been collected during the preceding summer: soft tules for bed mats; skins dressed with the hair or fur adhering, for blankets; rabbit-skin to be cut into strips and woven into fur robes and blankets; and feathers for the making of feather robes. Supplies of wood were gathered by both men and women, often from afar. Men climbed pine and juniper trees to knock off dead limbs and women gathered sagebrush, pine cones, and other materials available on the ground.

In December the winter run of trout appeared and some fishing was done in streams and open lakes. Fishing was continued, at a reduced level of productivity, throughout the winter by making holes in the ice. Men also hunted, making solitary forays when want threatened. All men were hunters—necessarily so for the economic welfare of the Modoc. There was no hunting specialization and no honors were received by the active and successful hunter. He was merely performing a duty in the proper and expected manner. The man who neglected his hunting or was careless in its execution was not criticized for being a poor hunter. He was merely looked upon as a lazy and careless man. It was his own family that suffered most because, primarily, the game a man took—and the roots, seeds, and berries that a woman gathered—belonged to the family. A man took pleasure and pride in distributing meat to his neighbors, but only in the summer time and only when the meat was fresh. That which was stored for winter was put into underground caches, a quarter mile or more from the village, and great care was taken to keep the location secret. The surface indications were obscured so thoroughly that most families used a secret sign to enable them to find the pit again. Even so, caches other than one's own were sometimes discovered, and theft was common—indeed expected under such circumstances. If the thief were apprehended a great altercation resulted but the object was the recovery of the food, not punishment for a wrong. Care was also taken to keep one's fellow villagers from knowing when stores were being brought from the family cache to the house. It was customary to retrieve the supplies at night and to camouflage the burden as a load of wood before carrying it to the village. By so doing the owner avoided the risk of having the food stolen from his house or the embarrassment of saying no to persons who might ask to share the supplies. People did ask, despite the fact that such requests were considered improper and were seldom granted. The only persons privileged to ask for food from another family during the late months of winter were the ill. In these circumstances the food was generally provided, if possible. However, a well person might properly buy food if he could find a seller. The courtesy of providing food to bona fide visitors was continued through the winter by most families but some simply stopped serving meals when others were temporarily present.

Despite the emphasis upon hunting and the importance of meat in the Modoc economy there was only one hunting ritual, the sweat bath; this preceded the quest for large game. Continence was not required as a precedent to the hunt and there were no ritualistic procedures in the handling of the animals killed. The Modoc did not share the bear ceremonialism of tribes to the north. Hunting songs were sung during the preparations for the venture but these were not spiritual or magical in character. The sweat-house prayers, however, were pleas for supernatural aid, as exemplified by the following: "I address myself to you, my Earth, and tell you that I am hungry. Listen to me, you, my Mountain, give me your lice. I address you, my Rocks, so that you will give me what I seek. I say, this is my world." The reference to lice was customary; the birds and animals were symbolically conceived as the "lice of the Earth." The prayers were recited as water was thrown on the hot rocks during the visit to the sweat house on the night preceding the hunt. Ordinarily several men were present but the sprinkling of the water and the saying of the prayers were individually done.

All regions of the tribal lands except the lava beds were utilized for deer hunting but the most productive areas were situated in the meadows and hills of south central Modoc territory, between Tule and Goose lakes, particularly Steele Meadow and Yokum Valley. This was fairly open country of about 4,700 feet elevation. Summer and fall hunting here was a profitable and enjoyable venture; consequently, parties of men regularly exploited the area. The hunting techniques, however, were strictly individual except on the special occasions described below. The average party consisted of five or ten men from a single village. All those who felt so inclined or were not otherwise engaged joined the group. These ventures were not planned ahead; they were spontaneous daily affairs. There was no leader; the men casually agreed upon a destination. When the party arrived, an equally casual discussion, during a few moments rest and smoking, settled the questions of particular areas in which individuals would hunt, and place and time of meeting for the return. In periods of especially good hunting an early meeting time was agreed upon. In poor times the hunters assembled for the return trip only at dusk. Old men often accompanied these parties and gave freely of their advice but did not engage in actual hunting. They remained at the base, enjoyed a day of talk and relaxation, and partook of a fine meal upon the return of the hunters, if the latter had been successful.

Each hunter stalked with bow and arrow, but variations of technique were numerous, the individual following his preference, or the procedure that he judged best suited to the circumstances. Some men covered a long but narrow area, proceeding more or less in a single direction. Others attempted to traverse all parts of a more concentrated area. All tried to keep to leeward of the spots where it was hoped that deer might be sighted. Dust was thrown upward to test wind direction. Little or no clothing was worn, apparently to minimize the risk of warning deer by wind-carried body odors. The sweat bath taken before the hunt was ostensibly for ritual purposes—praying for success—but incidentally it effectually increased the chances of success through elimination of body odor. Dogs and disguises were used by some hunters but these auxiliaries were more commonly associated with independent hunting ventures.

The appointed regathering was a matter of convenience only. A hunter desiring to follow the trail longer, or finding himself at a spot from which he could take a short cut home, might proceed on his own without the others giving it a thought. However, the gathering of hunters after a successful day was a festive affair, and in any event each man was eager to learn of the fortunes of the others. If a deer had been taken it was skinned and partially butchered immediately to provide a meal for the hunters. The liver and meat from the ribs were roasted and eaten. The hunters cooked their own pieces; women did not accompany these expeditions. The remainder of the carcass, which had been quartered, was carried back in the hide. If additional animals had been killed they were packed whole. Each deer was transported by the man who killed it, except that assistance was given if a man had shot more than one animal. Theoretically, the successful hunter was the owner of his kill and he took great pride in such ownership. He was thus marked as a competent hunter and he valued the attention and compliments of his friends. Also, he was able to play the role of benefactor of the village, for he could, and invariably did, distribute pieces of meat to all neighboring families. Indeed, all of the venison was thus distributed except head, tripe, lungs, heart, and hide, plus a cut or two of the better parts. The poorer portions were retained because the concepts of generosity marked them as unsuitable gifts. The hide, an item of great value, was kept. It was not food; different rules applied. Without food a man died; without a robe he merely shivered. Thus we see that the routine hunting party was essentially a community economic venture although the hunting techniques were purely individualistic and the rationalization was in terms of private property.

Deer stalking is not an efficient method of hunting. It was necessary for hunting parties to go out day after day, and for individuals to proceed quite alone whenever circumstances demanded. Otherwise the threat of starvation was ever present, especially during the winter. An attempt was made to accumulate sufficient venison during the summer hunting season to allow the drying and storage of a supply adequate for the winter. The nature of the Modoc habitat and the Modoc way of life precluded productive hunting of large game during the winter. It is true that some deer were taken in that season and that considerable effort was given to the hunting of antelope but the latter never quite compensated for a serious shortage of venison.

The winter hunting of antelope was a truly cooperative venture under the direction of an experienced hunter, with women playing important auxiliary roles. The chute and pound technique was employed. Although the procedure was rather crude and many animals were lost, those successfully impounded and killed augmented

significantly the winter meat supply. Sometimes an especially profitable drive netted ten or a dozen animals. A light covering of snow
on the ground was considered helpful to a successful drive. The
enclosure was formed on an open area of relatively flat ground.
(See accompanying illustration.) The wings from the opening were
merely piles of sagebrush at uniform intervals. They extended in
the direction of terrain that was lower or in some other way obscured, at least partially, from sight of the pound. The piles of
sagebrush at the points where the wings joined the enclosure were
considerably larger than the others. The circular form of the pound
itself was marked by similar but smaller mounds of sagebrush.

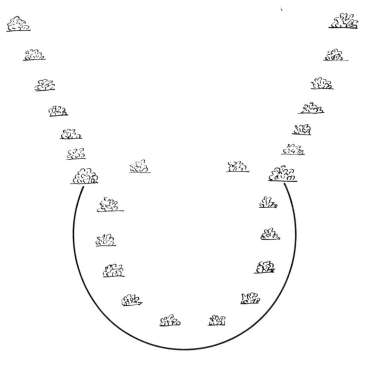

Chute and pound for antelope, formed of piles of sagebrush and a semi-
circular enclosure of rope

These served a double purpose. They not only formed a visual
boundary but were designed to be burned, at the appropriate moment, thus creating a barrier of fire. The firing was done with
torches carried by the women, who also held a rope encircling the

entire pound except for the entrance. The rope was made of tule and sagebrush-bark fibers and had clumps of brush fastened to it at intervals. The antelope were driven into the pound by the hunters who had sought them out and guided them into the chute by running and shouting. As the game entered the enclosure the women vigorously agitated the continuous rope which they held, causing the attached brush to wave and gyrate. While so doing, they shouted calls like those of the crow or raven. These actions, together with the fires, situated several feet inside the rope barrier, distracted and frightened the antelope so that the hunters were able to kill at least some of them with the clubs they carried. The chute and pound may also have been used for deer on rare occasions.

A related kind of cooperative drive was sometimes used for deer but appears to have played only a minor role compared to individual hunting. The venture required the services of from twenty to sixty men. It was essentially nothing more than a large game drive in which the firing of the brush was used as a supplementary device. The drive took place on a hill or low mountain and the object was to confine the game in an ever smaller circle until the top of the hill was reached. At this point the hunters closed in rapidly and killed as many animals as possible. The primary objective was to take deer but other game animals which were caught by the encircling activities were killed also if this did not mean neglecting the deer. An enclosure of sorts–merely a ring of men and women waving clumps of brush, or, possibly, holding a rope– was sometimes formed at the hill top upon the arrival of the game and the pursuing hunters.

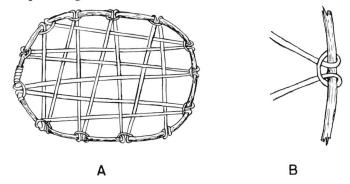

A   **B**

Snowshoes. (A) Pattern of webbing. (B) Technique of attaching webbing to frame

Individual hunters, wearing snowshoes, stalked both deer and antelope in hilly country where the game was at a disadvantage, especially when the snow was drifted or crusted. In milder weather the hunters hid in the brush or behind rocks near deer trails or waited at salt licks, fords, or watering places. The weapon for hunting in the snow was usually a club. At other times the bow and arrow were used. Artificial blinds were not employed nor was game driven over cliffs or into the water or onto the ice.

The antelope hunter sometimes wore a disguise consisting of an antelope headdress or even a whole skin. The same was done, more rarely, ·in deer and mountain-sheep hunting, the dress being that of the animal sought. Any one of these disguises was profitably used in the hunting of fowl. In summer, however, the hunter was usually naked or wore only a breechcloth, as suggested earlier. Occasionally an antelope hunter painted his body to resemble that animal.

Elk and mountain sheep were sought by individual hunters, using bows and arrows. However, as in the deer hunt, several men often went to the hunting grounds as a party, separating only for the actual hunting. Bear hunting was likewise an individual endeavor, except for the grizzly bear. The searching out of this animal and the pitting of the hunters' skill against the power of the great animal was as much a matter of sport as it was an economic activity. Three to six men ventured forth before dawn, but only in the summer. When a grizzly bear was sighted the fastest runner removed any clothing that he might be wearing and approached the animal. At the closest possible range the hunter released his arrow, then led the pursuing bear as near as he could to the hiding places of first one, then another, of his strategically situated companions. Each man hoped to get one effective arrow shot at the animal. If all were successful the grizzly bear was quite certain to collapse from its injuries before eluding the hunters who followed at top speed. Sometimes, of course, the plans went awry, and the man who shot the first arrow was then in a particularly vulnerable position. Resultant wounds were treated on the spot. The injured man's companions burned wood, preferably juniper, to coals, covered them with green vegetation, and placed the man so that his wounds would be exposed to the filtered heat, with the object of retarding or stopping the bleeding.

Black bears were frightened out of places of resting or of hibernation or sometimes were pulled out of a hole by twisting crossed poles into the animal's skin. Arrows were used to kill the animal when it emerged or was retrieved. Bears were never smoked out.

Juniper smoke was used, however, to drive cottontail rabbits from their lairs. They were also retrieved by twisting a pole into their fur, as were groundhogs. Jack rabbits were run down in the snow and clubbed, or were shot with arrows. The houses of beavers were torn down or burned and the animals killed by clubbing or with arrows. A net of the bag type was used for trapping beaver by suspending it through a hole in the ice. Two long parallel poles, resting on the ice, held the trap in a position favorable for entangling the beaver. The same trap was also used for otter. Small deadfalls were used for foxes.

Black bears and groundhogs were hunted with the aid of dogs. The Modoc dog was small and had a heavy coat of gray-white hair. They were scarce and highly prized, both as hunting dogs and as pets. (The Modoc did not eat dog meat, even in times of famine.) The dogs were trained for hunting by having powder blown into their noses. The powder consisted of dried and pulverized matter from a game animal, for example, the skin of a groundhog's foot. The efficacy of the treatment is questionable.

Nets, suspended vertically above the ground, were placed in localities where rabbits would become entangled in the mesh. Similar nets, with meshes varying according to the game sought, were used for taking geese, ducks, and other waterfowl. They were made of Indian hemp cordage, the height being about three feet, the length ten feet or longer. They were placed parallel to the river bank or lake shore about six feet out. The nets were held by poles driven vertically into the lake or river bottom; cross poles were not used. The nets were set at night, visited the following morning, then brought in to be set at a different place the next night. The game birds became entangled in the loosely hanging net while they fed at night. Decoys of stuffed bird skins or tailored buckskin were sometimes fastened to the base of the net. The same decoys were used by hunters using bows and arrows for taking waterfowl. These hunters also wore disguises made of tule and antelope head skins. Wearing disguises, hunters were sometimes successful in capturing sage hens and quails by approaching while the birds were "dancing." In winter, mud hens were grasped or clubbed when found on the ice.

Hunters employed numerous calls for the game they sought. A rabbit call was made with the lips and deer were called by holding a leaf in the lips and inhaling. A slingshot made of buckskin, sometimes with sinew thongs, was used in hunting rabbits and birds. It was also a favorite toy of children.

A further enumeration of the game hunted by the Modoc is provided in Appendix II together with additional miscellaneous information and a listing of animals kept as pets.

Men did the skinning and major butchering of large game but women assisted by cutting the meat in the manner customary for drying, storage, or immediate use. Women performed all these operations for small animals. The dressing of skins was a task shared by both, with the more arduous labor being performed by men. Large skins, if fresh, were soaked in water for a few hours before dressing; older skins required immersion for two or three days. Dehairing and defleshing were accomplished by draping the skin over a heavy post and scraping with an implement of deer leg bone or rib. The post, rounded on top, was set firmly in the ground at a slight angle. It extended only about four feet; the skin dresser knelt at his task. The skin was tied at the top of the post but the fastening was removed and replaced from time to time to permit the effective scraping of all parts. (See accompanying illustration.) Defleshing was accomplished by reversing the exposure of the skin and scraping with the same tools.

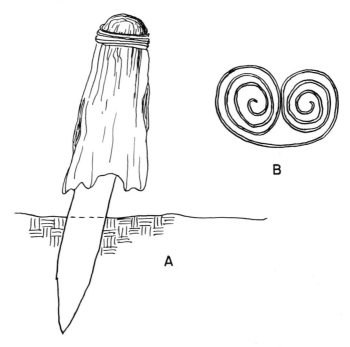

Skin dressing. (A) Defleshing and dehairing post. (B) Diagram of skin rolled for stretching

After thoroughly washing the dehaired and defleshed skin it was partially dried, then given a dressing of brain tissue, usually from a deer but alternatively from any large animal. The brain matter was used fresh if available. Otherwise, dried material from a stored supply was utilized. The drying had been accomplished by spreading the brains on pieces of sagebrush bark and exposing them to the air but not to the sun. They were returned to a plastic state by kneading in water.

The treated skin was tightly rolled and set aside. The next step in the dressing process could be carried out within a few days or postponed for months, possibly even a year. In either case, the skin was immersed in water for the time necessary to soften it thoroughly, two to four days. It was then pounded, twisted, and stretched. Smooth, round rocks of fine texture were used for pounding. Men sometimes chewed the skin as an auxiliary technique. Twisting and stretching were done by hand. Finally, the skin was tightly rolled from the two sides to the middle line (see Fig., page 190) and one end was tied to the trunk of a tree. The other end was fastened to a stout pole which was used for twisting the skin with great pressure. The twisting served to remove much of the water from the skin and also stretched it even further. After a time the skin was taken down, rolled in the opposite direction, and again wrung and stretched between the tree and the pole. Finally, it was spread in the sun, or near a fire, to complete the drying. During this stage it was periodically taken up to be further manipulated. The man spread it by holding with his feet, hands, and teeth, and stretched it to the limit of his strength, using both standing and sitting positions. Sometimes he used a stone scraper at various stages of this procedure. When the skin was thoroughly dry it was ready for use.

For especially heavy skins a scraping frame was used (see Fig., p. 192) with a scraping pole fashioned from mountain mahogany. The same frame served for the preparation of skins which were dressed without removing the hair. In the latter case, the skins were soaked by spreading them, flesh side down, on the surface of a pool of water. They were so fixed as to keep the flesh side in more or less constant contact with the water without the hair side being unduly wetted. A day or a day and a half were sufficient for the soaking. The defleshed side was then treated with brain tissue and the skin was set aside for drying. Later, the frame and wooden scraper were used for softening. Stretching was avoided. The skins so treated included fox, coyote, bobcat, and cougar.

Dehaired skins were usually smoked to make them more water resistant. Rotten wood was used as fuel; a second choice, less satisfactory, was pine cones. Bark was considered unsuitable. The

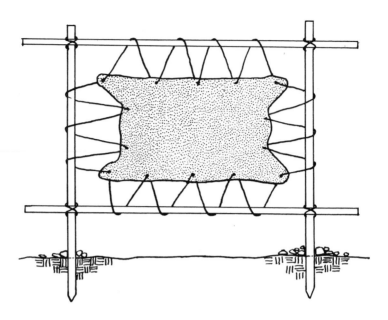

Skin-dressing frame for heavy hides

depression prepared for the fire was approximately eighteen inches in diameter, twelve inches deep. Over this a framework of light willow poles was erected to hold the skin. The skin was held in place by a cord fastened to the poles and carried around the skin. The wrapping was tight and firm at the base; rocks or stakes were not used to hold the bottom fast. Changes were made in the position of the skin as the smoking progressed so that pole marks or other irregularities would not develop. Three types of frame were used: four poles forming a cone; bent poles in hemispherical shape; and a tripod arrangement with one pole much longer than the others (see Fig., p. 193).

Fishing was a well-developed economic pursuit among the Modoc but it did not compare in importance to hunting. In this respect the Modoc contrasted greatly with the adjacent Klamath. It is true that salmon were absent in Modoc territory whereas they were available in the lands of the Klamath. However, there were numerous species of food fish in the streams and lakes of the Modoc and the quantities available were considerable, especially during the runs. Also, the Modoc traded with the Klamath for salmon and obtained some without payment when they visited their neighbors during the salmon runs in Sprague River. However, the quan-

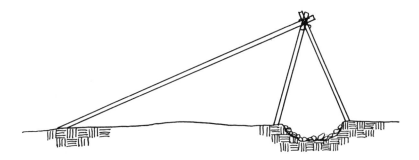

Framework for supporting skin while being smoked

tities involved were of little significance in the over-all Modoc
economy.

Fish taken by the Modoc were primarily suckers, secondarily
trout. The first sucker-fishing season was in March at which time
a large species appeared and was available for a short period.
Trout then appeared, first in Tule Lake and Bonanza River. These
highly prized fish sometimes reached a weight of fifteen pounds.
By late summer the trout were mostly gone but the sucker run
was at its height. Trout appeared again in December and were
caught through the ice during the winter months. The Modoc also
took advantage of the lesser fishes of their habitat—chubs, minnows, eels—and collected fresh water shellfish.

Suckers were taken with a net, about two feet deep, suspended
from an A-frame with slip rings. (See accompanying illustration.)
The side pieces of the frame were four to six feet long, giving the

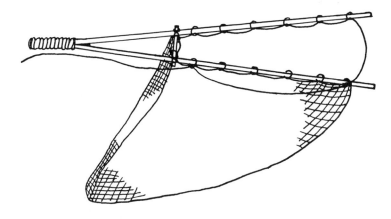

Triangular dip net with slip rings, on A-frame

net a considerable capacity. The twine for the net was spun from
Indian hemp by women; the weaving and construction of the frame
was by men. The nets were used in lakes when schools of fish were
seen, or in streams at spawning time. They were operated from
canoes at the bows, or from rafts. Women were permitted to pro-
pel the canoe or manage the raft but only men handled the net. The
larger nets required the services of two men.

A plain funnel trap made of willow poles fastened with Indian
hemp was used in stream rapids. It was a long trap of limited
diameter designed to keep the captured fish from turning about
and escaping. It was placed in the stream in such a position as
to leave the closed end almost above water and was anchored in
place with rocks. The trap was set at night, emptied and removed
in the morning. Sometimes an attempt was made to drive fish into
the opening. No double funnel traps, seines, or weirs were used
by the Modoc.

For the spearing of suckers or trout from shore positions a two-
pronged implement with detachable points was employed. (See accompanying illustration.) The main shaft, of any suitable wood such

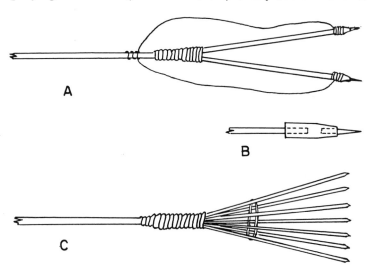

Fish spears. (A) Foreshafts of two-pronged spear. (B) Detail of point
of two-pronged spear. (C) Multipronged spear

as pine or fir, was eight to ten feet long. The foreshafts, of mountain mahogany, were attached to the main shaft with a wrapping of
Indian hemp cord reinforced with pitch. The foreshafts were fitted

with detachable points which, in turn, were connected to the main shaft by slack cords. The points were composite, the sockets being short tubular pieces of serviceberry wood, the points of bone. The points were inserted in the socket and made fast with a wrapping of sinew and pitch.

These spears were thrust from a concealed location over the edge of the water. They were not used from canoes or rafts. Spearing platforms were not utilized but rude huts or blinds were constructed in advantageous locations. These were tiny enclosures made of a few willow poles and a tule mat or two, the shape being an inverted-U or inverted-V in section. The fisherman sat inside, on a tule mat, with his spear poised just outside the opening, over the water. Sometimes the same implement was used while the fisherman waded near shore. It was also used in winter fishing for spearing through holes in the ice.

A multipronged spear for suckers was used exclusively from canoes or rafts. (See Fig., p. 194.) The main shaft, ten or fifteen feet long, was tipped with four to ten long, slender points. The points were preferably made of split pieces of deer leg bone but mountain mahogany was a second choice. The spreading points were held in place by a wooden ring fixed inside, near the end of the shaft. The fisherman used the spear to pin the sucker to the bottom of the shallow lake where it was held until dead. (The Modoc had no throwing spears.)

Chubs, minnows, trout, and eels were taken with hooks and gorgets of bone, attached to lines of Indian hemp. (See accompanying illustrations.) The two pieces forming the acute-angled hook were

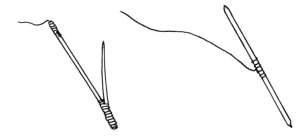

Fishhook and double gorget

fastened together with sinew and pitch. The poles were simple shafts of willow. The hooks, which were not barbed, were baited with insects (the devil fly was favored), ant larvae (for minnows), or worms. The use of worms was aboriginal—not learned from whites. Eels were caught with the hands as well as with hooks. Minnows were killed by biting; a club was used for other fish. An openwork basketry fish creel was sometimes carried. It was round at the top and tapered toward the bottom, in end view, making it wedge shaped. Around the top it was decorated with groundhog tail pendants or other ornaments. Lacking the creel, fish were carried in an ordinary basket or on a willow hoop, never on a pole.

Rafts and canoes have been mentioned above in connection with Modoc fishing. The canoes were few in number and crude in form despite the fact that numerous lakes and navigable streams were found in the tribal territory. Rafts, however, were plentiful and were found quite adequate for most fishing and transportation needs on the calm lakes.

Canoes were preferably of cedar. They were constructed, as dugouts, at locations where suitable trees were found as windfalls. Such areas were generally in the extreme western part of Modoc territory; therefore, the finished canoes had to be carried long distances. They were always small, however, averaging ten feet in length, twenty inches to two feet at the gunwales. Their capacity was one or two persons, never more. The shaping was accomplished by adzing, splitting, and burning. Horn wedges were used for splitting and breaking. Burning was hastened and partially controlled with the use of pitch. Only the inside was shaped. The walls were thick and the ends were blunt, with long, solid sections. The hull was never painted, either inside or out. Leaks were repaired by running melted pitch into the cracks from the inside. Canoes were individually owned by the builder or purchaser. However, they were freely available for use by others when not needed by the owner. Canoes were propelled by poling, the handler being seated at the bow, or with rudimentary paddles of cedar. (The bow was the forward end of the canoe. The boat was reversible but usually the narrower end was forward.) In the late nineteenth century there were only two canoes on Tule Lake. They were used near the shore, not for crossing. During the freezing weather of winter canoes were ordinarily sunk, bottom up, in a tule swamp.

Canoe paddle

Rafts were common. The usual size was ten feet long, six or eight feet wide. The framework, which included three crosspieces, was of pine. The frame was planked with pine, juniper, willow, or bark, usually a combination. The tying was done with skin thongs or tule rope. (See accompanying illustration. The tying is shown diagrammatically.)

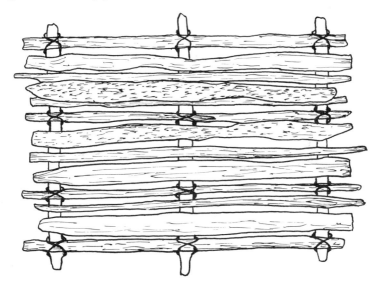

Raft (tying shown diagrammatically)

The search for vegetal foods occupied a large part of the Modoc woman's days, spring through autumn. Many of the movements of families and groups during the growing and ripening seasons were dictated by the succession of crops and the wide geographic spread of the many plants which had to be gathered of economic necessity. The total number of species utilized was impressively large but the physical character of the Modoc habitat was such that many kinds of plants were found only in limited numbers and in widely distributed patches. This was true even of the staples, epos and camas.

Epos was the most important plant food of the Modoc. (The word epos, from Sahaptin, has not come into extensive use and does not appear in most dictionaries. However, it is recognized in the local area as the English word for identification of the plant, and it appears in the ethnographic literature and in some botanical works, sometimes with the spelling ipos. There is no other common name in English. (The scientific name is *Carum oreganum* Wats.) It was the tuberous root of the plant that was used by the Modoc. It was gathered before blooming, usually in May, when the roots were soft and milky. The plants were found in elevations from 4,000 to 7,000 feet, in open places in the pine forests and in meadows and on rocky slopes. The season was very short, only three or four weeks. Modoc women were forced to work at top speed to harvest a sufficient quantity for current use and storage for the winter. Large groups of women went together early each morning to one and then another of the patches within working distance of the village. When these fields were exhausted the village moved to a new site, and so on, until the season was over. The productive days of the season amounted to only ten or fifteen because of time lost in traveling and in cleaning the plants. The cleaning had to be done while the roots were fresh, that is, every three or four days. The tubers were collected in conical, openwork burden baskets or in the same baskets as those used for cleaning the husks from the roots: round, openwork containers, large but shallow, of juniper withes. A successful day of digging netted one basketful. Each woman kept the product of her labors for the use of her family.

Camas was the root of second importance in the Modoc dietary. The bulbs were dug in June or July, depending upon the advancement of the season. The plants were found in moist meadows, scattered in the montane coniferous forests at elevations from 4,000 to 7,000 feet. The pattern of digging was much the same as for epos and the travel and logistics problems were similar. Most of the camas was kept for winter use. Toward this end the bulbs were partially dried and cleaned at the site of digging. This preliminary drying required several days or a week. As a consequence the women sometimes had to travel considerable distances from the village or the root-digging camp on the last days of a stay, the nearby fields having been exhausted meanwhile. The season lasted for about a month, at the end of which time the roots accumulated by each woman were carried to her winter home and cooked in an earth oven. After removal they were dried on tule mats, then placed in bags and stored in pits.

The roots of desert parsley were available in April and May—even earlier than epos. This parsley, a perennial plant with a turniplike tuber of large size, was found in the sagebrush scrub country; Tule Lake was a productive area. The early appearance and relative abundance of the plant gave it a prominent place in the Modoc dietary. The tubers were cooked and eaten fresh, also dried for winter.

Another plant extensively utilized by the Modoc is of especial interest because it is poisonous in the raw state. This is the so-called white camas, also known as death camas or deadly zygadene. A leaching process known by the Modoc rendered the bulbs edible. They were ready for harvesting soon after the camas season, in late July, thus prolonging the root-digging season, a significant economic advantage. The bulbs were gathered from moist, grassy places in the montane coniferous forests, carried to the village, and cleaned of their tunicate coverings. They were then dried and placed in tule sacks. Leaching was accomplished by immersing the sacks in a steadily flowing stream for three days, after which they were again dried and placed in storage.

The Modoc exploited seed-bearing plants of many species as a food resource. Their pattern contrasted greatly with the Klamath, however, whose major dependence was upon seeds of the water lily. The Modoc gathered water-lily seeds, too, but of more importance were the tiny seeds of a multitude of plants, in the typical manner of northern California Indians generally. Seeds were beaten from the plant with a snowshoe-shaped basketry plaque of closely woven juniper withes, fourteen to sixteen inches wide and half again as long. The self-handle was wrapped with buckskin.

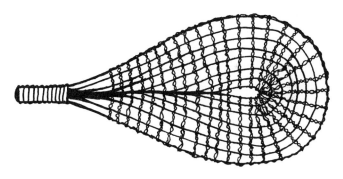

Seed beater

The hopper was a truncated conical burden basket of juniper or willow withes with a side handle and a lining of buckskin. Among the more important seed plants were the sunflower, buckwheat, willow dock, rye grass, plains mustard, lamb's-quarters, manna grass, blazing star, tarweed, balsam root, and water lily.

Pine nuts were of modest importance to the Modoc. Most families collected a half bushel or so for winter storage. Fruits were gathered in considerable quantity, the most used species being the

Sierra plum, twinberry, serviceberry, western chokecherry, blue elderberry, and strawberry.

The names of many additional food plants used by the Modoc, together with scientific names for all species will be found in Appendix II. (Frederick V. Coville, *Wokas, a Primitive Food of the Klamath Indians*, should be consulted for details concerning the collection and preparation of water-lily seeds.) Medicines are also listed in Appendix II.

APPENDIX I: TERRITORY AND VILLAGES

The boundaries of the Modoc tribal territory are described in chapter 1 and are presented graphically on the map accompanying this appendix. These boundaries were precisely defined and understood by the Modoc and transgression meant war. Automatically, this was the case with the Pit River tribes, the Paiute, and the Shasta, except during occasional short periods of truce. The Modoc were generally at peace with the Klamath although there was an underlying enmity which sometimes reached the surface. Nevertheless, the sharing of a language and frequent intermarriage resulted in a customary, though formal, amity between the two tribes. The formality was expressed, in part, in the rules governing intertribal visiting. Most such visiting was between related families. Mere friendship was only rarely the basis for visits. In either case, the visitors invariably were provided housing by the local tribe, specifically, by their relatives or friends. They were not allowed to establish their own camps and they never built their own houses.

Intertribal visits were for relatively long periods, usually a minimum of ten or fifteen days. Sometimes these sojourns were extended to a full year but it was generally understood that a longer period was not desirable. Such lengthy visits were not ordinarily projected as such; they developed through prolongation of trips originally planned for a shorter period. When visitors arrived from another tribe they never were asked how long they expected to stay. Similarly, they did not announce their intention of departing until two or three days before their actual leave-taking. (Of course, their intentions were sometimes obvious at an earlier time, even though unvoiced. Likewise, hosts were able to express, without words, the fact that their visitors' welcome had worn thin.)

During these sojourns the visitors jealously guarded their tribal identity. Whenever other persons were encountered, the first words exchanged conveyed their tribal and local identities. Indeed, the same thing was true, even in the home territory, between persons from separately named local areas. The formal greeting was, "What is your people?" The answer: "I am Gumbatwas," for example. "And you?" This greeting was exchanged even between persons who were acquainted with one another. (There were no alternative customary greetings.) The phrases were wholly formal and the Modoc used them automatically between close acquaintances just as they did with strangers. In the former instance there was no purposive effort to gain information, any more than in the English-language greeting, "How do you do?" (The "And you" phrase was usually omitted between close acquaintances.) However, meaningful information was conveyed between two tribesmen who had not seen one another for a period of time, because one or the other may recently have changed his place of residence. In such a case, the response was in terms of the new residence, even though it were to be temporary. Between strangers, and in intertribal situations, the information communicated was of prime significance.

The formal remark upon parting, in any situation, was, "Now you go back"; the response, "Yes, now I go back"; or the reverse.

Modoc tribal territory was divided into three geographic areas and the residents of each area were known by a distinctive name. The Gumbatwas were, literally, "people of the west." The root of the name was the word for west; the point of reference was Tule Lake. Thus, all Modoc living west of a line following the ridge between Lower Klamath Lake and Lost River Valley, to the northwestern corner of Tule Lake, then through the lake to its southeastern corner, then southeastward to the southern tribal boundary, were Gumbatwas.

All tribesmen living to the east of this line, except for the lower valley of Lost River, were Kokiwas, literally, "people of the far out country," referring to their remoteness from the more concentrated population centers of the lower Lost River Valley and the Lower Klamath Lake region. Many of their villages were located on the far reaches of Lost River, east of Lost River Gap (now Olene, Oregon) with a heavy concentration in Langell Valley.

Apparently the name of the river was different on the two sides of the gap, the designation (Ko´kiwat) in the Gumbatwas area being derived from, or giving its name to, the divisional population.

The Modoc of Lost River Valley from the gap to Tule Lake were Paskanwas, which means "river people," possibly a name derived from that of the lower river.

These divisions were strictly geographical, not ethnic nor political except quite incidentally. The minor cultural differences which distinguished one group from another were the consequence of response to the physical environment, either in terms of the resources available or the configuration of settlements and their positions with respect to ceremonial centers and neighboring tribes. In the political realm, a prominent Leader ordinarily received more recognition and wielded more power in his own division than in others but this was strictly a phenomenon of proximity. The most influential village Leader in a division was characteristically looked upon as a divisional Leader but this was a matter of personal prestige, not the power of an office.

Membership in an areal division was wholly a matter of residence. Superficially, a considerable ambiguity seems to have surrounded such membership; for example, a man could be a "member" of two divisions at the same time. However, the appearance is merely illusory and the resolution of the confusion reveals the true nature of the divisional groupings. They were, essentially, devices for providing a man with important identifying labels. We have already seen how this worked in the greetings exchanged by two persons upon meeting. More fundamentally, every man and woman had a basic divisional or areal affiliation. This was determined by his primary or earliest lengthy place of residence, and usually reflected his family and kinship ties. In these terms a man was, for example, a Gumbatwas. However, upon moving to a Kokiwas village, as either a temporary or permanent resident, his new fellow villagers consistently called him a Gumbatwas, but all other Modoc, including his former Gumbatwas associates and relatives, called him a Kokiwas. In the instance of a marriage of a Gumbatwas man to a Kokiwas woman, with residence in the Kokiwas area, their children, to the age of adulthood, were called Gumbatwas at home but Kokiwas by the Modoc of other divisions.

This being the nature of the system, it was possible and permissible to extend the pattern to even smaller regional aggregations, as was occasionally done by the Modoc of Lower Klamath Lake (see No. 1 in the list of villages, below). For the purposes of the moment, a Modoc often used the same device with respect to his village, thus conveying in a meaningful and economical way his temporary or adopted village connection as contrasted to his primary village affiliation, or the reverse. (It goes without saying that any Modoc family could establish residence, at will, in any part of Modoc territory.)

In the light of these facts it is clear that there was but one political entity superior to the village: the Modoc tribe.

The tribal name, Modoc, means "people to the south." It is of Klamath origin—unquestionably so despite numerous published guesses involving different derivations. Present day Modoc are puzzled as to how anyone could think otherwise, since they are "people to the south" only in Klamath terms, geographically as well as ethnically. (The Klamath used another variant of the term, "southerners," to designate Pit River Indians.)

The permanent villages of the Modoc generally consisted of three to seven earth-covered lodges with their attendant structures. Occasionally the number reached ten or fifteen, as was the case with a town near the mouth of Lost River. More commonly, when a local population expanded, a new village was established in a nearby location, as occurred again and again in Langell Valley. In most settlements one or two of the houses were considerably larger than the others. These were characteristically the homes of village Leaders or shamans and they served as places of gathering for religious or political purposes.

The Modoc family averaged five persons. The smaller earth-covered houses accommodated one to three families, the larger ones three or four. In the village listing, the adjectives—small, large, and very large—are used with moderately specific quantitative values. Small means two or three houses; large, six to eight houses; very large, more than eight. Where the size is not specified the number of houses was moderate or undetermined. All estimates are just that: approximations.

The village list refers to the mid-1800's. Most of these sites were occupied until about 1865, some much later. The list is incomplete but all the principal settlements of that period are included. Not all of the villages were occupied at the same time, because many were seasonal and some were alternate locations. However, in immediate prereservation times most of the winter villages here noted were occupied.

It will be observed that the areal divisions gave names to some villages within their limits. These were not necessarily the most important or most populous villages and in no case were they in

any sense capitol villages. Village names were sometimes duplicated within the Modoc territory, or between the Modoc and the
Klamath. This is to be expected because villages were frequently
named for topographic or other natural features that were similar
in various places.

I have Anglicized the village names sufficiently to permit spelling
them with letters of the English alphabet. They are, consequently,
easy to equate with the lists of Albert Gatschet *(The Klamath Indians of Southwestern Oregon)* and Livingston Farrand (in Frederick
W. Hodge, *Handbook of American Indians)* where some duplica-
tions occur. However, the names in my list represent villages,
not the dwellers therein. Consequently, I have not utilized the suf-
fixes that mean "the people of" (-kni and -was) which characteristically but erroneously have served to lengthen the terms earlier
published.

Two maps are presented here. One shows the Modoc tribal boundary and the locations of outlying villages. The other, on a larger
scale, locates the villages which were situated in the more populous central area. The numbers on both maps represent villages
and refer to the accompanying list. Some of the established cremation places and a portion of the ritual centers are also presented,
by means of symbols.

The tribal boundary map utilizes, as a base, the current state
maps of Oregon and California as prepared by the U.S. Geological
Survey, showing the present configurations of the lakes and rivers
on which the Modoc formerly lived. It will be seen that Tule Lake
and Lower Klamath Lake have been reduced greatly in size by recent draining for agricultural purposes. At the same time, Clear
Lake has been made a reservoir and much enlarged. Goose Lake
retains its former outline.

On the larger scaled village map these lakes and other geographic features are shown as they were during late Modoc oc-
cupation. The map is based upon the reconnaissance sheets of
the U.S. Geological Survey presenting the surveys of 1884 to
1887.

Gumbatwas Area

1. Aku´ast. A permanent village on the southwestern shore of
Lower Klamath Lake. The name of this village, with suffix (Aku-
astkni) was sometimes applied to all Modoc of the southwestern-
most part of the tribal territory (villages one through seven and

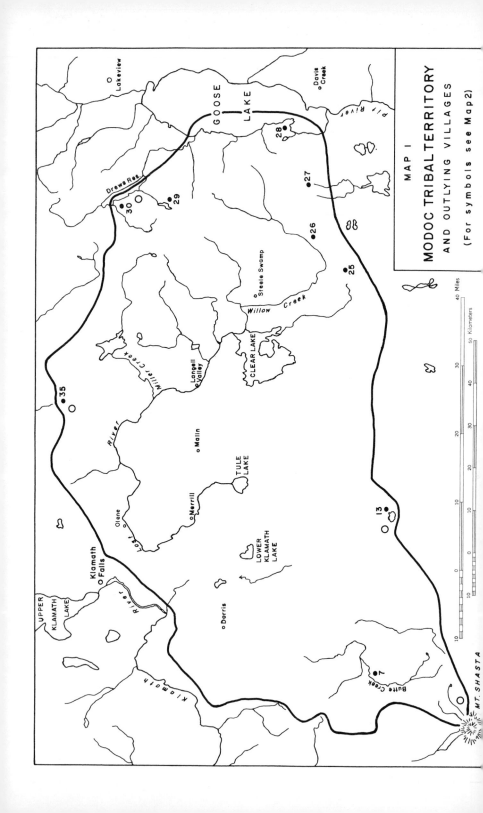

MAP I

MODOC TRIBAL TERRITORY

AND OUTLYING VILLAGES

(For symbols see Map2)

UPPER KLAMATH LAKE

Klamath Falls

LOWER KLAMATH LAKE

TULE LAKE

Dorris

Olene

Merrill

Malin

Langell Valley

CLEAR LAKE

Steele Swamp

Willow Creek

GOOSE LAKE

Lakeview

Davis Creek

Pit River

Drews Res.

M.T. SHASTA

Butte Creek

Lost River

Klamath River

Miller Creek

●7

●13

●25

●26

●27

●28

●29

●30

●35

40 Miles

50 Kilometers

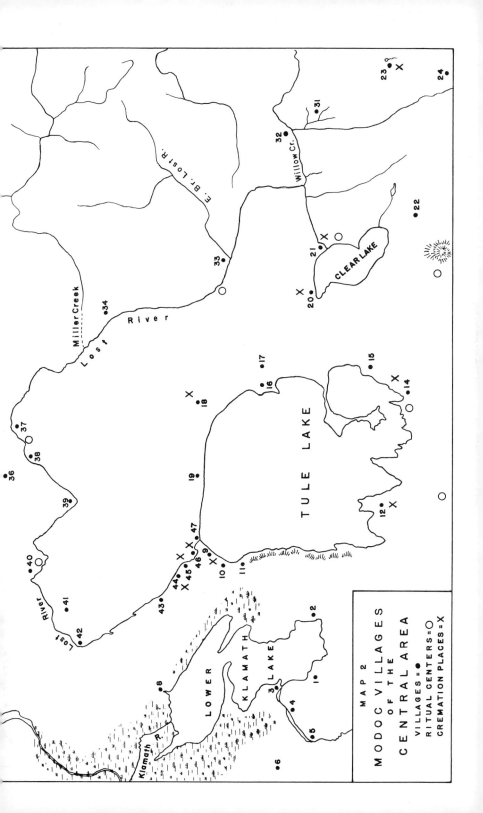

MAP 2

MODOC VILLAGES
OF THE
CENTRAL AREA

VILLAGES = •
RITUAL CENTERS = ○
CREMATION PLACES = X

the unlisted camps which dotted the territory during periods of hunting and gathering).

2. Shapa´sh. A summer village on the southeastern shore of Lower Klamath Lake.

3. Sputu´ish. A permanent village on Willow Creek (a tributary of Lower Klamath Lake, formerly called Cottonwood Creek or Hot Creek) near the lake.

4. Keuchi´s ("wolf rock"). A permanent village on Willow Creek, about two miles from Lower Klamath Lake (location approximate).

5. Aga´. A large permanent village on Willow Creek, near the foot of the mountains south of the present town of Dorris, California.

6. Yuwa´lna. A summer village near the present site of Dorris. Epos, plums, and chokecherries were gathered in the vicinity.

7. Nau´ki. This was a village site on Butte Creek to which the Modoc returned each summer for gathering epos and hunting antelope.

8. Stu´ikish ("canoe bay"). A summer village which regularly served as a base for gathering water-lily seeds. Located on the edge of the marshlands of the northeastern shore of Lower Klamath Lake.

9. Ka´lelk. A large permanent village on the northwestern shore of Tule Lake at the present Oregon-California boundary line. (A cremation place was located nearby.)

10. Pa´shka. A permanent village situated at the mouth of a small creek on the northwestern shore of Tule Lake.

11. Ala´lsi. A small permanent village on the western shore of Tule Lake at the northern end of Gillem Bluff.

12. Gu´mbat. A large permanent village on the south shore of Tule Lake. This village was particularly populous during the winter months. It gave its name to all the Modoc of the western portion of the tribal territory. The name (Gu´mbatwas) referred to the western position of these people with respect to Tule Lake but, as indicated, the principal village was on the south shore of the lake. The houses of the village were quite widely spread, some on the flats and some on a low butte. (A cremation place was situated near the village.)

13. Lani´shwi. A summer village site on Medicine Lake, near Mount Hoffman, maintained as a base for hunting and for mining obsidian at Glass Mountain.

Kokiwas Area

14. E´uslis ("lake place"). A permanent village on the south-eastern shore of Tule Lake (map location approximate). (A cremation place was located adjacent.)

15. Keshla´kchuish. An important summer village near present Scarface station. Epos was gathered in the rocky grounds of the vicinity.

16. Welwa´sh. This was a permanent village situated at a large spring on the eastern side of Tule Lake (map location approximate).

17. Wuka´. A permanent village situated in a valley immediately east of the preceding (No. 16), the separation apparently the result of varying preferences for house sites.

18. Le´ush. A large permanent village situated on a low butte immediately north of the present town of Malin, Oregon. This settlement was more populous in summer than winter because many root products were available in the vicinity. (A crematory was located nearby.)

19. Li´klis. A small summer village on the north shore of Tule Lake (map location approximate).

20. Ste´okas ("ridge"). A large permanent village on the north shore of Clear Lake (Tsa´psko). This settlement was important because it was in a desirable location for winter housing and also provided excellent summer resources of roots and seeds. (A cremation place was situated outside the town.)

21. Yama´ktsa. A permanent winter village on the northeastern shore of Clear Lake (map location approximate). (A crematory here, also.)

22. Chala´ks. A summer village northeast of Double Head (Saddle Mountain) which served as a base for hunting and gathering of epos.

23. Chiwulha´. A permanent village site at Pot Hole Spring west of Blue Mountain, where root digging was extensively pursued. (A cremation place was maintained here so that it would be unnecessary to carry corpses a long distance for disposal.)

24. Tanka´i. This was a summer village site on the South Fork of Willow Creek (a tributary of Lost River) at Boles Meadow. The Modoc returned here each summer for root digging and antelope hunting.

25. Ka´umpwis. A permanent village site that was utilized each summer for antelope hunting and root and seed gathering. It was

located at the north end of Fairchild Meadow, south of the bend of the South Fork of Willow Creek.

26. Tsktya´m. A summer village site between Bottle Creek and Beaver Creek, where antelope and small game were hunted and a variety of roots and seeds were gathered.

27. Chalklo´ki. Situated at the headwaters of Rattlesnake Creek, a tributary of Pit River, this summer village was the base for digging wild turnips, epos, and other roots, and for gathering seeds.

28. Lu´kmtsis ("big nose," referring to the shape of the peninsula jutting into Goose Lake). This was the only permanent Modoc village site on Goose Lake, temporary camps being used at other locations along the western shore. The village was situated on the peninsula opposite present Davis Creek, California. It was a major base for the hunting of deer, antelope, and waterfowl, and the gathering of roots and seeds.

29. Kina´n. This summer village, at Dog Lake, was used as a hunting base, particularly for deer.

30. Nja´ktis. A summer village, on Drew's Creek, for root digging, seed gathering, and hunting, particularly bears.

31. Hano´laksi. This summer village, a base for intensive gathering activities, was located on the South Fork of Willow Creek at Steele Meadow.

32. Sano´tks. A summer village at the confluence of the North and South Forks of Willow Creek.

33. Pe´owas. A small permanent village on Lost River near the mouth of the East Branch.

34. Ulga´na. This was a permanent village on Lost River near the present town of Langell Valley, one of many such villages lining the river both north and south of this site. A great many house pits were still visible in these locations in the early 1900's.

35. Ya´inaks. A summer village site near Keno Spring, south of Yainax Butte, where ceremonial and gambling activities took place.

36. Ka´wa. A summer village, possibly with a small winter population, situated near the present town of Dairy, Oregon (map location approximate).

37. Nushaltka´ga. A permanent village, especially populous during the fishing season, at the present site of Bonanza on Lost River.

38. Uglna´nksi. A summer fishing village on Lost River, west of Bonanza (map location approximate).

39. Niya´ntkis. A fishing village on Lost River between Bonanza and Olene (map location approximate).

Paskanwas Area

40. Tsotso´ksi. A large fishing village on Lost River near the present site of Olene, Oregon.

41. Yola´ksi. A permanent village at Nuss Lake, occupied principally in winter.

42. Lugosa´mnwapka. A fishing village on Lost River near Laki Peak (map location approximate).

43. Wa´isha. A large fishing village, also occupied in winter, at Stukel Ford on Lost River. This was the only possible crossing of the lower river except for the "natural bridge" (a rock ledge) near Tule Lake. The latter could be used only during low water.

44. Tolhaslo´oals. A small permanent village on the east side of Lost River near the site of present Merrill, Oregon. (The residents maintained their own cremation grounds.)

45. Wa´chamshwash. This very large village, situated on the west side of Lost River, one mile north of the natural bridge, consisted of ten to fourteen large earth-covered houses. (A crematory was located here.)

46. Nako´sh. A large permanent village at the natural bridge, one mile above the mouth of Lost River.

47. Koka´tat. A permanent village situated where Lost River entered Tule Lake.

APPENDIX II: FOODS AND MEDICINES

Plant Species

The following lists represent plant species identified with reasonable certainty. Most of the identifications are based upon plant specimens collected. The items represent subsistence or medical products, for the most part, but some plants used in the manufacture of small artifacts are included. The latter includes matting but excludes basketry, large items such as rafts, canoes and houses, and firewood.

The first list is alphabetical according to botanical names. For convenience in cross-referencing, the second list, which includes the Modoc names, is alphabetized according to common names.

Abies concolor (Gord. & Glendl.) Lindl.	White fir
Achillea borealis ssp. *californica* (Pollard) Keck	Yarrow
Agrostis exorata Trin.	Spike bent grass
Agrostis scabra Willd.	Tickle grass
Alectoria Fremontii Tuckerm.	Black lichen
Amaranthus blitoides S. Wats.	Amaranth
Amelanchier alnifolia Nutt.	Serviceberry
Apocynum cannabinum L. var. *glaberrinum* A. DC.	Indian hemp
Aralia californica Wats.	Spikenard
Arctostaphylos nevadensis Gray	Pinemat manzanita

Arctostaphylos Uva-ursi (L.) Spreng.	Kinnikinnick; bearberry
Artemisia tridentata Nutt.	Sagebrush
Balsamorhiza sagittata (Pursh) Nutt.	Arrow-leaved balsamroot
Beckmannia Syzigachne (Steud.) Fern.	Slough grass
Berberis Aquifolium (Pursh) Nutt.	Oregon grape
Berberis repens Lindl.	Barberry
Calochortus macrocarpus Dougl.	Sego lily
Calochortus uniflorus H. & A.	Star tulip
Camassia quamash (Pursh) Greene	Camas
Carex sp.	Sedge
Carum Gairdneri H. & A.	Epos; western false caraway
Carum oreganum Wats.	Epos; Oregon false caraway
Ceanothus sanguineus Pursh	Buckbrush
Cercocarpus ledifolius Nutt.	Mountain mahogany
Chenopodium Fremontii Wats.	Lamb's-quarters; goosefoot
Chrysothamnus nauseosus (Pall.) Britt.	Rabbit brush
Cicuta Douglasii (DC.) Coult. & Rose	Water hemlock
Daucus pusillus Michx.	Rattlesnake weed
Descurainia pinnata (Walt.) Britton	Tansy mustard
Elymus Triticoides Buckl.	Rye grass
Equisetum hiemale var. *californicum* Milde	Horsetail
Eriogonum umbellatum Torr. var. *stellatum* (Benth.) Jones	Buckwheat
Evernia vulpina (L.) Ach.	Yellow lichen
Fragaria platypetala Rydb.	Strawberry
Glyceria occidentalis (Piper) J. C. Nels	Manna grass
Helianthus Cusickii Gray	Sunflower
Helianthus Nuttallii T. & G.	Sunflower
Heracleum lanatum Michx.	Cow parsnip
Iris missouriensis Nutt.	Iris
Iris tenax Dougl. ssp. *klamathensis* Lenz	Iris

Juncus balticus Willd.	Rush
Juniperus occidentalis Hook.	Western juniper
Libocedrus decurrens Torr.	Incense cedar
Linum perenne L. ssp. *Lewisii* (Pursh.) Hult.	Flax
Lomatium Canbyi Coult. & Rose	Desert parsley
Lonicera conjugialis Kell.	Siamese twinberry
Lonicera involucrata Richards	Twinberry
Lycium Andersonii Gray	Thornwood
Madia glomerata Hook.	Tarweed
Mentha arvensis L. var. *villosa* (Benth.) S. R. Stewart	Woolly field mint
Mentha canadensis L. (Briq.)	Canada mint
Mentzelia albicaulis Dougl. ex Hook	Blazing star
Nicotiana attenuata Torr.	Tobacco
Nuphar polysepalum Engelm.	Water lily
Phragmites communis Trin. var. *Berlandieri* (Fourn.) Fern.	Common reed
Pinus Lambertiana Dougl.	Sugar pine
Pinus Murrayana Grev. & Balf.	Lodgepole pine
Pinus ponderosa Dougl. ex P. & C. Lawson	Yellow pine
Polygonum Douglasii Greene	Knotweed
Populus balsamifera L.	Balsam poplar
Populus tremuloides Michx.	Quaking aspen
Prunus emarginata (Dougl. ex Hook.) Walp.	Bitter cherry
Prunus subcordata Benth. var. *oregana* (Greene) W. Wight	Sierra plum
Prunus subcordata Benth. var. *rubicunda* Jeps.	Sierra plum
Prunus virginiana L. Var. *demissa* (Nutt.) Torr.	Western chokecherry
Ranunculus occidentalis Nutt.	Buttercup
Rhamnus Purshiana DC.	Cascara
Ribes aureum Pursh.	Flowering currant
Ribes cereum Dougl.	Squaw currant
Rosa californica Cham. & Schlecht	Wild rose
Rosa Woodsii Lindl. var. *ultramontane* (Wats.) Jeps.	Wild rose
Rubus leucodermis Dougl.	Blackcap

Rubus macropetalus Dougl.	Blackberry
Rumex lacustris Greene	Dock; sorrel
Rumex occidentalis Wats.	Western dock
Rumex salicifolius Weinm.	Willow dock
Sagittaria cuneata Sheldon	Arrowhead
Sagittaria latifolia Willd.	Wapato
Salix sp.	Willow
Salix lasiandra Benth.	Red willow
Sambucus coerulea Raf.	Blue elderberry
Scirpus acutus Muhl. ex Bigel.	Tule
Sisymbrium linifolium Nutt.	Plains mustard
Sium suave Walt.	Hemlock water parsnip
Sparganium eurycarpum Engelm.	Bur reed
Taxus brevifolia Nutt.	Western yew
Tetradymia canescens DC.	Gray tetradymia
Triglochin maritima L.	Arrow grass
Typha latifolia L.	Cattail
Urtica holosericea Nutt.	Hoary nettle
Urtica serra Blume	Sierra nettle
Vaccinium arbuscula (Gray) Merriam	Blueberry; bilberry
Vaccinium membranaceum Dougl.	Mountain huckleberry
Vaccinium occidentale Gray	Western huckleberry; western blueberry
Valeriana obovata (Nutt.) R. & S.	Tobacco root
Wyethia amplexicaulis Nutt.	Mule's ears
Zygadenus venenosis Wats.	Zygadene; "white camas"

English Common Names, Modoc Names, and English Binomials

Amaranth (ba´kai?)	*Amaranthus blitoides*
Arrowhead (tcuwa´q)	*Sagittaria cuneata*
Aspen, quaking	*Populus tremuloides*
Balsamroot, arrow-leaved (lba´)	*Balsamorhiza sagittata*
Barberry (babawe´sɑm)	*Berberis repens*
Bearberry (kemɑma´i)	*Arctostaphylos Uva-ursi*
Bilberry (qala´tc)	*Vaccinium arbuscula*
Blackberry (totanka´sɑm)	*Rubus macropetalus*
Blackcap (ma´sla)	*Rubus leucodermis*
Blazing star (lo´las)	*Mentzelia albicaulis*
Blueberry (i´wɑm)	*Vaccinium arbuscula*

Blueberry, western (i´wɑm)	*Vaccinium occidentale*
Buckbrush (dza´kulu)	*Ceanothus sanguineus*
Buckwheat (qa´lupka)	*Eriogonum umbellatum*
Bur reed (po´dtcaq)	*Sparganium eurycarpum*
Buttercup (ye´nɑmbado)	*Ranunculus occidentalis*
Camas (bo´kc)	*Camassia quamash*
"Camas, white" (sqa´o)	*Zygadenus venenosis*
Caraway, Oregon false (qa´s)	*Carum oreganum*
Caraway, western false (nda´lk)	*Carum Gairdneri*
Cascara	*Rhamnus Purshiana*
Cattail (pu´pɑsɑm; ktu´qs [root])	*Typha latifolia*
Cedar, incense (wolwa´nc)	*Libocedrus decurrens*
Cherry, bitter (dɑwιtcqa´s?)	*Prunus emarginata*
Chokecherry, western (dɑwιtcqa´s)	*Prunus virginiana*
Currant, flowering (tcɑ´mtcɑq)	*Ribes aureum*
Currant, squaw (tcmao´lɑq)	*Ribes cereum*
Dock (go´kca)	*Rumex lacustris*
Dock, western (go´kca)	*Rumex occidentalis*
Dock, willow (go´kca)	*Rumex salicifolius*
Elderberry, blue (clu´lusɑm; sapa´wal?)	*Sambucus coerulea*
Epos (qa´s; ndalk)	*Carum Gairdneri; C. oreganum*
Fir, white (cɑksa´lkιs; cι´ptkιs?)	*Abies concolor*
Flax (qo´lɑkɑmɑqs)	*Linum perenne*
Grass, arrow (gιlε´na)	*Triglochin maritima*
Grass, manna (kamtcoda´lιs)	*Glyceria occidentalis*
Grass, rye (gla´pi)	*Elymus triticoides*
Grass, spike bent (no´taq)	*Agrostis exorata*
Grass, tickle (no´taq)	*Agrostis scabra*
Goosefoot (kotca´nιks)	*Chenopodium Fremontii*
Hemlock, water (kawa´nks)	*Cicuta Douglasii*
Hemp, Indian (no´d)	*Apocynum cannabinum*
Horsetail (wa´tcaq)	*Equisetum hiemale*
Huckelberry, mountain (i´wɑm)	*Vaccinium membranaceum*
Huckleberry, western (i´wɑm)	*Vaccinium occidentale*
Iris (qa´qɑqlɑqo´)	*Iris missouriensis; I. tenax*
Juniper, western (qa´lu)	*Juniperus occidentalis*
Kinnikinnick (kemɑma´i?)	*Arctostaphylos Uva-ursi*

Knotweed (ka´pionks)	*Polygonum Douglasii*
Lamb's-quarters (kotca´nɩks)	*Chenopodium Fremontii*
Lichen, black (qa´l)	*Alectoria Fremontii*
Lichen, yellow (ga´da)	*Evernia vulpina*
Lily, sego (yα´nc)	*Calochortus macrocarpus*
Lily, water (wo´qas)	*Nuphar polysepalum*
Mahogany, mountain (yokma´kam)	*Cercocarpus ledifolius*
Manzanita, pinemat (patca´i?)	*Arctostaphylos nevadensis*
Mint, Canada (matca´sαm)	*Mentha canadensis*
Mint, woolly field (lulα´t)	*Mentha arvensis*
Mustard, plains (tci´pas)	*Sisymbrium linifolium*
Mustard, tansy (tci´pas)	*Descurainia pinnata*
Mule's ears	*Wyethia amplexicaulis*
Nettle, hoary (cle´dz)	*Urtica holosericea*
Nettle, Sierra (cle´dz)	*Urtica serra*
Oregon grape (balbale´nαm?)	*Berberis Aquifolium*
Parsley, desert (le´xαs)	*Lomatium Canbyi*
Parsnip, cow (bu´tcu)	*Heracleum lanatum*
Parsnip, hemlock water (qa´ansαm)	*Sium suave*
Pine, lodgepole (wa´qu)	*Pinus Murrayana*
Pine, sugar (kte´lo)	*Pinus Lambertiana*
Pine, yellow (lala´go)	*Pinus ponderosa*
Plum, Sierra (tumα´lo)	*Prunus subcordata*
Poplar, balsam (ko´oc)	*Populus balsamifera*
Rabbit brush	*Chrysothamnus nauseosus*
Rattlesnake weed (mα´s)	*Daucus pusillus*
Reed, common (tcu´l)	*Phragmites communis*
Rose, wild (tcuwɩ´di)	*Rosa californica; R. Woodsii*
Rush (qoda´isαm; tcɩ´nau)	*Juncus balticus*
Sagebrush (cqo´t; bu´lxwɩ)	*Artemisia tridentata*
Sedge (bɛ´ɛni)	*Carex*
Serviceberry (tcα´q)	*Amelanchier alnifolia*
Slough grass (tca´pto)	*Beckmannia Syzigachne*
Sorrel (go´kca)	*Rumex lacustris*
Spikenard (ba´was)	*Aralia californica*
Strawberry (qoqatcqαtcαlɛ´nαm; dzu´widzi´ks)	*Fragaria platypetala*
Sunflower (bα´mdαq; lαba´lαm)	*Helianthus Cusickii; H. Nuttallii*
Tarweed (go´ewa)	*Madia glomerata*
Tetradymia, gray (qeqe´tqetsαm)	*Tetradymia canescens*

Thornwood (la´)	*Lycium Andersonii*
Tobacco (qatklɑ´m)	*Nicotiana attenuata*
Tobacco root (ko´l)	*Valeriana obovata*
Tule (ma´i; kla´na?)	*Scirpus acutus*
Tulip, star	*Calochortus uniflorus*
Twinberry (o´tam)	*Lonicera involucrata*
Twinberry, siamese (o´tam)	*Lonicera conjugialis*
Wapato (tcuwa´q)	*Sagittaria latifolia*
Willow (ya´c)	*Salix*
Willow, red (tqu´a)	*Salix lasiandra*
Yarrow (la´lualsɑm)	*Achillea borealis*
Yew, western (tsobɩ´nksɑm)	*Taxus brevifolia*
Zygadene (sqa´o)	*Zygadenus venenosis*

Food Plants

Roots: arrowhead; bur reed; camas; "white camas" (after leaching); false caraway; cattail; epos; sego lily; desert parsley; sedge; spikenard; tobacco root; tule; star tulip; wapato.

Seeds: amaranth; balsamroot; blazing star; buckwheat; cattail; dock; goosefoot; grasses (arrow, rye, spike bent, tickle); knotweed; lamb's-quarters; water lily; plains mustard; tansy mustard; desert parsley; lodgepole pine; sugar pine; common reed; rush; slough grass; sorrel; sunflower; tarweed; yarrow.

Fruits: bilberry; blackberry; blackcap; bitter cherry; chokecherry; flowering currant; squaw currant; blue elderberry; mountain huckleberry; western huckleberry; pinemat manzanita; Sierra plum; wild rose; serviceberry; strawberry; twinberry; siamese twinberry.

Stems and shoots: bur reed; cattail; cow parsnip; dock; rush; sedge; tule.

Lichen and bark: black lichen; yellow lichen; lodgepole pine cambium layer; yellow pine inner bark; also, tetradymia root bark as a "chewing gum."

Leaves: hemlock water parsnip.

Fibers and Raw Materials

Fibers: buckbrush; cattail; flax; Indian hemp; juniper; hoary nettle; Sierra nettle; rabbit brush; rush; sagebrush; sedge; slough grass; tule.

Raw materials (only the principal use is noted): buckbrush (dye); quaking aspen; incense cedar (fire drill hearths); elderberry (tubing); white fir (dye, from the bark); horsetail (abrasive); juniper (bows); yellow lichen (dye); mountain mahogany (products requiring dense wood); balsam poplar; sagebrush (fire drill); thornwood (products requiring hard wood); yew (bows).

Medicines

For colds, coughs, pulmonary congestion: buckbrush (infusion); incense cedar (resin chewed); juniper (infusion from leaves; smoke inhaled); mint (infusion from leaves); cow parsnip (root chewed; infusion from root drunk).

For mouth and throat soreness, infection: barberry (salve from root); incense cedar (resin chewed); white fir (resin chewed); juniper (smoke inhaled); lodgepole pine (resin chewed).

For bruises and swellings: rye grass (poultice); cow parsnip (salve); mule's ears (poultice); yellow pine (resin); rabbit brush (poultice for blisters); rattlesnake weed (poultice).

For wounds, sores: buckwheat (leaves); white fir (resin); cow parsnip (salve, to stop bleeding); sugar pine (resin); yellow pine (resin).

For aches, pains: buckbrush (leaves chewed, applied as poultice, for rheumatism); Canada mint (salve from root); cow parsnip (infusion drunk for headache); sagebrush (pulp applied; infusion drunk).

For fever: sagebrush (infusion of leaves).

For gastrointestinal disturbances: buckbrush (seeds, as emetic); buttercup (infusion of roots, as laxative); cascara (infusion of bark or leaves, as laxative; berries eaten as emetic); mint (infusion of leaves); rattlesnake weed (infusion); sagebrush (leaves chewed; leaves boiled, eaten).

For urinary disturbances: juniper (infusion of leaves or berries).

For the eyes: barberry (infusion of leaves, as lotion); iris (infusion of root, as lotion); mint (infusion from leaves, as lotion; leaves as compress); cow parsnip (root compress); lodgepole pine (resin); tetradymia (infusion from root, as lotion).

Plants Identified Only by Modoc Names

Foods: bɛ´u (seeds, parched, ground on metate); ga´tagx (seeds); klu´(root, similar to desert parsley); ko´lsampala (seeds, parched, ground on metate, boiled to make mush); kpo´k (berries, fresh or dried); mɛ´tckal (seeds, parched, ground); mɑ´lwɑns (seeds);

na´uli (roots, pit roasted); pni´ (root, onionlike odor, pit roasted); puta´m (berries, fresh or dried); qɑnɑ´lɩx (root, a "choice food" in spring); qɛqɛ´tɑnaq (root); qtcu´mian (seeds); sto´plam (seeds, dried and pulverized); tca´ucɑm (seeds); tsaia´nkɩs (berries, fresh or dried).

Medicines: balbale´nɑm (infusion from flowers, for headaches; sprinkled on head or fumes inhaled); geka´tnaq (irislike root; infusion for eyes; salve for wounds; root sucked for sore mouth); klane´lɑm (raw root eaten for cold or sore throat); ko´gum (poultice for swelling); lɑmɛ´ndsɑm (poultice from boiled, dried, and reboiled roots; infusion as gargle); tca´ucɑm (poultice from roots, for bruises); tcɩtcɩ´lsɑm (high mountain plant; root chewed and juice swallowed, or infusion drunk, for chronic lung congestion and cough).

Fiber: steho´las (a coarse swamp grass).

Perfume: wɑ´n (strands of the plant used as a necklace).

Game Food

Land game: antelope; badger; black bear; grizzly bear; beaver; bobcat; chipmunk; cougar; coyote; blacktailed deer; whitetailed deer; mule deer; elk; fisher; gray fox; silver fox; lynx; mink; otter; porcupine; cottontail rabbit; jack rabbit; snowshoe rabbit; raccoon; mountain sheep; skunk; flying squirrel; pine squirrel; timber wolf; woodchuck (ground hog).

Fowl: brant (several species); crane (several species); curlew; duck (several species); goose; gull; loon; mudhen; pelican; prairie chicken; quail; sage hen; swan.

Pets

Most of the following pets were kept for short times only; blackbirds; young coyotes; ducks; young eagles; geese; magpies; mink; raccoons; rabbits (cottontail, especially); swans; young wolves; woodchucks.

APPENDIX III: BIOGRAPHICAL NOTES

Sally George, born about 1845. Mrs. George was the highly respected and well-informed widow of Dr. George, the eminent shaman. She had served Dr. George as singer and assistant and she remembered the songs and rituals of his ceremonial and curing activities. Mrs. George spoke no English and was totally blind; she lived entirely in the past. She occupied a small house near the residence of her son, Usee George. She took her meals with her son and his family.

Mrs. George was better informed on old Modoc culture, especially the subtle and ritual aspects, than any other person living at the time of our research. She was intelligent, alert, and reasonably cooperative. Usee George and Cora Lynch served as interpreters.

Usee George, born about 1870, near Tule Lake. Usee George was an invaluable informant and a faithful and talented interpreter. He had traveled throughout the Modoc lands in the course of his active life and had been curious enough to acquire a great store of knowledge about his country, his people, and their practices. From his father, the famous shaman, he had learned the secrets of religion and society, and from direct participation he was well acquainted with the economy and material culture of the tribe. His mother was still alert, her memory unimpaired, while our research was underway and Usee occupied evenings and other free time, week after week, discussing with her the subjects we were investigating with the two of them. He loved the old life and deplored its passing. Sometimes—not too often—he was unavailable, having sought solace (or visions?) in alcohol.

Peter Sconchin, born about 1850, near Tule Lake. Sconchin was the last surviving Modoc participant in the war with the whites, 1872-73. He had served as a full-fledged fighting man. He was possibly more of a liability than an asset to his fellow warriors for he was a clumsy man and not very intelligent. He proved valuable as an informant, however, because he was conscientiously honest, he could express himself directly in English—albeit quite broken English—he had lived the old Modoc culture while it was yet quite undisturbed, and he had participated in the Modoc War. With Sconchin it was necessary to exert more than the usual amount of care and attention in applying the checks and safeguards which are integral to the methodology of field research in ethnology, but the efforts paid dividends.

Peter Sconchin was the son of John Sconchin, the second in command during the Modoc War, and paternal nephew of Old Sconchin, the head chief of the Modoc until 1864, the year of the signing of a treaty with the United States government. (Lesser chiefs recognized at this date were Dr. George, Ben Drew, and Moose Cusket. All lived in the same village at that time. Local authority in other villages was vested in the resident leaders.) In 1869, when the tribe was removed to the Klamath Indian Reservation, a child had been born to Peter and his wife. Following the war, Peter and other survivors were sent to the Quapaw Reservation in Oklahoma. This was 1873. While in Oklahoma he was married briefly to a white woman. He returned to the Klamath Reservation in 1887 and that year married Lizzie, his fifth and last wife.

By 1930 Peter had become quite deaf. Interviews with him had to be conducted at a shouting level but he didn't seem to be disturbed by this fact. Peter liked to have his wife present when being interviewed because she was able to sense when he did not understand a statement or a phrase. She enunciated in a manner which was easy for him to understand. Indeed, Peter leaned on his wife in many ways. He was uncomfortable when she was not present. He was essentially a very weak man and he often depended upon his wife to clarify his roughly expressed statements. Such "clarification" had to be rejected, however, for purposes of the research, because Mrs. Sconchin was culturally a Klamath and her elaborations were usually derived from Klamath experience.

Peter's weakness was unquestionably complex in origin. It would be hazardous to guess what kind of a man he was before the barbarous events of the Modoc War. Here was a bloody conflict which was futile and wholly without reason. Both sides were equally blameworthy. Both sides behaved stupidly, purposelessly, and in a quite indefensible manner. Both sides betrayed their friends—for money, or for nothing. Modoc military tactics were superb but futile. Tactics of the United States forces were notable for their absence. The Modoc, fifty-three warriors, with their wives, children, and old people, retreated to the lava beds of northern California and held off their pursuers for over six months. Under cover of darkness and morning fog they stole out for water and supplies, moving under the very noses of the enemy, one thousand to fifteen hundred in humber! (The end of the war saw thirteen Modoc lost in battle, hundreds of their adversaries dead.)

The Modoc killed two unarmed members of a peace party when the latter carried out a rendezvous after being three times warned by friendly Indians that they must not go because they would never return alive. The United States soldiers killed helpless old people and took scalps. Final defeat of the Modoc was hastened by traitors who sold their services to the United States. Peter, his father, and his uncle were among the fifty-three warriors. His father was executed as an aftermath of the struggle. Peter's uncle faced his doomed brother before the gallows and disowned him in a blistering speech of denunication—disowned him, not because he had been guilty of treachery and needless bloodshed, but rather because he had tears in his eyes as he faced death.

In time of peace as well as war, Peter lived in a world of violence. As did all Modoc! A prominent man within Peter's intimate social circle—a tribal leader who shall be nameless in deference to living relatives—on successive occasions killed a brother, a son, and a wife. The last two murders, at least, were in fits of anger at trivial annoyances. The son was disturbing his father in the work of skinning an animal. The father stabbed the boy with a skinning knife. The wife was killed when she laughed at her husband in the presence of guests. Again the weapon was a knife. Apparently there was no retaliation against the aggressor in any of these cases except that a brother attacked him with a club when he killed the woman.

In later life, Peter devised his own religion, a rather original and well-integrated kind of sun worship. The basic idea apparently was borrowed from his father's blind brother but Peter's formulation undoubtedly represented the profoundest of his thinking. (Several examples of the prayers he composed are presented in the chapter on World View.) At the same time he rejected shamanism and spoke out on every available occasion against both the beliefs and the practices of the old religion. He was also antagonistic to Christianity but that religion nevertheless influenced markedly certain aspects of his thinking and reasoning.

Lizzie Sconchin, born about 1860, at Yainax. Her mother was Modoc, her father Klamath. She was reared as a Klamath and remained a Klamath, culturally speaking, throughout her life. It is true that she learned a great deal about Modoc customs from her mother, and that she was the wife of a prominent Modoc man, Peter Sconchin, for many years. It is also true that she was an intelligent woman who could distinguish between Klamath and Modoc cultural variants when she put her mind to it. However, her orientation often shifted without her being aware of the fact. As a consequence, her services were useful only as a kind of interpreter and aid in interviews with her husband whose hearing and comprehension were both deficient.

Evaline Sconchin, born about 1850, at Steolas, a native village on the east side of Tule Lake, where she continued to live until reservation days. The advanced age of this informant precluded extensive interviewing but she was cooperative and alert, and her memory was fairly good. She persisted in the old ways to the extent of wearing a basketry hat, sitting and eating only on the floor, giving many hours of her day to basket weaving and the hours of the evening to recollections of the old life and the admonishment of her younger relatives and visitors to retain the traditional values and, so far as possible, the practices, too. Her recent ancestry was exclusively Modoc but she spoke both Modoc and Klamath. She did not acquire English.

Celia Lynch, born about 1860 at the native village of Steopgas, between Tule Lake and Clear Lake. This intelligent and alert informant supplied a considerable bulk of information, covering numerous aspects of the old culture, particularly women's activities, dances, rituals, and religious practices. She spoke very little English. An interpreter was used for all ethnographic recording.

Elmer Lynch, born about 1880, son of Celia Lynch. Served as an interpreter, a role in which he was highly competent, and provided minor bits of ethnographic information.

Cora Lynch, born about 1875. Cora, the wife of Usee George, had only a shallow knowledge of the aboriginal culture but could be relied upon to provide accurate information on subjects familiar to her. She also served occasionally as an interpreter.

Jenny Clinton, born about 1858, on the western shore of Tule Lake. Her father was Modoc-Shasta, her mother full Modoc. Her knowledge of the old life was limited by the fact that she was moved to Oklahoma when quite young, her family having been with the insurgents during the Modoc War. She returned to the Klamath Reservation in 1903 and thereafter attempted a limited adjustment to white patterns of living. She embraced Christianity, having come under the influence of the Quakers in Oklahoma. From 1883 to 1922 she was married to Daniel Clinton, for whom she bore nine children. The fact that all of her children died while young turned her further toward a visionary type of Christianity and she became a "woman preacher." In her version of the religion, she incorporated numerous elements of native belief and declared that the famous Modoc shamans were prophets of the Bible. Jenny spoke fluently both Modoc and English.

Anderson Faithful, born about 1872, on Lost River near the present site of Merrill, Oregon. His recent ancestry was entirely Modoc but he spent much time with the Klamath during his youth. For this reason, and because he had no direct acquaintance with the tribal culture prior to the Modoc War, he was of limited use as an informant. He spoke English with moderate facility, Modoc with fluency.

Mary Chiloquin, born about 1880, near Tule Lake, sister of Anderson Faithful. Mary served both as informant and interpreter; her English was good. Her immediate ancestry was Modoc but her maternal grandmother was Shasta. She was married to a Modoc-Shasta man. Although young, she retained many old customs such as mat and basketry making, and the gathering and cooking of water-lily seeds in the old manner. Much of her knowledge of the aboriginal culture came from her mother who lived until 1934. She was well acquainted with the whole Modoc country and provided valuable geographical information.

Stonewall Jackson, born about 1855, was an ex-Pit River slave who had been captured as a boy and reared as a Modoc. He was a useful informant with a wide scope of knowledge. Having attended and participated in a wide range of ceremonies, he showed special competence on the subject of ritualism.

Arthur Chester was a young Modoc who served with distinction as an interpreter.

Leaders and Shamans

Chief Sconchin or *Old Sconchin*, so-called to distinguish him from his brother, John Sconchin, was the head chief of the Modoc during the pre-Modoc War days when the old system of leadership had been modified, as a reaction to the presence of whites, to recognize "chieftainships." Chief Sconchin remained on the Klamath Reservation, at Yainax, during the Modoc War. With him were the great bulk of the Modoc tribe, all of whom remained peaceful throughout the war. Chief Sconchin showed great powers of leadership in keeping his people out of the war but he was unsuccessful in his several efforts to stop the fighting and bring the insurgent remnant back into the tribe.

Captain Jack was the first in command of the insurgents during the Modoc War. His ancestry included prominent Modoc leaders of the past but he was not himself a "chief" or even a civil leader. Rather, he was simply the war leader of fifty-three Modoc men and their families. He was executed by the United States military as an aftermath of the war.

John Sconchin was the younger brother of Chief Sconchin and the second in command during the war. He was the father of Peter Sconchin (informant) who also served in the war. John Sconchin was executed along with Captain Jack.

Jakalunus was the most notable shaman ever known to the Modoc. He was the father of Anderson Faithful's mother. He practiced in the late eighteenth and early nineteenth centuries. Anecdotes relating to his shamanistic power and his activities are recounted in the chapter on Shamanistic Practice.

Curly-headed Doctor was a highly accomplished and respected Modoc shaman during the immediate prewar years. He joined the insurgents and played a prominent role during the war both by power of his oratory and through the performance of rituals for the purpose of protecting the insurgents and bringing misfortunes to the United States troops. The fact that the troops suffered disaster after disaster raised the Indians' estimation of Curly-headed Doctor to a very high level. He died in Oklahoma in 1890.

Doctor George was considered by his Modoc tribesmen to be the greatest shaman since Jakalunus. His curing powers were tremendously respected and he was an unusually accomplished ceremonial leader. Indeed, he was responsible for numerous ritual innovations which would have expanded Modoc religion markedly if the culture had not reached the point of decline at that time. Doctor George was the husband of Sally George and the father of Usee George (both informants). He died about 1930.

BIBLIOGRAPHY OF RELATED WORKS

Bancroft, Herbert Howe. *The Native Races of the Pacific States.*
Vol. 1. San Francisco: A. L. Bancroft and Co., 1883.
————. *History of Oregon.* San Francisco: The History Pub-
lishers, 1888.
Barrett, S. A. "The Material Culture of the Klamath Lake and
Modoc Indians of Northeastern California and Southern Oregon,"
*University of California Publications in American Archaeology
and Ethnology,* V, No. 4, 1910.
Colville, Frederick V. "Notes on the Plants Used by the Klamath
Indians of Oregon," *Contributions from the U. S. National Her-
barium,* V, No. 2, 1897.
————. "Wokas, A Primitive Food of the Klamath Indians," *Re-
ports, United States National Museum* (1902), pp. 725-39.
Culin, Stewart. "Games of North American Indians," *Annual Re-
port, Bureau of American Ethnology,* XXIV, 1907.
Curtin, Jeremiah. *Myths of the Modocs.* Boston: Little, Brown
and Co., 1912.
Curtis, Edward S. *The North American Indian,* Vol. XIII. Nor-
wood, Mass., 1924.
Dubois, Cora. "The 1870 Ghost Dance," *Anthropological Records,*
III, No. 1. University of California, 1939.
Gatschet, Albert S. "The Klamath Indians of Southwestern Ore-
gon," *Contributions to North American Ethnology,* II, Washing-
ton, D. C., 1890.
Hodge, F. W., ed. "Handbook of American Indians," *Bulletin,
Bureau of American Ethnology,* XXX. Washington, D. C., 1907.

Howard, O. O. *My Life and Experiences among Our Hostile Indians*. Hartford, Conn., 1907.

Kniffen, Fred B. "Achomawi Geography," *University of California Publications in American Archaeology and Ethnology*, XXIII, No. 5, 1928.

Kroeber, A. L. "Handbook of the Indians of California," *Bulletin, Bureau of American Ethnology*, LXXVIII. Washington, D. C., 1925.

Meacham, A. B. *Wigwam and Warpath*. Boston: John P. Dale and Co., 1875.

Merriam, C. Hart. "The Classification and Distribution of the Pit River Tribes of California," *Smithsonian Miscellaneous Collections*, LXXVIII, No. 3, 1926.

Miller, Joaquin. *Life amongst the Modocs*. London, 1873.

Murray, Keith A. *The Modocs and Their War*. Norman, Okla.: University of Oklahoma Press, 1959.

Nash, Philleo. "The Place of Religious Revivalism in the Formation of the Intercultural Community on the Klamath Reservation," in Fred Eggan, ed., *Social Anthropology of North American Tribes*. Chicago: University of Chicago Press, 1937.

Payne, Doris Palmer. *Captain Jack, Modoc Renegade*. Portland, Ore.: Binford and Mort, 1938.

Powers, Stephen. "The California Indians," *The Overland Monthly* (No. VIII: The Modocs), June 1873, pp. 535-45.

————. "Tribes of California," *U. S. Geographic and Geological Survey*, III (1877), 252-66.

Ray, Verne F. *Cultural Relations in the Plateau of Northwestern America*. Los Angeles: The Southwest Museum, 1939.

————. "Culture Element Distributions: XXII. Plateau," *Anthropological Records*, VIII, No. 2. University of California, 1942.

————. "The Klamath Oppose Liquidation," *American Indian*, IV (1948), 15-22.

————, and others. "Tribal Distribution in Eastern Oregon and Adjacent Regions," *American Anthropologist*, XL, No. 3, 1938.

Riddle, Jeff C. *The Indian History of the Modoc War and the Causes That Led to It*. San Francisco, 1914.

Spier, Leslie. "The Ghost Dance of 1870 among the Klamath of Oregon," *University of Washington Publications in Anthropology*, II, No. 2, 1927.

————. "Klamath Ethnography," *University of California Publications in American Archaeology and Ethnology*, XXX, 1930.

Steward, Julian H. "Basin-Plateau Aboriginal Sociopolitical Groups," *Bulletin, Bureau of American Ethnology*, CXX, 1938.

Stewart, Omer C. "The Northern Paiute Bands," *Anthropological Records*, II, No. 3. University of California, 1939.

————. "Culture Element Distributions: XIV. Northern Paiute," *Anthropological Records*, IV, No. 3. University of California, 1941.

Swanton, John R. "The Indian Tribes of North America," *Bulletin, Bureau of American Ethnology*, CXLV, Washington, D.C., 1952.

Voegelin, Carl F. "Notes on Klamath, Modoc and Achumawi Dialects," *International Journal of American Linguistics*, XII, No. 2 (1946), 96-101.

Voegelin, Erminie. "Culture Element Distributions: XX. Northeast California," *Anthropological Records*, VII, No. 2. University of California, 1942.

INDEX

Abortion, 101
Achomawi: relationship with Modoc, x. *See also* Pit River Indians
Adoption, 105
Adultery, 11-12, 91
Aged: care of, 157, 180
Aisis (mythological character), 19
Animals: in prayer, 21, 27-28; in world view, 24-25; in omens, 25; in moon's phases, 26; taboos at pregnancy, 96
Antelope: hunting of, 185-86; enclosure for hunting, 186-87, 188; and location of villages, 208, 209, 210, 220
Ant spirit, 67
Apron: description of, 165
Armor, 144
Assembly: mechanics of, 9-10, 137

Ball-kicking game, 130-31
Basin. *See* Great Basin culture area
Basket game: in intertribal gambling, 124-28, 129
Bathing: in crisis quests, 77, 78, 79, 80; at pregnancy, 96; in childhood, 107; for body care, 176
Bears: hunting of, x, 188, 210, 220; beliefs about, 24-25, 26
Bear spirit, 41
Beaver Creek, 210
Berries, 208, 212-20 *passim*
Bible: in dream, 23; prophets of, 225

Birds: hunting of, x, 189, 210, 220; in omens, 25; avoidance of, at pregnancy, 96; as spirits *See* under specific names
Birth: practices of, xii, 97-100
Blood revenge. *See* Feuds
Blue Mountain, 209
Body signs: in omens, 26
Boles Meadow, 209
Bonanza, 210, 211
Bonanza River, 193
Bottle Creek, 210
Boundaries. *See* Territory
Breechcloth: description of, 166
Buckskin. *See* Skins
Burial. *See* Cremation
Butte Creek, 208
Buzzard spirit, 46, 60, 101

California: tribes of, 162, 173, 178, 199
California culture area: relation to Modoc, v, x, xi, xii, 22
Camas, x, 181; gathering of, 197, 198-99
Canoes: kinds of, xii; in fishing, 194; description of, 196
Captain Jack, 94, 226
Cascade Divide, x
Cascade Range, ix
Chalk, 174
Charley, Doctor. *See* Doctor Charley
Charms: in good luck, 26

231

PUBLICATIONS OF THE AMERICAN ETHNOLOGICAL SOCIETY

Law and Status among the Kiowa Indians. Jane Richardson. (Monograph I) 1940. 142 pages, bibliography. Out of print

Rank and Warfare among the Plains Indians. Bernard Mishkin. (Monograph III) 1940. 73 pages, bibliography. Out of print

Disease, Religion and Society in the Fiji Islands. Dorothy M. Spencer. (Monograph II) 1941. 92 pages, chart. Out of print

An Analysis of Inca Militarism. Joseph Bram. (Monograph IV) 1941. 93 pages, bibliography. Out of print

A Primitive Mexican Economy. George M. Foster. (Monograph V) 1942. 123 pages, plates, maps, bibliography. Out of print

The Effects of White Contact upon Blackfoot Culture, with Special Reference to the Role of the Fur Trade. Oscar Lewis. (Monograph VI) 1942. 79 pages, maps, bibliography. Out of print

Arapesh. R. F. Fortune. (Publication XIX) 1942. 243 pages. $5.00

Prayer: The Compulsive Word. Gladys A. Reichard. (Monograph VII) 1944. 121 pages, figures, bibliography. Out of print

Changing Configurations in the Social Organization of a Blackfoot Tribe during the Reserve Period (The Blood of Alberta, Canada). Esther S. Goldfrank. (Monograph VIII) 1945. 81 pages, plates, bibliography. (Bound with IX). Out of print

Observations on Northern Blackfoot Kinship. L. M. Hanks, Jr., and Jane Richardson. (Monograph IX) 1945. 37 pages, figures. (Bound with VIII). Out of print

Map of North American Indian Languages. Compiled and drawn by C. F. Voegelin and E. W. Voegelin. (Publication XX) 1945. Wall size, color. Out of print

The Influence of Islam on a Sudanese Religion. Joseph Greenberg. (Monograph X) 1946. 83 pages, figures, map, bibliography. Out of print

Alaskan Eskimo Ceremonialism. Margaret Lantis. (Monograph XI) 1947. 143 pages, maps, bibliography. Out of print

Economics of the Mount Hagen Tribes, New Guinea. Abraham L. Gitlow. (Monograph XII) 1947. 122 pages, plates, figures, maps, bibliography. Out of print

Ceremonial Patterns in the Greater Southwest. Ruth M. Underhill (Monograph XIII) 1948. 74 pages, bibliography, index. (Bound with XIV)

Factionalism in Isleta Pueblo. David H. French. (Monograph XIV) 1948. 54 pages, bibliography. (Bound with XIII) $2.50

The Negro in Northern Brazil: A Study in Acculturation. Octavio da Costa Eduardo. (Monograph XV) 1948. 139 pages, map, bibliography. Out of print

Bali: Rangda and Barong. Jane Belo. (Monograph XVI) 1949. 71 pages, plates, figures, bibliography. $2.75

The Rubber-Ball Games of the Americas. Theodore Stern. (Monograph XVII) 1950. 129 pages, plate, maps, bibliography. Out of print

Fighting with Property: A Study of Kwakiutl Potlatching and Warfare 1792-1930. Helen Codere. With Tribal and Linguistic Map of Vancouver Island and Adjacent Territory, drawn and compiled by Vincent F. Kotschar. (Monograph XVIII) 1950. 143 pages, figures, maps, charts, bibliography. $3.00. Out of print

The Cheyenne in Plains Indian Trade Relations 1795-1840. Joseph Jablow. (Monograph XIX) 1951. 110 pages, maps, bibliography, index. $2.50

The Tsimshian: Their Arts and Music. The Tsimshian and Their Neighbors, by Viola E. Garfield; Tsimshian Sculpture, by Paul S. Wingert; Tsimshian Songs, by Marius Barbeau. (Publication XVIII) 1951. 302 pages, plates, figures, maps, music, bibliography, index. $6.00. Out of print

Navaho Grammar. Gladys A. Reichard. (Publication XXI) 1951. 407 pages, bibliography. $7.00

Buzios Island: A Caiçara Community in Southern Brazil. Emilio Willems in cooperation with Gioconda Mussolini. (Monograph XX) 1952. 124 pages, figures, maps, bibliography. $2.75

Chichicastenango: A Guatemalan Village. Ruth Bunzel. (Publication XXII) 1952. 464 pages, figures, bibliography. $7.00

Changing Military Patterns on the Great Plains (17th Century through Early 19th Century). Frank Raymond Secoy. (Monograph XXI) 1953. 120 pages, maps, bibliography. $2.75

Bali: Temple Festival. Jane Belo. (Monograph XXII) 1953. 78 pages, plates, chart, bibliography. $2.75

Hungarian and Vogul Mythology. Géza Róheim. With appendixes by John Lotz. (Monograph XXIII) 1954. 96 pages, map, bibliography. Out of print

The Trumaí Indians of Central Brazil. Robert F. Murphy and Buell Quain. (Monograph XXIV) 1955. 120 pages, plates, map, bibliography. $2.75. Out of print

The Deeply Rooted: A Study of a Drents Community in the Netherlands. John Y. Keur and Dorothy L. Keur. (Monograph XXV) 1955. 208 pages, plates, maps, bibliography. Out of print

The Tlingit Indians: Results of a Trip to the Northwest Coast of America and the Bering Straits. Aurel Krause. Translated by Erna Gunther. 1956. 320 pages, plates, figures, map, bibliography, index. $4.50

Village and Plantation Life in Northeastern Brazil. Harry William

Hutchinson. 1957. 209 pages, plates, maps, charts, bibliography, index. $3.50. Out of print

Malaya. Norton Ginsburg and Chester F. Roberts, Jr. 1958. 54€ pages, maps, charts, bibliography, index. $6.75

Social Stratification in Polynesia. Marshall D. Sahlins. 1958. 32(pages, figures, bibliography. $4.50

Status Terminology and the Social Structure of North America Indians. Munro S. Edmonson. 1958. 92 pages, charts, bibliography. $3.00

A Community in the Andes: Problems and Progress in Muquiyauyc Richard N. Adams. 1959. 266 pages, maps, figures, bibliography, index. $4.75

Land and Polity in Tibet. Pedro Carrasco. 1959. 318 pages, maps bibliography, index. $5.75

Eskimo Childhood and Interpersonal Relationships: Nunivak Biogrc phies and Genealogies. Margaret Lantis. 1960. 232 pages, ma figures, charts, bibliography. $5.00

Caribbean Studies: A Symposium. Vera Rubin, ed. (2nd ed. 1960. 124 pages, map, references, notes on contributors. $3.(

West Indian Family Structure. M. G. Smith. 1962. 320 page 100 pages of tables included. $6.00

Point Hope: An Eskimo Community in Transition. James W. Van Stone. 1962. 163 pages, maps, illustrations, bibliography. $5. 2

Papago Indian Pottery. Bernard L. Fontana, William J. Robinso Charles W. Cormack, and Ernest E. Leavitt, Jr. 1962. 1 pages, maps, drawings, photographs. $5.75

Primitive Pragmatists: The Modoc Indians of Northern Californi Verne F. Ray. 1963. 256 pages, maps, figures. $5.00